MW01707866

The History, Construction and Dynamics of Motorcycles

Silas Singer

The role of the book within our culture is changing. The change is brought on by new ways to acquire & use content, the rapid dissemination of information and real-time peer collaboration on a global scale. Despite these changes one thing is clear--"the book" in it's traditional form continues to play an important role in learning and communication. The book you are holding in your hands utilizes the unique characteristics of the Internet -- relying on web infrastructure and collaborative tools to share and use resources in keeping with the characteristics of the medium (user-created, defying control, etc.)--while maintaining all the convenience and utility of a real book.

Contents

Articles

Overview

Motorcycle

A **motorcycle** (also called a **motorbike**, **bike**, or **cycle**) is a single-track, engine-powered, two-wheeled motor vehicle. Motorcycles vary considerably depending on the task for which they are designed, such as long distance travel, navigating congested urban traffic, cruising, sport and racing, or off-road conditions.

A 1954 Triumph T110 650 cc motorcycle

A Ural motorcycle with sidecar

Motorcycles are one of the most affordable forms of motorised transport in many parts of the world and, for most of the world's population, they are also the most common type of motor vehicle. There are around 200 million motorcycles (including mopeds, motor scooters and other powered two and three-wheelers) in use worldwide, or about 33 motorcycles per 1000 people. This compares to around 590 million cars, or about 91 per 1000 people. Most of the motorcycles, 58%, are in the developing countries of Asia—Southern and Eastern Asia, and the Asia Pacific countries, excluding Japan—while 33% of the cars (195 million) are concentrated in the United States and Japan. As of 2002, India with an estimated 37 million motorcycles/mopeds was home to the largest number of motorised two wheelers in the world. China came a close second with 34 million motorcycles/mopeds.

History

Main article: Motorcycle history

The first internal combustion, petroleum fueled motorcycle was the *Petroleum Reitwagen*. It was designed and built by the German inventors Gottlieb Daimler and Wilhelm Maybach in Bad Cannstatt, Germany in 1885. This vehicle was unlike either the safety bicycles or the boneshaker bicycles of the era in that it had zero degrees of steering axis angle and no fork offset, and thus did not use the principles of bicycle and motorcycle dynamics developed nearly 70 years earlier. Instead, it relied on two outrigger wheels to remain upright while turning. The inventors called their invention the *Reitwagen* ("riding car"). It was designed as an expedient testbed for their new engine, rather than a true prototype vehicle. Many authorities who exclude steam powered, electric or diesel two-wheelers from the definition of a motorcycle, credit the Daimler *Reitwagen* as the world's first motorcycle.

Replica of the Daimler-Maybach *Petroleum Reitwagen*.

If a two-wheeled vehicle with steam propulsion is considered a motorcycle, then the first was the French Michaux-Perreaux steam bicycle of 1868. This was followed by the American Roper steam velocipede of 1869, built by Sylvester Howard Roper of Roxbury, Massachusetts. Roper demonstrated his machine at fairs and circuses in the eastern U.S. in 1867, and built a total of 10 examples.

In 1894, Hildebrand & Wolfmüller became the first series production motorcycle, and the first to be called a motorcycle (German: *Motorrad*). In the early period of motorcycle history, many producers of bicycles adapted their designs to accommodate the new internal combustion engine. As the engines became more powerful and designs outgrew the bicycle origins, the number of motorcycle producers increased.

Until World War I, the largest motorcycle manufacturer in the world was Indian, producing over 20,000 bikes per year. By 1920, this honour went to Harley-Davidson, [*citation needed*] with their motorcycles being sold by dealers in 67 countries. By the late 1920s or early 1930s, DKW took over as the largest manufacturer.

After World War II, the BSA Group became the largest producer of motorcycles in the world, producing up to 75,000 bikes per year in the 1950s.[*citation needed*] The German company NSU held the position of largest manufacturer from 1955 until the 1970s.[citation needed]

NSU Sportmax streamlined motorcycle, 250 cc class winner of the 1955 Grand Prix season

In the 1950s, streamlining began to play an increasing part in the development of racing motorcycles and the "dustbin fairing" held out the possibility of radical changes to motorcycle design. NSU and Moto Guzzi were in the vanguard of this development both producing very radical designs well ahead of their time. NSU produced the most advanced design, but after the deaths of four NSU riders in the 1954–1956 seasons, they abandoned further development and quit Grand Prix motorcycle racing. Moto Guzzi produced competitive race machines, and by 1957 nearly all the Grand Prix races were being won by streamlined machines.[citation needed] The following year, 1958, full enclosure fairings were banned from racing by the FIM in the light of the safety concerns.

From the 1960s through the 1990s, small two-stroke motorcycles were popular worldwide, partly as a result of East German Walter Kaaden's engine work in the 1950s.

Today, the motorcycle industry is mainly dominated by Japanese companies such as Honda, Kawasaki, Suzuki, and Yamaha, although Harley-Davidson and BMW continue to be popular and supply considerable markets. Other major manufacturers include Piaggio group of Italy, KTM, Triumph and Ducati.

In addition to the large capacity motorcycles, there is a large market in smaller capacity (less than 300 cc) motorcycles, mostly concentrated in Asian and African countries. An example is the 1958 Honda Super Cub, which went on to become the biggest selling vehicle of all time, with its 60 millionth unit produced in April 2008. Today, this area is dominated by mostly Indian companies with Hero Honda emerging as the world's largest manufacturer of two wheelers. Other major producers are Bajaj and TVS Motors. For example, its Splendor model has sold more than 8.5 million to date.

Technical aspects

Construction

See also: Motorcycle construction and Motorcycle design

A Suzuki GS500 with a clearly visible frame (painted silver).

Motorcycle construction is the engineering, manufacturing, and assembly of components and systems for a motorcycle which results in the performance, cost, and aesthetics desired by the designer. With some exceptions, construction of modern mass-produced motorcycles has standardised on a steel or aluminium frame, telescopic forks holding the front wheel, and disc brakes. Some other body parts, designed for either aesthetic or performance reasons may be added. A petrol powered engine typically consisting of between one and four cylinders (and less commonly, up to eight cylinders) coupled to a manual five- or six-speed sequential transmission drives the swingarm-mounted rear wheel by a chain, driveshaft or belt.

Fuel economy

Motorcycle fuel economy varies greatly with engine displacement and riding style ranging from a low of 29 mpg_{-US} (8.1 L/100 km; 35 mpg_{-imp}) reported by a Honda VTR1000F rider, to 107 mpg_{-US} (2.20 L/100 km; 129 mpg_{-imp}) reported for the Verucci Nitro 50 cc Scooter. A specially designed Matzu Matsuzawa Honda XL125 achieved 470 mpg_{-US} (0.50 L/100 km; 560 mpg_{-imp}) "on real highways - in real conditions." Due to lower engine displacements (100 cc–200 cc), motorcycles in developing countries offer good fuel economy.[citation needed] In the Indian market, the second best selling company, Bajaj, offers two models with superior fuel economy: XCD 125 and Platina. Both are 125 cc motorbikes with a company-claimed fuel economy of 256 mpg_{-US} (0.919 L/100 km; 307 mpg_{-imp}) and 261 mpg_{-US} (0.901 L/100 km; 313 mpg_{-imp}), respectively.[citation needed]

Electric motorcycles

Main article: Electric motorcycle

Very high fuel economy equivalents can be derived by electric motorcycles. Electric motorcycles are nearly silent, zero-emission electric motor-driven vehicles. Operating range and top speed suffer because of limitations of battery technology.[citation needed] Fuel cells and petroleum-electric hybrids are also under development to extend the range and improve performance of the electric motors.

Dynamics

Main article: Bicycle and motorcycle dynamics

Different types of motorcycles have different dynamics and these play a role in how a motorcycle performs in given conditions. For example, one with a longer wheelbase provides the feeling of more stability by responding less to disturbances. Motorcycle tyres have a large influence over handling.

Motorcycles must be leaned in order to make turns. This lean is induced by the method known as countersteering, in which the rider steers the handlebars in the direction opposite of the desired turn. Because it is counter-intuitive this practice is often very confusing to novices—and even to many experienced motorcyclists.

Short wheelbase motorcycles, such as sport bikes, can generate enough torque at the rear wheel, and enough stopping force at the front wheel, to lift the opposite wheel off the road. These actions, if performed on purpose, are known as wheelies and stoppies respectively. If carried past the point of recovery the resulting upset is known as an "endo" (short for "end-over-end"), or "looping" the vehicle.

Accessories

Main article: Motorcycle accessories

Various features and accessories may be attached to a motorcycle either as OEM (factory-fitted) or after-market. Such accessories are selected by the owner to enhance the motorcycle's appearance, safety, performance, or comfort, and may include anything from mobile electronics to sidecars and trailers.

Social aspects

Main article: Motorcycling

Popularity

In numerous cultures, motorcycles are the primary means of motorised transport. According to the Taiwanese government, for example, "the number of automobiles per ten thousand population is around 2,500, and the number of motorcycles is about 5,000." In places such as Vietnam, motorised traffic consist of mostly motorbikes due to a lack of public transport and low income levels that put automobiles out of reach for many.

Motorbikes are the primary form of transportation in Vietnam.

The four largest motorcycle markets in the world are all in Asia: China, India, Indonesia, and Vietnam. The motorcycle is also popular in Brazil's frontier towns. Amid the global economic downturn of 2008, the motorcycle market grew by 6.5%.

Recent years have seen an increase in the popularity of motorcycles elsewhere. In the USA, registrations increased by 51% between 2000 and 2005. This is mainly attributed to increasing fuel prices and urban congestion. A Consumer Reports subscribers' survey of mainly United States motorcycle and scooter owners reported that they rode an average of only 1000 miles (1600 km) per year, 82% for recreation and 38% for commuting. Americans put 10000–12000 miles (16000–19000 km) per year on their cars and light trucks.

Subcultures

See also: Motorcycle club, Outlaw motorcycle club, and Category:Motorcycling subculture

Sunbeam motorcycle owners rally, 2008.

A Hells Angels wall mural in Southampton, UK

Around the world, motorcycles have historically been associated with subcultures. Some of these subcultures have been loose-knit social groups such as the cafe racers of 1950s Britain, and the Mods and Rockers of the 1960s. A few are believed to be criminal gangs.

Social motorcyclist organisations are popular and are sometimes organised geographically, focus on individual makes, or even specific models. Example motorcycle clubs include: American Motorcyclist Association, Harley Owners Group and BMW MOA. Some organisations hold large international motorcycle rallies in different parts of the world that are attended by many thousands of riders.

Whereas many social motorcycle organisations raise money for charities through organised events and rides, some other motorcycle organisations exist only for the direct benefit of others. Bikers Against Child Abuse (BACA) is one example. BACA assigns members to individual children to help them through difficult situations, or even stay with the child if the child is alone or frightened.

In recent decades, motorcyclists have formed political lobbying organisations in order to influence legislators to introduce motorcycle-friendly legislation. One of the oldest such organisations, the British Motorcycle Action Group, was founded in 1973 specifically in response to helmet compulsion, introduced without public consultation. In addition, the British Motorcyclists Federation (BMF), originally founded in 1960 as a reaction to the public perception of motorcyclists as leather-jacketed hooligans, has itself moved into political lobbying. Likewise, the U.S. has ABATE, which, like most such organisations, also works to improve motorcycle safety, as well as running the usual charity fund-raising events and rallies, often for motorcycle-related political interests.

At the other end of the spectrum from the charitable organisations and the motorcycle rights activists are the Outlaw Motorcycle Gangs. These are defined by the Provincial Court of Manitoba as: "Any group of motorcycle enthusiasts who have voluntarily made a commitment to band together and abide by their organisations' rigorous rules enforced by violence, who engage in activities that bring them and their club into serious conflict with society and the law". The Federal Bureau of Investigation (FBI) and Criminal Intelligence Service Canada have designated four MCs as Outlaw Motorcycle Gangs (OMGs), which are the Pagans, Hells Angels, Outlaws MC, and Bandidos, known as the "Big Four".

Mobility

While people choose to ride motorcycles for various reasons, those reasons are increasingly practical, with riders opting for a powered two-wheeler as a cost-efficient alternative to infrequent and expensive public transport systems, or as a means of avoiding or reducing the effects of urban congestion. In places where it is permitted, lane splitting, also known as filtering, allows motorcycles to use the space between vehicles to move through stationary or slow traffic.

A couple ride on a motorcycle in Udaipur, India. Annual sales of motorcycles in India are expected to exceed 10 million by 2010.

In the UK, motorcycles are exempt from the £8 per day London congestion charge other vehicles must pay to enter the city during the day. Motorcycles are also exempt from toll charges at some river crossings, such as the Severn Bridge, Dartford Crossing, and Mersey Tunnels. Some cities, such as Bristol, allow motorcycles to use bus lanes and provide dedicated free parking. In the United States, those states that have high-occupancy vehicle lanes also allow for motorcycle travel in them. Other countries have similar policies.

In New Zealand motorcycle riders are not required to pay for parking that is controlled by a barrier arm; the arm does not occupy the entire width of the lane, and the motorcyclist simply rides around it. Many car parks controlled in this way supply special areas for motorcycles to park, so as not to unnecessarily consume spaces.

In many cities that have serious parking challenges for cars, such as San Francisco, US and Melbourne, Australia, motorcycles are generally permitted to park on the sidewalk, rather than occupy a space on the street which might otherwise be used by a car.[*citation needed*]

Safety

Main articles: Motorcycle safety and Motorcycle safety clothing

Motorcycles have a higher rate of fatal accidents than automobiles. United States Department of Transportation data for 2005 from the Fatality Analysis Reporting System show that for passenger cars, 18.62 fatal crashes occur per 100,000 registered vehicles. For motorcycles this figure is higher at 75.19 per 100,000 registered vehicles – four times higher than for cars. The same data shows that 1.56 fatalities occur per 100 million vehicle miles travelled for passenger cars, whereas for motorcycles the figure is 43.47 – 28 times higher than for cars (37 times more deaths per mile travelled in 2007). Furthermore for motorcycles the accident rates have increased significantly since the end of the 1990s, while the rates have dropped for passenger cars.

The two major causes of motorcycle accidents in the United States are: motorists pulling out or turning in front of motorcyclists and violating their rights-of-way and motorcyclists running wide through turns. The former is sometimes called a SMIDSY, an acronym formed from the motorists' common response of "Sorry mate, I didn't see you". The latter is more commonly caused by operating a motorcycle while intoxicated. Motorcyclists can anticipate and avoid some of these crashes with proper training, increasing their conspicuousness to other traffic, and separating alcohol and riding.

The United Kingdom has several organisations which are dedicated to improving motorcycle safety by providing advanced rider training over and above what is necessary to pass the basic motorcycle test. These include the Institute of Advanced Motorists (IAM) and the Royal Society for the Prevention of Accidents (RoSPA). Along with increased personal safety, riders with these advanced qualifications often benefit from reduced insurance costs.

In South Africa, the Think Bike campaign is dedicated to increasing both motorcycle safety and the awareness of motorcycles on the country's roads. The campaign, while strongest in the Gauteng province, has representation in Western Cape, KwaZulu Natal and the Free State. It has dozens of trained marshals available for various events such as cycle races and is deeply involved in numerous other projects such as the annual Motorcycle Toy Run.

Motorcycle Safety Education is offered throughout the United States by organisations ranging from state agencies to non-profit organisations to corporations. The courses, designed by the Motorcycle Safety Foundation (MSF), include a Basic Rider Course, an Intermediate Rider Course and an Advanced Rider Course.

An MSF rider course for novices

In the UK (except Northern Ireland) and some Australian jurisdictions, such as Victoria, New South Wales, the

Australian Capital Territory, Tasmania and the Northern Territory, it is compulsory to undertake a rider training course before being issued a Learners Licence.

In Canada, motorcycle rider training is compulsory in Quebec and Manitoba only, but all provinces and territories have Graduated Licensing programs which place restrictions on new drivers until they have gained experience. Eligibility for a full motorcycle licence or endorsement for completing a Motorcycle Safety course varies by province. The Canada Safety Council, a non-profit safety organisation, offers the Gearing Up program across Canada and is endorsed by the Motorcycle and Moped Industry Council. Training course graduates may qualify for reduced insurance premiums.

Types

Main article: Types of motorcycles

There are three major types of motorcycle: street, off-road, and dual purpose. Within these types, there are many different sub-types of motorcycles for many different purposes.

Street bikes include cruisers, sportbikes, scooters and mopeds, and many other types. Off-road motorcycles include many types designed for dirt-oriented racing classes such as motocross and are not street legal in most areas. Dual purpose machines like the dual-sport style are made to go off-road but include features to make them legal and comfortable on the street as well.

A boulevard cruiser (front) and a sportbike (background)

Each configuration offers either specialised advantage or broad capability, and each design creates a different riding posture.

Motorcycle rider postures

The motorcyclist's riding position depends on rider body-geometry (anthropometry) combined with the geometry of the motorcycle itself. These factors create a set of three basic postures.

- Sport — the rider leans forwards into the wind and the weight of the upper torso is supported by air pressure as long as the motorcycle is travelling at speed, typically above 50 mph (80 km/h). The footpegs are below the rider or to the rear. The reduced frontal area cuts wind resistance and allow higher speeds. However, at low-speed this position throws the weight of the rider onto the arms instead, and this is quickly tiring to the wrists of unfamiliar riders. Moreover, the sports position makes it more difficult for the rider to look around and foot through traffic. Many sport bikes have narrow, swept-back handlebars, or clip-ons (short stubs clamped to the telescopic fork tubes). Following the style of racing bikes, most have full-fairings and often come with almost complete engine enclosure, although motorcycles with a sport riding position are becoming more diverse with the marketing of factory naked bikes, streetfighters, retro cafe racers, and other blends of styles, having varying riding positions somewhere in the range from sport to standard.

- Standard — the rider sits upright or leans forwards slightly. The feet are below the rider, not too far to the front or back. These are straightforward, versatile motorcycles that are not too specialised for one task, but don't excel in one area either. The standard posture is used with touring and commuting as well as dirt and dual-sport bikes, and is good for beginners. The rider enjoys the benefits of freedom of head movement, good visibility in all directions, and easier use of the feet while moving through stationary traffic.
- Cruiser — the rider sits at a lower seat height with the upper torso upright or leaning slightly rearwards. Legs are extended forwards, sometimes out of reach of the regular controls on cruiser pegs. The low seat heights can be a consideration for new or short riders. Handlebars tend to be high, and wide. Harley-Davidsons are exemplars of this style. The emphasis is on comfort, while compromising cornering ability because of low ground clearance and the greater likelihood of scraping foot pegs, floor boards, or other parts if turns are taken at the speeds other types of motorcycles can do.

Factors of a motorcycle's ergonomic geometry that determine the seating posture include the height, angle and location of footpegs, seat and handlebars. Factors in a rider's physical geometry that contribute to seating posture include torso, arm, thigh and leg length, and overall rider height.

Legal definitions and restrictions

Main article: Legal definition of motorcycle

A motorcycle is broadly defined by law in most countries for the purposes of registration, taxation and rider licensing as a powered two-wheel motor vehicle. Most countries distinguish between mopeds of 49 cc and the more powerful, larger, vehicles (scooters do not count as a separate category). Many jurisdictions include some forms of three-wheelers as motorcycles.

Environmental impact

In 2007 and 2008, motorcycles and scooters, due to good fuel efficiency, attracted interest in the United States from environmentalists and those affected by increased fuel prices. Piaggio Group Americas supported this interest with the launch of a "Vespanomics" website and platform, citing lower per-mile carbon emissions of 0.4 lb/mile (113 g/km) less than the average car, a 65% reduction, and better fuel economy.

Other sources, however, claim that while motorcycles produce much less pollution in terms of greenhouse gases, a motorcycle can in some cases emit 10–20 times the quantity of nitrogen oxides (NOx) when compared to the NOx emissions of a car. This is because many motorcycles lack a catalytic converter to reduce NOx emissions, and while catalytic converters have been used in cars long enough that they are now commonplace, they are a relatively new technology in motorcycles. Many newer motorcycles (such as later models of the Yamaha R1 and Suzuki GSXR1000, as well as most BMWs which have included catalytic converers since the 1990s) now have factory fitted catalytic converters. Along with other technologies that have taken longer to appear in motorcycles (e.g. fuel injection, anti-lock brake systems),[citation needed] catalytic converters are becoming increasingly commonplace.

United States Environmental Protection Agency 2007 certification result reports for all vehicles versus on highway motorcycles (which also includes scooters), the average certified emissions level for 12,327 vehicles tested was 0.734. The average "Nox+Co End-Of-Useful-Life-Emissions" for 3,863 motorcycles tested was 0.8531, for a difference of about 16%, not the claimed 10X factor. Likewise, if one looks at how many of the 2007 motorcycles tested were also catalytic equipped, 54% of them, 2,092, were equipped with a catalytic converter.

United States emissions limits

The following table shows maximum acceptable legal emissions of the combination of hydrocarbon and nitrous oxides, as well as carbon monoxide, for new Class III motorcycles (280 cc or larger displacement) sold in the United States.

Tier	Model year	HC+NOx (g/km)	CO (g/km)
Tier 1	2006–2009	1.4	12.0
Tier 2	2010 and later	0.8	12.0

The maximum acceptable legal emissions of hydrocarbon and carbon monoxide for new Class I and II motorcycles (50 cc–169 cc and 170 cc–279 cc respectively) sold in the United States are as follows:

Model year	HC (g/km)	CO (g/km)
2006 and later	1.0	12.0

Europe

European emission standards for motorcycles are similar to those for cars. New motorcycles must meet Euro III standards, while cars must meet Euro V standards. Therefore, the difference in total pollution between motorcycles and cars that pass European emission standards would be small, certainly much smaller than the 10X factor claimed by the referenced *LA Times* article. Motorcycle emissions controls are being updated and it has been proposed to update to Euro IV in 2012 and Euro V in 2015

See also

- List of motorcycle manufacturers
- Fédération Internationale de Motocyclisme (FIM) - the governing body for international motorcycle sport, which also lobbies for the rights and interests of motorcyclists.

External links

- Motorcycles [1] at the Open Directory Project
- About Motorcycles [2] - comprehensive motorcycle information and news

Motorcycling

Motorcycling is the act of riding a motorcycle. A variety of subcultures and lifestyles have been built up around motorcycling.

A motorcycle ride up Kitt Peak in Arizona

Benefits

Robert M. Pirsig's book *Zen and the Art of Motorcycle Maintenance* (1974) was a paean celebrating motorcycling. Pirsig contrasted the sense of connection experienced by motorcyclists with the isolation of drivers who are "always in a compartment", passively observing the passing landscape. In contrast, Pirsig argues that a motorcyclist is "completely in contact with it all... in the scene." The process and experience of motorcycling forces the rider into the present. The

A motorcycle rider in Arizona

environment of the road engulfs the senses, and the need for constant awareness fills the mind. The total involvement in motorcycling leaves little room for worrying about tomorrow, or second-guessing yesterday.

A motorcyclist wearing a full-face helmet with a visor

Many motorcyclists ride as a way to relieve stress, to "clear the mind." Despite the fact that *Zen and the Art of Motorcycle Maintenance* speaks very little about motorcycle maintenance, or Zen, some enthusiasts believe the link to be a natural one. Zen is a branch of Mahayana Buddhism which strongly emphasizes the practice of moment-by-moment awareness and of "seeing deeply into the nature of things by direct experience." Motorcycling demands moment-by-moment awareness and, unlike driving, rewards the rider with direct experience.

Hunter S. Thompson's book *Hell's Angels* includes an ode to the joys of pushing a motorcycle to its limits on the open road: he states that "with the throttle screwed on there is only the barest margin, and no room at all for mistakes... that's when the strange music starts, [and]... fear becomes exhilaration [and the]... only sounds are the wind and a dull roar floating back from the mufflers. Similarly, T. E. Lawrence wrote of the "lustfulness of moving swiftly" and the "pleasure of speeding on the road" on a motorcycle, which he compared to the sensation of "feel[ing] the earth moulding herself under me", coming alive, and "heaving and tossing on each side like a sea."

Milan Kundera also noted that "speed is the form of ecstasy the technical revolution has bestowed on man"; unlike a runner, "when man delegates the faculty of speed to a machine" such as a motorbike, "from then on, his own body is outside the process, and he gives over to a speed that is noncorporeal, nonmaterial, pure speed, speed itself, ecstasy speed." Not all motorcyclists have a "need for speed", but many do. Speed draws many people to motorcycling, because the power-to-weight ratios of even low-power motorcycles rivals that of an expensive sports car. The power-to-weight ratio of high power sport bikes is well beyond any mass-production automobile. All for a fraction of the price of those automobiles.

High speeds on a motorcycle can also be more exhilarating than high speeds in an automobile. Not only is the sensation of speed greater since the rider is not separated from the environment of the road, but motorcycles negotiate turns by leaning. And the greater the speed, the greater the lean, sometimes to the point of scraping parts of the motorcycle on the road. Some riders will point proudly to the worn-away parts of their motorcycle, proof that they take turns so fast that they must lean the motorcycle over to the limits of its capabilities.

Disadvantages

Motorcycling is a more dangerous means of transport than other road alternatives: the relative risk of a motorcycle rider being killed or seriously injured per kilometre travelled was around 54 times higher in Great Britain in 2006 than for car drivers. However, motorcycling is less dangerous than many other popular outdoor recreational activities, including horseback riding.

To address motorcycle safety issues, motorcycle-specific training and personal protective equipment is important for motorcyclists' survival on the road, and mandated in many countries and several U.S. states and counties.

Subcultures

See also Category:Motorcycling subculture

These range from mainstream motorcycle clubs, which include long-distance riding clubs, amateur racers, and trail riders to those involved with motorcycling's "extreme sports" motocross riding, drag racing, and trick stunt enthusiasts.

The motorcycling lifestyle spans across different motorcycling groups but transcends many countries and cultures.

Repairing

Motorcyclists will refer to maintenance or repair of a motorcycle as *wrenching*, as in "turning a wrench." UK motorcyclists refer to a wrench as a "spanner", and the activity of working on the bike is similarly known as "spannering". Melissa Holbrook Pierson points out that the do-it-yourself self sufficiency is "part of [motor]bikes' allure in an increasingly monolithic, unfixable world." She also claims that motorcyclists "become a member of a community, linked first and foremost to anyone who rides; when another [motor]bike passes, you...[w]ave, and perhaps [give] a thumbs-up."

Historically, motorcycle maintenance was a necessary skill for riders, since the materials and technology used in motorcycles often meant that repairs had to be done on the road-side miles from home. Modern motorcycles are as reliable as automobiles, but the feeling that many riders have that their motorcycle is more than just a means of transportation leads them to want to do any wrenching on the bike themselves. This drive to wrench reaches its zenith with rat bikes. Riders of rats often eschew paying anyone else to work on their motorcycles on principle, and therefore do all their own maintenance.

External links

- Season of the Bike [1] "The difference between driving a car and climbing onto a motorcycle is the difference between watching TV and actually living your life."
- IHIE Guidelines for Motorcycling [2] - these authoritative Guidelines are the first in the UK, setting out comprehensive, practical guidance for highway engineers, traffic engineers, road safety officers and transport planners on providing a safer transport environment for motorcycles, mopeds and scooters.
- Motorcycling [3] at the Open Directory Project

History

Motorcycle history

Motorcycle history begins in the second half of the 19th century. Motorcycles are descended from the "safety bicycle," a bicycle with front and rear wheels of the same size and a pedal crank mechanism to drive the rear wheel. Despite some early landmarks in its development, motorcycles lack a rigid pedigree that can be traced back to a single idea or machine. Instead, the idea seems to have occurred to numerous engineers and inventors around Europe at around the same time.

The 1900 Werner Brothers patented motorcycle

Early Pioneers

Steam power

In the 1860s Pierre Michaux, a blacksmith in Paris, founded 'Michaux et Cie' ("Michaux and company"), the first company to construct bicycles with pedals called a velocipede at the time, or "Michauline" . The first steam powered motorcycle can be traced to 1867, when Pierre's son Ernest Michaux fitted a small steam engine to one of the 'velocipedes'.

Lucius Copeland 1894

The design went to the USA when Pierre Lallement, a Michaux employee who also claimed to have developed the prototype in 1863, filed for the first bicycle patent with the U.S. patent office in 1866. In 1868 an American, Sylvester Howard Roper of Roxbury, Massachusetts developed a twin cylinder machine from the French velocipede design, with a charcoal fired boiler between the wheels. (Roper's contribution to motorcycle development ended suddenly when he died demonstrating one of his machines in Cambridge, Massachusetts on June 1st 1896).

Also in 1868, a French engineer Louis-Guillaume Perreaux patented a similar steam powered single cylinder motorcycle with a petrol burner and twin belt drives, which was possibly invented independently of Roper's. Although the patent is dated 1868, nothing indicates the invention had been operable before 1871.

In 1881, Lucius Copeland of Phoenix, Arizona designed a much smaller steam boiler which could drive the large rear wheel of a 'farthing-penny' "Star" cycle at 12mph. In 1887 Copeland formed the Northrop Manufacturing Co. to priduce the first successful 'Moto-Cycle' (actually a three wheeler).

Petroleum power

The inspiration for the earliest dirt bike, and arguably the first motorcycle, was designed and built by the German inventors Gottlieb Daimler and Wilhelm Maybach in Bad Cannstatt (since 1905 a city district of Stuttgart) in 1885. The first petroleum-powered vehicle, it was essentially a motorized bicycle, although the inventors called their invention the *Reitwagen* ("riding carriage"). They had not set out to create a vehicle form but to build a simple carriage for the engine, which was the focus of their endeavours.

Replica of the 1885 Daimler-Maybach *Reitwagen*

First commercial products

In the decade from the late 1880s, dozens of designs and machines emerged, particularly in France, Germany and England, and soon spread to America. During this early period of motorcycle history, there were many manufacturers since bicycle makers were adapting their designs for the new internal combustion engine.

In 1894, the Hildebrand & Wolfmüller became the first motorcycle available to the public for purchase. However, only a few hundred examples of this motorcycle were ever built. Soon, as the engines became more powerful and designs outgrew the bicycle origins, the number of motorcycle-oriented producers increased.

The first known motorcycle in the United States was said to be brought to New York by a French circus performer, in 1895. It weighed about 200 lb (91 kg) and was capable of 40 mph (64 km/h) on a level surface. However, that same year, an inventor from the United States E.J. Pennington demonstrated a motorcycle of his own design in Milwaukee. Pennington claimed his machine was capable of a speed of 58 mph (93 km/h), and is credited with inventing the term "motor cycle" to describe his machine.

The 20th century

Before World War II

A 1913 FN (Fabrique National), Belgium, 4cylinders and shaft drive

In 1901 English quadricycle and bicycle maker Royal Enfield introduced its first motorcycle, with a 239 cc engine mounted in the front and driving the rear wheel through a belt. In 1898, English bicycle maker Triumph decided to extend its focus to include motorcycles, and by 1902, the company had produced its first motorcycle—a bicycle fitted with a Belgian-built engine. In 1903, as Triumph's motorcycle sales topped 500, the American company Harley-Davidson started producing motorcycles.

In 1901, the Indian Motorcycle Manufacturing Company, which had been founded by two former bicycle racers, designed the so-called "diamond framed" Indian Single, whose engine was built by the Aurora Firm in Illinois per Indian's specifications. The Single was made available in the deep blue. Indian's production was up to over 500 bikes by 1902, and would rise to 32,000, its best ever, in 1913.

During this period, experimentation and innovation were driven by the popular new sport of motorcycle racing, with its powerful incentive to produce tough, fast, reliable machines. These enhancements quickly found their way to the public's machines.

A 1923 BMW R32, with a shaft-drive, boxer twin engine

Chief August Vollmer of the Berkeley, California Police Department is credited with organizing the first official Police Motorcycle Patrol in the United States in 1911. By 1914, motorcycles were no longer just bicycles with engines; they had their own technologies, although many still maintained bicycle elements, like the seats and suspension.

Until the First World War, Indian was the largest motorcycle manufacturer in the world. After that, this honor went to Harley-Davidson, until 1928 when DKW took over as the largest manufacturer. [[|BMW Motorrad|BMW motorcycles]] came on the scene in 1923 with a shaft drive and an opposed-twin or "boxer" engine enclosed with the transmission in a single aluminum housing.

By 1931, Indian and Harley-Davidson were the only two American manufacturers producing commercial motorcycles. This two-company rivalry in the United States remained until 1953, when the Indian Motorcycle factory in Springfield, Massachusetts closed and Royal Enfield took over the Indian name.

There were over 80 different makes of motorcycle available in Britain in the 1930s, from the familiar marques like Norton, Triumph and AJS to the completely obscure, with names like New Gerrard, NUT, SOS, Chell and Whitwood, about twice as many motorcycle makes competing in the world market during the early 21st century.

In 1937, Joe Petrali set a new land speed record of 136.183 mph (219.165 km/h) on a modified Harley-Davidson 61 cubic inch (1,000 cc) overhead valve-driven motorcycle. The same day, Petrali also broke the speed record for 45 cubic inch (737 cc) engine motorcycles.

In Europe, production demands, driven by the buildup to World War II, included motorcycles for military use, and BSA supplied 126,000 BSA M20 motorcycles to the British armed forces, starting in 1937 and continuing until 1950. Royal Enfield also produced motorcycles for the military, including a 125 cc lightweight motorcycle that could be dropped (in a parachute-fitted tube cage) from an aircraft.

After World War II

After the Second World War, some American veterans found a replacement for the camaraderie, excitement, danger and speed of life at war in motorcycles. Grouped into loosely organized clubs, motorcycle riders in the U.S. created a new social institution—the motorcyclists or "bikers"—which was later skewed by the "outlaw" persona Marlon Brando portrayed in the 1954 film *The Wild One*.

In Europe, on the other hand, post-war motorcycle producers were more concerned with designing practical, economical transportation than the social aspects, or "biker" image. Italian designer Piaggio introduced the Vespa in 1946, which experienced immediate and widespread popularity. Imports from the UK, Italy and Germany, thus found a niche in U.S. markets that American bikes did not fill.

The BSA Group purchased Triumph Motorcycles in 1951 to become the largest producer of motorcycles in the world claiming "one in four". The German NSU was the largest manufacturer from 1955 until the 1970s when Honda became the largest manufacturer—a title now claimed by Indian bike firm Hero Honda, which specialises in small motorcycles throughout India and similar markets.

British manufacturers Triumph, BSA, and Norton retained a dominant position in some markets until the rise of the Japanese manufacturers (led by Honda) in the late 1960s and early 1970s. The role of the motorcycle shifted in the 1960s, from the tool of a life to a toy of a lifestyle. It became part of an image, of status, a cultural icon for individualism, a prop in Hollywood B-movies.

A 1962 Triumph Bonneville represents the popularity of British motorcycles at that time

The motorcycle also became a recreational machine for sport and leisure, a vehicle for carefree youth, not essential transportation for the mature family man or woman, and the Japanese were able to produce modern designs more quickly, more cheaply, and of better quality than their competitors. Their motorbikes were more stylish and more reliable, so the British manufacturers fell behind as mass-market producers.

The Honda Motor Co., which was officially founded in Japan on September 24, 1948, introduced their SOHC inline 4-cylinder 750 in 1969, which was inexpensive and immediately successful. It was not a high-performance bike, but it established the across-the-frame-4 engine configuration as a design with huge potential for power and performance. Despite being much more complex than any other mass-market motorcycle, it was the most reliable large motorcycle on the road.[*citation needed*]

Shortly after the introduction of the SOHC, Kawasaki demonstrated the potential of the four-cycle four-cylinder engine with the introduction of the KZ900. The only motorcycle that outperformed the KZ900 was another Kawasaki, the H1, a much smaller and lighter 3-cylinder, two-cycle engine.[*citation needed*] The H1 was prone to fouling, and was considered dangerous by many riders.[*citation needed*]

The Suzuki Motor Co., Ltd., Kawasaki Heavy Industries and the Yamaha Motor Corporation each started producing motorcycles in the 1950s. Meanwhile, the sun was setting on British dominion over the big-displacement motorbike market.

Japanese dominance

The Honda CB750 revolutionized motorcycle marketing and was emblematic of Japanese dominance

The excellence of Japanese motorcycles caused similar effects in all "Western" markets: many Italian bike firms either went bust or only just managed to survive. As a result BMW's worldwide sales sagged in the 1960s, but came back strongly with the introduction of a completely redesigned "slash-5" series for model year 1970.

From the 1960s through the 1990s, small two-stroke motorcycles were popular worldwide, partly as a result of the East German Walter Kaaden's engine work in the 1950s, later acquired by Suzuki via stolen plans supplied by MZ rider Ernst Degner, who defected to the West on 13th September 1961 after retiring from the 125cc Swedish Grand Prix at Kristianstad.

Harley-Davidson (HD) in the U.S. at the time suffered from the same problems as the European firms, but its unique product range, American tariff laws and nationalism-driven customer loyalty allowed it to survive. One alleged flaw, however, was retaining the characteristic HD 45° engine vee-angle, which causes excess vibration as well as the loping HD sound.

A factory full fairing was introduced by BMW motorcycles in the R100RS of 1977, the first factory fairing produced in quantity. In 1980, BMW stimulated the "adventure touring" category of motorcycling with its R80G/S. In 1988, BMW was the first motorcycle manufacturer to introduce anti-lock-brakes (ABS) on its sporting K100RS-SE and K1 models.

The present

Today the Japanese manufacturers, Honda, Kawasaki, Suzuki, and Yamaha dominate the large motorcycle industry, although Harley-Davidson still maintains a high degree of popularity, particularly in the United States.

Recent years have seen a resurgence in the popularity around the world of many other motorcycle brands, including BMW, Triumph and Ducati, and the emergence of Victory as a second successful mass-builder of big-twin American cruisers.

In November 2006, the Dutch company E.V.A. Products BV Holland announced that the first commercially available diesel-powered motorcycle, its Track T-800CDI, achieved production status. The Track T-800CDI uses a 800 cc three-cylinder Daimler Chrysler diesel engine. However, other manufacturers, including Royal Enfield, had been producing diesel-powered bikes since at least 1965.

Currently, the largest motorcycle market is the small machines market for the developing world, hence the claim from Indian Hero Honda to be the world's new biggest bike firm. India has also been the home to the Enfield Cycle Company's Royal Enfield, since 1995. Enfield India still makes updated versions of the 1955 Royal Enfield Bullet motorcycle.

Motorcycle traffic in Bangkok

There is a large demand for small, cheap motorcycles in the "developing world", and many of the firms meeting that demand now also compete in "developed" markets, such as China's Hongdou which makes a version of Honda's venerable CG 125.

Motorcycle taxis are the developing world's limousines. Scooters, mopeds and motorcycles offer a fast, cheap and risky way around snarled traffic and scarce mass transit, as they can easily squeeze through jams.

See also

- Motorcycle
- Motorcycle manufacturers
- Motorcycling
- Police motorcycle
- Safety bicycle
- History of electric motorcycles and scooters

Further reading

Early history and use in the United Kingdom

- Pennell, Joseph (February 8 1901). "Some Experiences Of Motor Bicycles" [1]. *Journal of the Society of Arts* **XLIX** (2,516). Retrieved 2009-08-15.
- Hiscox, Gardner Dexter (1902). *The Automobile: A Practical Treatise On The Construction Of Modern Motor Cars Steam, Petrol, Electric And Petrol-Electric: Chapter XXI. Motor Bicycles (1903 ed.)* [2]. London: Cassell And Company, Limited. pp. 751–763. Retrieved 2009-08-15.
- Lavergne, Gerard (1902). *The Automobile: Its Construction And Management (Various Chapters)* [3]. London: Cassell And Company, Limited. Retrieved 2009-08-15.
- Wilson, A. J. (1903). *Motor Cycles And How To Manage Them, 6th ed.* [4]. London: Iliffe & Sons Limited. Retrieved 2009-08-15.

Early history and use in the United States

- Lockert, Louis (1899). *Petroleum Motor-Cars: Chapter VIII "Motor Bicycles"* [5]. New York: D. Van Nostrand Company. pp. 64–75. Retrieved 2009-08-15.
- "The Automobile Bicycle" [6]. *The Literary Digest* **XIX** (16): 463–464. October 14 1899. Retrieved 2009-08-15.
- Hiscox, Gardner Dexter (1900). *Horseless Vehicles, Automobiles, Motor Cycles Operated By Steam, Petrol, Electric And Petrol-Electric: Chapter XI. Automobile Bicycles And Tricycles* [7]. New York: Munn & COmpany. pp. 175–215. Retrieved 2009-08-15.
- "Interesting Notes. Single Motor Bicycles" [8]. *The School Journal* **LX** (22): 632. June 2 1900. Retrieved 2009-08-15.
- Krarup, M.C. (November 1900). *The Field For Motorcycles: Motorcycling Vs. Motoring* [9]. **XXXVII**. pp. 207–212. Retrieved 2009-08-15.
- Bill, L. H. (August 1902). "The Poor Man's Automobile" [10]. *Overland Monthly, and Out West Magazine* **XL** (2): 197–198. Retrieved 2009-08-15.
- Burr, H. Walter (December 1902). *Up Mount Hamilton On A Motor Cycle* [11]. **XL**. pp. 556–561.
- "Possibilities of the Motorcycle" [12]. *The Automobile* **XIII** (4): 123. July 27 1903. Retrieved 2009-08-15.

- Hiscox, Gardner Dexter (1904). *Mechanical Appliances, Mechanical Movements And Novelties Of Construction: Road And Vehicle Devices, Types Of Motor Bicycles* [13]. New York: The Norman W. Henley Publishing Company. pp. 215–216. Retrieved 2009-08-15.
- "Motor Bicycles for Medical Men" [14]. *The Medical World* **XXIII** (10). October 1905. Retrieved 2009-08-15.
- Cummings, C. E. (February 1906). "An Idyl Of The Tireless Bike" [15]. *Recreation* **XXIV** (2): 127–130. Retrieved 2009-08-15.
- Bashore, S. D. (July 1906). "The Motor Cycle For Physicians" [16]. *The Texas State Journal of Medicine* **II** (3): 92–93. Retrieved 2009-08-15.
- "Mail Collection By Motor Van" [17]. *The Commercial Vehicle* **III** (7). July 1908. Retrieved 2009-08-15. "An experiment is being conducted by the Post-office ... with the use of a motorcycle van ... of the "Indian" type".
- "Development Of The Motor Cycle Van: Increasing Use Of This Type Of Light Package Delivery Motor Vehicle Noted Both Here And Abroad" [18]. *The Commercial Vehicle* **III** (10): 227–228. October 1908. Retrieved 2009-08-15.

External links

- The Art of the Motorcycle [19] at the Orlando Museum of Art.
- The Future of Motorcycles - An Opinion [20] - Before the future, we have to understand the past.

Inventors

Gottlieb Daimler

Gottlieb Daimler	
 Gottlieb Daimler	
Born	March 17, 1834 Schorndorf, Württemberg
Died	March 6, 1900 (aged 66)
Nationality	German
Occupation	Engineer, industrialist, automotive pioneer
Known for	Daimler-Motoren-Gesellschaft (Daimler Motor Company, DMG)

Gottlieb Daimler (German pronunciation: [ˈɡɔtliːp ˈdaɪmlɐ]; March 17, 1834 – March 6, 1900) was an engineer, industrial designer and industrialist, born in Schorndorf (Kingdom of Württemberg, a federal state of the German Confederation), in what is now Germany. He was a pioneer of internal-combustion engines and automobile development. He invented the first high-speed petrol engine and the first four-wheel automobile.

Daimler and his lifelong business partner Wilhelm Maybach were two inventors whose goal was to create small, high speed engines to be mounted in any kind of locomotion device. In 1885 they designed a precursor of the modern petrol (gasoline) engine which they subsequently fitted to a two-wheeler, considered the first motorcycle and, in the next year, to a stagecoach, and a boat. Daimler baptized it the Grandfather Clock engine (Standuhr) because of its resemblance to an old pendulum clock.

In 1890, they founded Daimler Motoren Gesellschaft (DMG). They sold their first automobile in 1892. Daimler fell ill and took a break from the company. Upon his return he experienced difficulty with the other stockholders that led to his resignation in 1893. This was reversed in 1894. Maybach resigned at the same time, and also returned. In 1900 Daimler died and Wilhelm Maybach quit DMG in 1907. In 1924, the DMG management signed a long term co-operation agreement with Karl Benz's Benz & Cie., and in 1926 the two companies merged to become Daimler-Benz AG, which is now part of Daimler AG.[*citation needed*]

Early life (1834 to 1852)

Gottlieb Wilhelm Daimler was the son of a baker named Johannes Däumler (Daimler) and his wife Frederika, from the town of Schorndorf near Stuttgart, Württemberg. By the age of 13 (1847), he had completed six years of primary studies in Lateinschule where he had taken additional drawing lessons on Sundays and expressed an interest in engineering. The next year, he started studying gunsmithing, building with his teacher, Riedel, a double-barreled gun.

In 1852 when eighteen, Daimler decided to take up mechanical engineering, and left his hometown. He worked at several firms, including Armstrong-Whitworth, before ending up at Deutz.

The Otto four-stroke engine (1876)

In 1872 (at age 38), Daimler and Maybach moved to work at the world's largest manufacturer of stationary engines at the time, the Deutz-AG-Gasmotorenfabrik in Cologne. It was half-owned by Nikolaus Otto, who was looking for a new technical director. As directors, both Daimler and Otto focused on gas-engine development while Maybach was chief designer.

In 1876, Otto invented the four-stroke cycle, also known as the Otto Cycle, a system characterized by four piston strokes (intake, compression, power, and exhaust). Otto intended that his invention would replace the steam engines predominant in those years, even though his engine was still primitive and inefficient. Otto's engine was patented in 1877, but the patent was soon challenged and overturned. Unbeknownst to Otto, Daimler, and Maybach, in Mannheim during 1878 Karl Benz was concentrating all his efforts on creating a reliable two-stroke gas engine based on the same principle. Benz finished his engine on December 31, 1878, and was granted a patent for his engine in 1879.

Meanwhile, serious personal differences arose between Daimler and Otto, reportedly with Otto being jealous of Daimler, because of his university background and knowledge. Daimler was fired in 1880, receiving 112 goldmarks in Deutz-AG shares in compensation for the patents of both Daimler and Maybach. Maybach resigned later.

Daimler Motors: small, high-speed engines (1882)

Daimler's summer house (Cannstatt)

After leaving Deutz-AG, Daimler and Maybach started to work together. In 1882, they moved back to Stuttgart in southern Germany, purchasing a cottage in Cannstatt's Taubenheimstrasse, with 75,000 goldmarks from the compensation from Deutz-AG. In the garden, they added a brick extension to the roomy glass-fronted summer house and this became their workshop. Their activities alarmed the neighbors who reported them to the police as suspected counterfeiters. The police obtained a key from the gardener and raided the house in their absence, but found only engines.

Daimler and Maybach spent long hours debating how best to fuel Otto's four-stroke design, and turned to a byproduct of petroleum. The main distillates of petroleum at the time were lubricating oil, kerosene (burned as lamp fuel), and benzine, which up to then was used mainly as a cleaner and was sold in pharmacies.

The grandfather clock engine (1885)

In late 1885,[*citation needed*] Daimler and Maybach developed the first of their petrol engines, which featured:

- a single horizontal cylinder of 264 cc (16 cu in) (58×100 mm, 2.28×3.94 in)
- air cooling
- large cast iron flywheel
- hot tube ignition system (patent 28022)
- cam operated exhaust valves, allowing high speed operation
- 0.5 hp (370 W)
- 600[*citation needed*] rpm running speed, beating previous engines, which typically ran at about 120 to 180 rpm
- weight of around 50 kg (110 lb)
- height of 76 cm (30 in)

In 1885, they created a carburetor which mixed gasoline with air allowing its use as fuel. In the same year Daimler and Maybach assembled a larger version of their engine, still relatively compact, but now with a vertical cylinder of 100 cm^2 displacement and an output of 1 hp at 600 rpm (patent DRP-28-022: "non-cooled, heat insulated engine with unregulated hot-tube ignition"). It was baptized the *Standuhr* (Grandfather Clock), because Daimler thought it resembled an old pendulum clock. This is probably the same internal-combustion engine referred to by the American author and historian Henry Brooks Adams, who describes the "Daimler motor" and its great speed from his visit to the 1900 Paris

Exposition in his autobiography.

In November 1885, Daimler installed a smaller version of this engine in a wooden bicycle, creating the first motorcycle (Patent 36-423impff & Sohn "Vehicle with gas or petroleum drive machine"). It was named the *Reitwagen* ("riding car"). Maybach rode it for three kilometers (two miles) alongside the river Neckar, from Cannstatt to Untertürkheim, reaching 12 kilometres per hour (7 mph).

The first motorcycle (1885)

Also in 1885, but unknown to Maybach and Daimler, only sixty miles away in Mannheim, Karl Benz built the first true automobile using an integral design for a motorized vehicle with one of his own engine. He was granted a patent for his *motorwagen* on January 29, 1886.

On March 8, 1886, Daimler and Maybach secretly brought a stagecoach made by Wilhelm Wafter into the house, telling the neighbors it was a birthday gift for Mrs. Daimler. Maybach supervised the installation of a larger 1.1 hp 462 cc (28 cu in) (70×120 mm, 2.76×4.72 in) version of the Grandfather Clock engine into this stagecoach and it became the first four-wheeled vehicle to reach 16 kilometres per hour (10 mph). The engine power was transmitted by a set of belts. As with the motorcycle, it was tested on the road to Untertürkheim where nowadays the Gottlieb-Daimler-Stadion is situated.

Driven by Daimler's desire to use the engine as many ways as possible, Daimler and Maybach used the engine in other types of transport including:

- on water (1887), by mounting it in a 4.5 metres (15 ft) long boat and achieving a speed of 6 knots (11 km/h; 6.9 mph). The boat was called *Neckar* after the river where it was tested. (patent DRP 39-367). Boat engines would become Daimler's main product for several years. The first customers expressed fear the petrol engine could explode, so Daimler hid the engine with a ceramic cover and told them it was "oil-electrical".
- street-cars and trolleys.
- in the air in Daimler's balloon, usually regarded as the first airship, where it replaced a hand-operated engine designed by Dr. Friedrich Hermann Wölfert of Leipzig. With the new engine, Daimler successfully flew over Seelberg on August 10, 1888.

They sold their first foreign licenses for engines in 1887 and Maybach went as company representative to the 1889 Paris Exposition to show their achievements.

First Daimler-Maybach automobile built (1889)

Steel Wheel Automobile 1889

· high speed four-stroke petrol engine
· fuel vaporization
· 2 cylinders V-configured
· mushroom shaped valves
· water-cooled
· 4 speed toothed gearbox
· pioneer axle-pivot steering system

Engine sales increased, mostly for use in boats, and in June 1887, Daimler bought another property at Seelberg hill, Cannstatt. It was located some distance from the town on Ludwigstraße 67 because Cannstatt's mayor did not approve of the workshop. Built at a cost 30,200 goldmarks, the new premises had room for 23 employees. Daimler managed the commercial issues while Maybach ran the engine design department.

In 1889, Daimler and Maybach built their first automobile that did not involve adapting a horse-drawn carriage with their engine, but which was somewhat influenced by bicycle designs. There was no production in Germany, but it was licensed to be built in France and presented to the public in Paris in October 1889 by both engineers. The same year, Daimler's wife, Emma Kunz, died.

The Phoenix engine (1890 to 1900)

In 1890 Daimler Motoren Gesellschaft (Daimler Engines Company) or DMG, was founded with Maybach as chief designer. Its purpose was the construction of small, high-speed engines for use on land, water, and air transport. The three uses were expressed by Daimler in a sketch that became the basis for a logo with a three-pointed star.

Daimler and Maybach were struggling financially, as they were not selling enough engines or making enough money from their patents. Two financiers and munitions makers, Max Von Duttenhofer and William Lorenz, along with the influential banker Kilian von Steiner agreed to inject some capital and converted the company on November 28, 1890 into a public corporation named the Daimler Motoren Gesellschaft, DMG.

Many German historians consider this Daimler's "pact with the devil". DMG expanded, but it changed. The newcomers, not believing in automobile production, ordered the creation of additional stationary building capacity, and considered merging DMG with Otto's *Deutz-AG*.

Daimler and Maybach preferred plans to produce automobiles and reacted against Duttenhofer and Lorenz. Maybach was denied a seat on the board and on February 11, 1891, he left the company. He continued his design work as a freelance in Cannstatt from his own house, with Daimler's support, moving to the closed Hermann Hotel in the autumn of 1892. He used its ballroom and winter garden as workshops, employing twelve workers and five apprentices.

First automobile sold (1892)

In 1892, DMG finally sold its first automobile. Gottlieb Daimler, aged 58, had heart problems and suffered a collapse in the winter of 1892-1893. His doctor prescribed a trip to Florence, where he met Lina Hartmann, a widow 22 years his junior who was the owner of the hotel where he was staying. They married on July 8, 1893, honeymooning in Chicago during its World Fair.

The disputes with Lorenz continued. Daimler attempted to buy 102 extra shares to get a majority holding, but was forced out of his post as technical director. The company was 400,000 goldmarks in debt. The other directors threatened to declare bankruptcy if Daimler didn't sell them all his shares and all his personal patent rights from the previous thirty years. Daimler accepted the offer, receiving 66,666 goldmarks, and resigned in 1893.

In 1894 at the Hermann Hotel, Maybach together with Daimler and his son Paul designed a third engine called the "Phoenix" and had DMG make it. It featured:

- four cylinders cast in one block arranged vertically and parallel
- camshaft operated exhaust valves
- a spray nozzle carburetor, patented by Maybach in 1893
- an improved belt drive system

It became famous around the world. When fitted to a car it won the petrol engine category of the first car race in history, the Paris to Rouen 1894.

The ill-defined relationship between the inventors and DMG harmed the image of DMG's technical department. This continued until 1894 when the British industrialist Frederick Simms made it a condition of his 350,000 mark purchase of a Phoenix engine license, which would stabilize the company finances, that Daimler, now aged sixty, should return to DMG. Gottlieb Daimler received 200,000 goldmarks in shares, plus a 100,000 bonus. Simms received the right to use the name "Daimler" as his brand name for the engines. In 1895, the year DMG assembled its 1,000th engine, Maybach returned as chief engineer, receiving 30,000 shares.

During this period, they agreed to licenses to build Daimler engines around the world, which included:

- France, from 1890, by Panhard et Levassor and Peugeot
- the United States, from 1891, by American and German piano maker Steinway & Sons
- the United Kingdom, from 1896, by Frederick Simms as the Daimler Motor Company
- Austria, by Austro Daimler

Daimler died in 1900, and in 1907 Maybach resigned from DMG.

Honours

Gottlieb Daimler was accepted into the Automotive Hall of Fame in 1978. Between 1993 and July 2008 Daimler had a stadium named after him in Stuttgart, Germany. The Gottlieb-Daimler-Stadion was the venue for six matches in the 2006 FIFA World Cup. It is now called Mercedes-Benz Arena.

Gottlieb Daimler's motto was *Das Beste oder nichts* ("The best or nothing at all"; "Nothing but the best").

See also

- German inventors and discoverers
- the British Daimler Motor Company (later acquired by Jaguar)

External links

- Gottlieb Daimler and Karl Benz-Foundation [1]
- Mercedes Benz USA [2]
- Mercedes Benz Canada [3]
- Encarta article [4] (Archived [5] 2009-10-31)
- German Wikipedia (German)
- The workaholic who made the automotive revolution possible [6]

Wilhelm Maybach

Wilhelm Maybach	
 Wilhelm Maybach in 1900	
Born	February 9, 1846 Heilbronn, Baden-Württemberg
Died	December 29, 1929 (aged 83) Stuttgart
Nationality	German
Occupation	Engineer and industrialist
Known for	Daimler Motoren Gesellschaft, Maybach-Motorenbau GmbH

Wilhelm Maybach (German pronunciation: [ˈvɪlhɛlm ˈmaɪbax]; 9 February 1846 – 29 December 1929) was an early German engine designer and industrialist. During the 1890s he was hailed in France, then the world centre for car production, as the "King of constructors".

From the late 19th century Wilhelm Maybach, together with Gottlieb Daimler, developed light, high-speed internal combustion engines suitable for land, water, and air use. These were fitted to the world's first motorcycle, motorboat, and after Daimler's death, to a new automobile introduced in late 1902, the Mercedes model, built to the specifications of Emil Jellinek.

Maybach rose to become technical director of the Daimler Motoren Gesellschaft, also known as Daimler Motor Company or DMG, but he did not get on well with its chairmen. As a result Maybach left DMG in 1907 to found Maybach-Motorenbau GmbH together with his son Karl in 1909; they manufactured Zeppelin engines. After the signing of the Versailles Treaty in 1919 the company started producing large luxury vehicles, branded as "Maybach". The company joined the German war effort in

1940, ceasing automotive production in favour of tank engines. including those for Tiger tanks.

In 1998 Daimler-Benz merged with Chrysler Corporation to become DaimlerChrysler. The new company revived the *Maybach* brand name as a luxury make in 2002.

Early life and career beginnings (1846 to 1869)

Wilhelm Maybach was born in Heilbronn, Baden-Württemberg in 1846, the son of a carpenter and his wife Luise. He had four brothers. When he was eight years old the family moved from Löwenstein near Heilbronn to Stuttgart. His mother died in 1856 and his father in 1859.

After his relatives published an announcement in the *Stuttgarter Anzeiger* newspaper, a philanthropic institution at Reutlingen took in Maybach as a student. Its founder and director, Gustav Werner, discovered Maybach's technical inclination and helped to stimulate his career by sending him to the school's engineering workshop. At 15 years old (1861), Maybach was heading for a career in Industrial design and took extra classes in physics and mathematics at Reutlingen's public high school.

By the time he was 19 years old, he was a qualified designer working on stationary engines. His workshop manager, Gottlieb Daimler, then 29, noticed his efforts and took him on as his main assistant, a post he held until Daimler's death in 1900.

Daimler and Otto's four-stroke engine (1869 to 1880)

In 1869, Maybach followed Daimler to Maschinenbau-Gesellschaft Karlsruhe AG in Karlsruhe, a manufacturer of heavy locomotives. Daimler was on the Executive Committee and they spent long nights discussing new designs for engines, pumps, lumber machinery, and metalworking.

In 1872, Daimler moved to Deutz-AG-Gasmotorenfabrik in Cologne, then the world's largest manufacturer of stationary gas engines. Nikolaus Otto, part owner of the company, focused on engine development with Daimler. Maybach joined them as Chief Designer.

In 1876, Nikolaus Otto patented the Otto cycle engine. It was a four-stroke cycle gas internal combustion engine with intake, compression, power, and exhaust strokes. Otto's patent on this engine was later challenged and overturned.

Also in 1876, Maybach was sent to show Deutz's engines at the Philadelphia World's Fair (USA). On returning to Cologne in 1877, he concentrated on improving the four-stroke design to get it ready for its impending commercial launch.

In 1878, Maybach married Bertha Wilhelmine Habermaas a friend of Daimler's wife, Emma Kunz. Her family members were landowners who ran the post office in Maulbronn. On 6 July 1879 Karl Maybach was born, the first of their three sons.

In 1880, Daimler and Otto had serious disagreements which resulted in Daimler leaving Deutz-AG. Daimler received 112,000 goldmarks in Deutz-AG shares as compensation for patents granted to him and Maybach. Maybach also left shortly afterwards, and followed his friend to found a new company in Cannstatt.

Daimler Motors: fast and small engines (1882)

In 1882, Maybach moved to Taubenheimstrasse in Cannstatt, Stuttgart where Daimler had purchased a house with 75,000 goldmarks from his Deutz compensation. They added a brick extension to the glass-fronted summer house in the garden, which became their workshop.

Daimler's summer house (Cannstatt)

Their activities alarmed the neighbours who suspected they were engaged in counterfeiting. The police police raided the property in their absence using the gardener's key, but found only engines.

In 1884, Maybach's second son, Adolf was born.

The Grandfather Clock engine (1885)

By the end of 1885, Maybach and Daimler developed the first of their engines, which is regarded as a precursor to all modern petrol engines. It featured:

- single horizontal cylinder
- air cooling
- large cast iron flywheel
- revolutionary hot tube ignition (Patent 28022)
- exhaust valve controlled by a camshaft allowing high speeds
- a speed of 600 rpm, when at the time most engines could only achieve about 120 to 180 rpm.

In 1885, they created the first carburetor, which mixed evaporated gasoline with air to allow its efficient use as fuel. It was used that year on a larger but still compact version of the engine, now with a vertical cylinder, that featured:

- 1 Horsepower at 600 rpm output
- 100 cc engine displacement
- non cooled insulated cylinder with unregulated hot-tube ignition (patent DRP-28-022)

Daimler baptized it the *Standuhr* (Grandfather Clock) because of its resemblance to a pendulum clock.

Replica of the *Reitwagen*

In November 1885, Daimler installed a smaller version of the engine into a wooden bicycle, creating the first motorcycle (patent 36-423 - Vehicle with gas or petroleum engine), and Maybach drove it three kilometers from Cannstatt to Untertürkheim, reaching 7.5 mph (12 km/h). It became known as the *Reitwagen*.

On 8 March 1886, the inventors took a stagecoach built by Wilhelm Wimpff & Sohn inside the house, telling the neighbours that it was a birthday gift for Mrs. Daimler. Maybach supervised the installation of an enlarged 1.5 hp Grandfather Clock engine into the coach, and installed a belt drive to the wheels. The vehicle reached 10 mph (15 km/h) when tested on the road to Untertürkheim.

Maybach and Daimler went on to prove the engine in many other ways including:

- On water (1887). It was mounted in a 4.5-metre-long boat which achieved 6 knots (11 km/h). The boat was called the *Neckar* after the river it was tested on and was registered as patent number DRP 39-367. Motor boat engines would become their main product until the first decade of the 1900s.
- More road vehicles including street cars
- In the air. They built the first motorized airship, a balloon based on designs by Dr. Friedrich Hermann Wölfert from Leipzig. They replaced his hand operated drive system and flew over Seelberg successfully on 10 August 1888.

By 1887 they were licensing their first patents abroad, and Maybach represented the company at the great Paris Exposition Universelle (1889).

First Daimler-Maybach automobile built (1889)

Steel Wheel Automobile 1889

· high speed four-stroke petrol engine
· fuel vaporization
· 2 cylinders V-configured
· mushroom shaped valves
· water-cooled
· 4 speed toothed gearbox
· pioneer axle-pivot steering system

Sales increased, mostly from the Neckar motorboat. In June 1887, Daimler bought land in the Seelberg Hills of Cannstatt. The workshop was some distance from the town on Ludwig Route 67, because Cannstatt's mayor objected to the presence of the workshop in the town. It covered 2,903 square meters and cost 30,200 goldmarks. They initially employed 23 people. Daimler managed the commercial issues and Maybach the design department.

In 1889 they built their first automobile to be designed from scratch rather than as an adaptation of a stagecoach. It was publicly launched by both inventors in Paris in October 1889.

Daimler's engine licenses began to be taken up throughout the world, starting the modern car industry in:

- France, 1890, Panhard & Levassor and Peugeot
- United Kingdom, 1896, Daimler Motor Company
- United States of America, 1891, Steinway
- Austro-Daimler in Austria, starting in 1899

Daimler's "pact with the devil", DMG, and the Phoenix engine (1890 to 1900)

Resources were scant to keep the business going as neither the engine sales nor the worldwide proceeds from their patents were yielding enough money. Fresh capital was injected by bringing in the financiers Max von Duttenhofer and William Lorenz, former munitions makers, who were associated with Kilian von Steiner owner of a German investment bank. The company was taken public.

In 1890, Daimler and Maybach together founded the Daimler Motoren Gesellschaft, the Daimler Motor Company or DMG for short, which was dedicated to the construction of small high speed internal combustion engines for land, water, or air transport. Maybach was Chief Designer. After spending long hours debating which fuel was best to use in Otto's four-stroke engine, which had normally used methane gas as a fuel, they turned to petroleum which until then had been used mainly as a cleaner and sold in pharmacies.

The company's re-foundation took place on 28 November 1890. This has been regarded as a "pact with the devil" by some German historians, as the following decade was chaotic for Daimler and Maybach. DMG continued to expand, selling engines from Moscow to New York, and additional stationary engine-making capacity was added, but the belief continued that automobile production wouldn't be profitable. The new chairmen planned to merge *DMG* and *Deutz-AG*, in spite of Gottlieb's disagreement with Nikolaus Otto.

Daimler and Chief Engineer Maybach preferred to produce automobiles and reacted against Duttenhofer and Lorenz in particular. Maybach was rejected as a member of the Board of Management and left the company on 11 February 1891, and continued his design work from his own house, financed by Gottlieb Daimler. In late 1892, he set up a shop in the ballroom of the former Hermann

Hotel and Winter Garden where he employed 17 workers, five of which were paid by Daimler.

In 1894 Maybach designed his third engine model, together with Daimler and his son Paul. Used in the Phoenix, it gained worldwide attention, pioneering the use of four cylinders in the automobile and featuring:

- single block casting of cylinders, arranged vertically and parallel to each other
- camshaft controlled exhaust valves
- spray-nozzle carburetor (patented by Maybach in 1893)
- improved belt drive

Some of these cars gained first place in the petrol engine category in the first auto race in history, the Paris to Rouen 1894.

Maybach's creations are considered some of the finest motors of the second half of the 19th century. His inventions became indispensable for any model by any automaker in the world. He became recognised as the backbone of France's early automobile industry where he was hailed as the "King of Constructors".

Daimler was forced out of his post as Technical Director at DMG and resigned in 1893, which damaged DMG's prestige. However, in 1894, a British industrialist, Frederick Simms, purchased the rights to the Phoenix engine for 350,000 marks and stabilised the companies finances. He also made it a condition that Daimler was re-employed. In 1895 DMG assembled its 1,000th engine, and Maybach also returned as Chief Engineer, obtaining 30,000 Goldmark worth of shares through his original contract with Gottlieb Daimler.

Maybach patented more automobile inventions including:

- a revolutionary cooling system, tubular radiator with fan
- the honeycomb radiator

Around this time though Maybach suffered two setbacks. His teenage second son, Adolf, suffered a schizophrenia attack and spent the rest of his life in various mental institutions (In 1940 he was murdered by the Nazis as part of the Euthanasia Program). In 1900, Gottlieb Daimler died of heart disease.

Daimler-Mercedes engine of 1900

Mercedes 35 hp (1902)

· Large wheelbase. Wide track
· Pressed steel framework. Lightweight metals
· Low center of gravity (lower engine)
· 75 km/h (45 mph). 35 hp (950 rpm) · 300 to 1000 rpm (driver controlled)
· Light and high performance engine: 4 in-line cylinders · Bore/stroke ratio: 116x140 mm · Displacement: 5918 cc · Cylinder heads part of the castings · Two carburetors, one for each cylinder pair · Driver controlled intake valve throttling · Two camshafts
· 4-forward/1-reverse transmission
· Low voltage ignition magnetos
· Aluminium crankcase (pioneer), horizontally divided
· Honeycomb radiator
· Comfortable ride

Between April and October 1900, Maybach designed a completely new kind of car inspired by racing which would be called the Mercedes 35 hp when released in 1902. It featured:

- long wheelbase
- wide track
- low height
- unheard-of power from its 35 hp engine allowing it to reach 40 mph (64,4 km/h).

Emil Jellinek, a successful Austrian dealer and racing driver on the French Riviera who greatly admired Maybach's work, promised to buy a shipment of 36 automobiles for 550,000 goldmarks if Maybach could design a great race car for him following his specifications.

The prototype was finished in December 1900 and, in 1901 went on to have a string of racing successes. Its engine was baptized Daimler-Mercedes (Spanish for mercy) after Mercedes Jellinek, Emil's 10–year–old daughter. European high society bought the car in large numbers making it the commercial success that convinced the company directors there was a future in automobiles. Production increased greatly and DMG rapidly increased in size and number of employees. DMG officially registered the Mercedes trademark in June 1902.

In 1902, a fire destroyed DMG's Cannstatt facilities and the company moved to Stuttgart-Untertürkheim. Maybach continued with his innovations:

- a 6-cylinder/70 hp engine (1903–04)
- a pioneer aircraft engine: a high speed racing engine of 120 hp, with overhead inlet and exhaust valves and double ignition (1906)

DMG demoted him to an "Inventor's Office" causing him to leave the company again in 1907. DMG replaced him with Paul Daimler. That same year, the German Engineers Association (VDI) recognized Wilhelm Maybach as an honorary member.

Zeppelin engines (1908)

In 1900, Maybach had had his first contact with Count Ferdinand von Zeppelin who sought to improve the engines of the Zeppelin LZ1 airship. Maybach built some engines for him based on sketches of a 150 hp unit created by his son, Karl, while at DMG.

In 1908, Count Zeppelin attempted to sell his models *LZ3* and *LZ4* to the government. On 5 August, *LZ4* exploded against a row of trees after attempting an emergency landing when its engines failed. This was far from being the end for the airship project as 6.25 million goldmarks were raised in a donation campaign after the accident. Count Zeppelin founded the Luftschiffbau Zeppelin GmbH, the company that built the Zeppelin airships.

Maybach had to hold off joining the new company for a while as he was still in litigation with DMG so Karl took his place. On 23 March 1909, a deal was finally signed, creating an engine subsidiary to Luftschiffbau Zeppelin at Bissingen/Enz, in Württemberg. Wilhelm Maybach was Technical Assistant and Karl was Technical Manager. Their first designs reached 72 km/h (44.73873 mph).

Wilhelm Maybach moved his company to Friedrichshafen and renamed it *Luftfahrzeug-Motoren-GmbH*. Karl and Wilhem held 20% of the shares with an arrangement for Karl to inherit. They kept supplying *Zeppelin*, but worked on other airship engines too. In 1912, the company adopted the name Maybach-Motorenbau GmbH (Maybach Engine Construction Company). In 1916, they developed a 160 hp aircraft engine which sold 2000 units before the end of World War I. In 1916, Wilhelm Maybach was awarded an Honorary Doctorate by the Technical University of Stuttgart.

Maybach automobiles (1922)

After the First World War, the Versailles Treaty of 1919 prohibited airship production in Germany so Maybach turned to making high-speed diesel engines for naval and railroad use, and petrol engines for automobiles, but not complete automobiles.

Many of the small automakers in Germany built their own engines for cost reasons and only the Dutch Spyker company was interested in taking Maybach engines. Wilhelm Maybach turned down the contract because he could not agree to its conditions. Instead, he opted to build complete automobiles and the factory began to produce Maybach limousines in 1921.

The first model, the Maybach W3, was shown at the 1921 Automobile Exposition in Berlin and featured

- 6 cylinder engine
- 4-wheel brakes
- new transmission system
- maximum speed of 105 km/h (65 mph)

It was produced until 1928, selling 300 units, mostly with sedan bodies; the two-seat sport version was less successful. The Maybach W5 followed, with the top speed increased to 135 km/h (84 mph); 250 units sold in 1927 and 1929.

Next Maybach produced the V12 car:

- the first 12-cylinder German automobile
- lightweight aluminium engine based on his airship work
- light alloy pistons
- 7-litre capacity
- high torque and power - 150 hp (110 kW) at 2,800 rpm

Only a few dozen were sold due to the German postwar economic crisis. In 1930, its successor, the DS7-Zeppelin, also featured a 12 cylinder engine of 7 liters.

In August 1929, the Zeppelin LZ-127 used five Maybach-V12 petrol engines of 550 hp (410 kW) each.

Neither Wilhelm nor Karl owned a Maybach automobile. Wilhelm never even owned a car. "He, who created the basics for the modern automobilism, rarely utilized a car for his personal purposes. He walked or took the tram. Although he could have afforded one, he did not own a car."

Final years of DMG (1924–1929)

By 1924 DMG was suffering from the post war economic crisis and under pressure from the banks, it began the process that would result in a merger with Karl Benz's *Benz & Cie., Rheinische Gasmotorenfabrik Mannheim* in 1926 to form Daimler-Benz AG.

Wilhelm Maybach died at the age of 83 in Stuttgart on 29 December 1929.

Legacy

- Wilhelm Maybach was accepted into the Automotive Hall of Fame in 1996.
- Three technical Schools in Germany are named *Wilhelm Maybach*: Stuttgart, Heilbronn, and Berlin-Spandau.
- In 2002, Daimler AG began to produce models under the Maybach name.
- In 2005, in honor of his grandfather Karl and his great-grandfather Wilhelm, Ulrich Schmid-Maybach founded the Wilhelm and Karl Maybach Foundation.

See also

- Gottlieb Daimler
- Daimler Motoren Gesellschaft
- Mercedes 35 hp (1900)
- Mercedes Simplex
- Maybach
- Maybach Foundation
- Mercedes (car)
- Mercedes-Benz
- Karl Benz
- German inventors and discoverers

External links

- Maybach Manufaktur [1]
- A biography of Wilhelm Maybach (in German) [2]
- Maybach UK Site [3]
- Maybach Foundation [4]

Bibliography

- Niemann, Harry: Mythos Maybach, 4. Aufl., Stuttgart 2002
- Niemann, Harry: Maybach - der Vater des Mercedes, 3. Aufl., Stuttgart 2000
- Niemann, Harry: Wilhelm Maybach - König der Konstrukteure, 1. Aufl., Stuttgart 1995
- Rathke, Kurt: Wilhelm Maybach - Anbruch eines neuen Zeitalters, 1. Aufl., Friedrichshafen 1953
- Rauck, Max J.: Wilhelm Maybach: der grosse Automobilkonstrukteur. Baar 1979.
- Dokumentarfilm im Auftrag der Mercedes-Benz AG 1995: Wilhelm Maybach - König der Konstrukteure [5]

Hildebrand & Wolfmüller

Manufacturer	Hildebrand & Wolfmüller
Production	1894–1897
Engine	1489 cc (90.9 cu in) two-cylinder water cooled four-stroke, surface carburetor
Bore / Stroke	90 × 117 mm (3.5 × 4.6 in)
Top speed	28 mph (45 km/h)
Power	2.5 bhp (1.9 kW) @ 240 rpm
Ignition type	Hot tube
Transmission	Direct drive via connecting rods
Frame type	Steel tubular
Brakes	spoon brake, friction against front tire
Tires	pneumatic, front 26 in (66 cm), rear 22 in (56 cm)
Weight	110 lb (50 kg) (dry)

The **Hildebrand & Wolfmüller** was the world's first production motorcycle. Heinrich and Wilhelm Hidebrand were steam-engine engineers before Alois Wolfmüller agreed to finance them to produce their internal combustion *Motorrad* in Munich in 1894.

Alternate claims

The Hildebrand & Wolfmüller is credited as the world first because other possible claimants tend to be based on a bicycle chassis (e.g. de Dion-Bouton and Orient Aster, and the E. R. Thomas) or were never put into production. Or both, e.g. Gottlieb Daimler's Reitwagen of 1885 was a one-off test-bed for an experimental engine in a bicycle chassis. The Felix Millet designed 'Motocyclette,' of 1893 used an aviation-style radial five-cylinder engine, but never went into mass-production.

Gottlieb Daimler is sometimes known as the "Father of the Motorcycle"Wikipedia:Avoid weasel words but supportersWikipedia:Avoid weasel words of H & M point out that his Einspur "boneshaker" motor bike was actually a "hybrid" motor-driven bicycle with a wooden bicycle frame, and wooden wheels.[*citation needed*]

Mechanical Details

The motorcycle featured a water-cooled engine (the coolant tank/radiator of which is prominent over and around the rear wheel) mounted in a purpose-designed tubular frame. The rear wheel was directly driven from the connecting rods (a similar arrangement to that of steam locomotives). There was no flywheel other than the rear wheel, and it needed heavy rubber bands to provide the return impulse.

The Hildebrand & Wolfmüller patent of 20 January 1894, No. 78553 describes a 1489 cc (90.9 cu in) two-cylinder, four-stroke engine, with a bore and stroke of 90 × 117 mm (3.5 × 4.6 in). It produced 1.9 kW (2.5 bhp) @ 240 rpm propelling a weight of 50 kg (110 lb) up to a maximum speed of 45 km/h (28 mph).

Examples exist today in the Deutsches Zweirad- und NSU-Museum in Neckarsulm, Germany, the Science Museum in London, The Henry Ford in Detroit, Michigan, the Wells Auto Museum in Wells, Maine, and the Museum Lalu Lintas in Surabaya, Indonesia.

Production run

Several hundred examples of this motorcycles were built but with a high initial purchase price and fierce competition from improving designs (this model was entirely "run and jump" with neither clutch nor pedals) it is not thought to have been a great commercial success. The Hildebrand & Wolfmüller factory closed in 1919 after WWI.

External links

- Hildebrand and Wolfmüller restored motorcycle [1]

Construction and Design

Motorcycle construction

Motorcycle construction is the engineering, manufacturing, and assembly of components and systems for a motorcycle which results in the desired performance, cost and aesthetics. Construction of modern motorcycles has standardized on the key components listed below.

Chassis

The chassis of a motorcycle includes the frame and suspension, along with the front forks, of the vehicle.

Frame

Main article: Motorcycle frame

The frame is typically made from welded aluminium or steel (or alloy) struts, with the rear suspension being an integral component in the design. Carbon fibre and titanium are used in a few very expensive custom frames.

The frame includes the head tube that holds the front fork and allows it to pivot. Some motorcycles include the engine as a load-bearing (or *stressed*) member; this has been used all through motorcycle history but is now becoming more common.

Oil-in-Frame (OIF) chassis, where the lubricating oil is stored in the frame of the motorcycle, was used for Vincent motorcycles of the 1950s, and for a while during the 1970s on some NVT British motorcycles. It was widely unpopular and generally regarded as a bad idea at the time. Today it is a used on some "thumpers" (single-cylinder four-strokes) that usually have dry-sump lubrication requiring an external oil tank. It has since gained some cachet in the modern custom bike world too because of the space savings it can afford and the reference to an earlier era.

Buell motorcycles employ a similar design — the oil is held in the swingarm, while the fuel is held in the frame.

Suspension

Main article: Suspension (motorcycle)

Modern designs have the two wheels of a motorcycle connected to the chassis by a suspension arrangement, however 'chopper' style motorcycles often elect to forgo rear suspension, using a rigid frame.

The front suspension is usually built into the front fork and may consist of telescoping tubes called fork tubes which contain the suspension inside or some multibar linkage that incorporate the suspension externally.

The rear suspension supports the *swingarm*, which is attached via the *swingarm pivot bolt* to the frame and holds the axle of the rear wheel. The rear suspension can consist of several shock arrangements:

- Dual shocks, which are placed at the far ends of the swingarm
- Traditional monoshock, which is placed at the front of the swingarm, above the swingarm pivot bolt
- Softail style suspension, where the shock absorbers are mounted horizontally in front of the swingarm, below the swingarm pivot bolt and operate in extension.

Front fork

Main article: Motorcycle fork

A motorcycle fork is the portion of a motorcycle that holds the front wheel and allows one to steer. For handling, the front fork is the most critical part of a motorcycle. The combination of rake and trail determines how stable the motorcycle is.

A fork generally consists of two fork tubes (sometimes also referred to as forks), which hold the front wheel axle, and a triple tree, which connects the fork tubes and the handlebars to the frame with a pivot that allows for steering.

Engine

Main article: Motorcycle engine

Almost all commercially available motorcycles are driven by conventional gasoline internal combustion engines, but some small scooter-type models use an electric motor, and a very small number of diesel models exist (e.g., the USMC M1030 M1 version of the Kawasaki KLR650 and the Dutch-produced Track T-800CDI).

The displacement is defined as the total volume of air/fuel mixture an engine can draw in during one complete engine cycle. In a piston engine, this is the volume that is swept as the pistons are moved from top dead centre to bottom dead centre. To the layperson this is the "size" of the engine. Motorcycle engines range from less than 50 cc (cubic centimetres), commonly found in many small scooters, to 5735 cc, a Chevrolet V8 engine, currently used by Boss Hoss in its cruiser style motorcycle.

Opposed twin engine on a Ural

Motorcycles have mostly, but not exclusively, been produced with one to four cylinders, and designers have tried virtually every imaginable layout. The most common engine configurations today are the single and twin, the V-twin, the opposed twin (or boxer), and the in-line triple and in-line four. A number of others designs have reached mass production, including the V-4, the flat 6-cylinder, the flat 4-cylinder, the in-line 6-cylinder, and the Wankel engine. Exotic engines, such as a radial piston engine, sometimes appear in custom built motorcycles, though two firms Megola and Redrup put radial engined motorcycles into production.

A Sokół 1000 V-twin engine

Engines with more cylinders for the same displacement feel smoother to ride. Engines with fewer cylinders are cheaper, lighter, and easier to maintain. Liquid-cooled motorcycles have a radiator which is the primary way their heat is dispersed. Coolant or oil is constantly circulated between this radiator and the cylinder when the engine is running. Air-cooled motorcycles rely on air blowing past fins on the engine case to disperse heat. Liquid cooled motorcycles have the potential for greater power at a given displacement, tighter tolerances, and longer operating life, whereas air cooled motorcycles are potentially cheaper to purchase, less mechanically complex and lighter weight.

An air cooled engine contracts and expands with its wider temperature range, requiring looser tolerances, and giving shorter engine life. The temperature range of an air cooled two stroke is even more extreme and component life even shorter than in an air cooled four stroke.

As applied to motorcycles, two-stroke engines have some advantages over equivalent four-strokes: they are lighter, mechanically much simpler, and produce more power when operating at their best. But four-stroke engines are cleaner, more reliable, and deliver power over a much broader range of engine speeds. In developed countries, two-stroke road-bikes are rare, because—in addition to the reasons above—modifying them to meet contemporary emissions standards is prohibitively expensive. Almost all modern two-strokes are single-cylinder, liquid-cooled, and under 600 cc.

In November 2006, the Dutch company E.V.A. Products BV Holland announced that its diesel-powered motorcycle, the Track T-800CDI, achieved production status. The Track T-800CDI uses a 800 cc three-cylinder Daimler Chrysler diesel engine. Other manufacturers, including Royal Enfield, had been producing diesel-powered bikes since at least the 1980s. Also, Intelligent Energy, a British alternative-fuel company, is developing a motorcycle powered by a detachable hydrogen-powered fuel cell, which it calls an Emissions Neutral Vehicle (ENV). According to reports, the vehicle can sustain speeds of 50 mph (80 km/h) while making virtually no noise, and can run for up to four hours without refueling.

Transmission

The transmission on this 1921 ABC motorcycle is located behind the engine and shifts by a long hand-operated lever on its right side.

Modern motorcycles (excepting scooters) all change gears (of which they will increasingly have five or six) by foot lever. The weight of the largest touring motorcycles (sometimes in excess of 360 kg or 800 lbs) is such that they cannot effectively be pushed backwards by a seated rider, and they are fitted with a reverse gear as standard. In some cases, including the Honda Gold Wing and BMW K1200LT, this is not really a reverse gear, but a feature of the starter motor which when reversed, performs the same function. In earlier times pre WWII, hand-operated gear changes were common, a lever was provided to the side the fuel tank. British and many other motorcycles after WWII used a lever on the right but today gear-changing is standardised on a foot-operated lever to the left.

All two-wheelers use a sequential gearbox. On a motorcycle either first or second gear can be selected from neutral, but higher gears may only be accessed in order - it is not possible to shift from second gear to fourth gear without shifting through third gear. A five-speed of this configuration would be known as "one down, four up" because of the placement of the gears with relation to neutral. Neutral is to be found "half a click" away from first and second gears, so shifting directly between the two gears can be made in a single movement.

Traditional scooters still have manual gear-changing by a twist grip on the left hand side of the handlebar, with a clutch on a lever also rotating. Increasingly they may be fitted with a continuously variable transmission or CVT instead, a kind of automatic transmission (as once used in the DAF car) that is stepless. Step-through motorcycles often have a three-speed foot change, but the clutch is automatic.

The clutch is typically an arrangement of plates stacked in alternating fashion, one geared on the inside to the engine and the next geared on the outside to the transmission input shaft. Whether wet (rotating in engine oil) or dry, the plates are squeezed together by a spring, causing friction build up between the plates until they rotate as a single unit, driving the transmission directly. A lever on the handlebar exploits mechanical advantage through a cable or hydraulic arrangement to release the clutch spring, allowing the engine to freewheel with respect to the transmission.

Final drive

Power transfer from the gearbox to the rear wheel is accomplished by different methods.

A shaft final drive is housed within a rear swingarm of a BMW R1200GS

Chain drive uses sprockets and a roller chain, which requires both lubrication and adjustment for elongation (stretch) that occurs through wear. The lubricant is subject to being thrown off the fast-moving chain and results in grime and dirt build up. Chains do deteriorate, and excessive wear on the front and rear sprockets can be dangerous. In a chain drive the power is transmitted into the real wheel via a cush drive. Virtually all high performance racing motorcycles use chain drive.

A belt drive is still subject to stretch but operates very quietly, cleanly, and efficiently. However, belt drives are limited in the amount of power they can transmit. A toothed belt is frequently used.

A shaft drive is usually completely enclosed; the visual cue is a tube extending from the rear of the transmission to a bell housing on the rear wheel. Inside the bell housing a bevelled gear on the shaft mates with another on the wheel mount. This arrangement is superior in terms of noise and cleanliness and is virtually maintenance free, with the exception of occasional fluid changes. However, the additional gearsets are a source of power loss and added weight. A shaft-equipped motorcycle may also be susceptible to shaft effect.

Wheels

The wheel rims are usually steel or aluminium (generally with steel spokes and an aluminium hub) or mag-type cast or machined aluminium. At one time, motorcycles used spoke wheels built up from separate components, but, except for dirtbikes, one-piece wheels are more common now. Performance racing motorcycles often use carbon-fibre wheels, but the expense of these wheels is prohibitively high for general usage.

Wire wheels have a central hub connected to the rim of the wheel via spokes made of wire. These spokes are generally quite solid and will not easily bend as would typical wire cord. Nevertheless, they mechanically function as wires under tension, holding the rim true and providing strength to the wheel. Cast magnesium disks, produced by one-step hot forging from magnesium alloys ZK60 and MA-14, are also used for many motorcycle wheels.

Tires

Main article: Motorcycle tyres

Motorcycles mainly use pneumatic tires. However, in some cases where punctures are common (some enduros), the tyres are filled with a "mousse" which is unpunctureable. Both types of tyre come in many configurations. The most important characteristic of any tyre is the contact patch, the small area that is in contact with the road surface while riding. There are tyres designed for dirtbikes, touring, sport and cruiser bikes.

Dirtbike tyres have knobbly, deep treads for maximum grip on loose dirt, mud, or gravel; such tyres tend to be less stable on paved surfaces. Touring tyres are usually made of harder rubber for greater durability. They may last longer, but they tend to provide less outright grip than sports tyres at optimal operating temperatures. The payoff is that touring tyres typically offer more grip at lower temperatures, meaning they can be more suitable for riding in cold or winter conditions whereas a sport tyre may never reach the optimal operating temperature.

Sport/performance tyres provide amazing grip but may last 1,000 miles (1,600 km) or less. Cruiser and "sport touring" tyres try to find the best compromise between grip and durability. There is also a type of tyre developed specifically for racing. These tyres offer the highest of levels of grip for cornering. Because of the high temperatures at which these tyres typically operate, use on the street is unsafe because the tyres will typically not reach optimum temperature before a rider arrives, thus providing almost no grip *en route*. In racing situations, racing tyres would normally be brought up to temperature in advance by the use of tyre warmers.

Brakes

Front disk brakes with an ABS sensor ring on a BMW R1200RT

There are generally two independent brakes on a motorcycle, one set on the front wheel and one on the rear. However, some models have "linked brakes" whereby both can be applied at the same time using only one control.

Front brakes are generally much more effective than rear brakes: roughly two thirds of stopping power comes from the front brake—mainly as a result of weight transfer being much more pronounced compared to longer or lower vehicles, because of the motorcycle's short wheelbase relative to its center of mass height. This can result in brake dive.

Brakes can either be drum or disc based, with disc brakes being more common on large, modern or more expensive motorcycles for their far superior stopping power, particularly in wet conditions. There are many brake-performance-enhancing aftermarket parts available for most motorcycles, including brake pads of varying compounds and steel-braided brake lines.

In 1981, BMW introduced an antilock braking system (ABS) on a motorcycle. Other manufacturers have since also adopted this technology, although Harley Davidson only offers it on some police motorcycles and not on civilian motorcycles. ABS is normally found on motorcycles of 500 cc or greater engine capacity, although it is available on motor scooters down to 49 cc.

Instruments

Most road motorcycles have an instrument panel, usually consisting of speedometer, odometer and tachometer. Fuel gauges are becoming more common, but traditionally a reserve tank arrangement is used with a petcock (petrol tap) on the side of the motorcycle allowing the rider to switch to a reserve fuel supply when the main fuel supply is exhausted. There is not actually a separate reserve tank: The intake for the petcock has two pipes, one extending higher into the fuel tank than the other. When fuel no longer covers the longer pipe the engine will lose power/splutter and the rider switches the petcock to the "reserve" setting, which accesses the shorter pipe. Riders whose bikes lack a fuel gauge (most machines prior to the past few years) usually learn how far they can go with a full tank of fuel, and then use a trip meter if available to judge when they must refill the tank.

See also

- Bicycle and motorcycle dynamics
- Motorcycle accessories
- Motorcycle saddle
- Shaft effect

External links

- How Motorcycles Work [1] by Bill Harris
- Motorcycle Glossary [2] - definitions of motorcycle terms

Motorcycle design

Motorcycle design can be described as activities that define the appearance, function and engineering of motorcycles.

Professionally it is a branch of industrial design, similar to automotive design using identical techniques and methodology, but confined by a set of conventions about what is acceptable to the buying public. These conventions have been defined by the acceptance of the industry and media as a whole to the assumption that the public will only purchase machines that bear more than a passing resemblance to competition machines of whatever kind. In some large OEM motorcycle manufacturers, the term designer can also be applied to the project leader or chief engineer charged with laying down the principle architecture of the vehicle. In recent years it has also become associated with custom or "chopper" builder culture.

Motivations

In general, motorcycle design appears to follows standard industrial doctrine of designing products that fulfill market demands, satisfy engineering and economic requirements to produce safe and profitable vehicles. But in reality these demands are engineered by a number of vested interests starting with the sporting promoters, the motorcycling press and ending with the motorcycle manufacturers themselves.

The market has been educated by the media and the industry to think that the present state of design development comes from a gradual development of the motorcycle from its original concept as a motorised bicycle, discarding on the way any developments that prove to be inherently unsafe or unsaleable. But this is totally untrue. In the 1950s interest in various forms of streamlining developed and by 1957 all the leading manufacturers that competed in road racing were using a form of full streamlining that covered the front wheel. Some were developing new and radical designs that would enclose the rider. But all this progress was brought to a halt by the governing body of motorcycle sport (the FIM) and other commercial interests. These were mainly those who thought the sport might lose money and those who were reluctant to spend on wind tunnel research and new designs. It was claimed that many of the new designs were unsafe but in reality many of the most radical designs were in fact safer, even in those early days. Nevertheless a ban was imposed on any design that might enclose the wheels or the rider.

Thus enforcing on motorcycle design the exposed vulnerability of the rider and machine that had already cost so many lives. It is obvious that having to design all the brake, suspension and steering components to aesthetically look good before they can be used will retard progress. Then there is the protection afforded by a smooth, rounded streamline shell to the rider and pedestrian in a collision. When the emphasis on safety and crash testing for cars arrived, the design of motorcycles was and still is in a straitjacket which allows the manufacturers to conveniently abrogate their responsibility for any effort to protect the rider. The possibility of fitting new safety devices like those that are now used in cars was there then and still is especially in designs such as the NSU flying hammock. Due to the highly emotive and often symbolic nature of motorcycles as social and cultural instruments, the practice of designing one has now become just as much an exercise in intuitive human psychology as rendering the relevant observations into metal and plastic.

Professional Design

Professional motorcycle designers almost always hold degrees in industrial design, industrial design engineering or similar, and have training in styling, modeling, as well as knowledge in aspects of technology associated with single track vehicles. Although no degree as a specialisation exists per se, the majority of candidates graduate through colleges and universities with established transportation design courses, and are trained as automotive designers.

Most OEM motorcycle manufacturers, such as Honda, Suzuki, Kawasaki, BMW, Ducati, Piaggio and others have in-house design studios dedicated to this purpose, while others such as Yamaha and KTM depend on specialised independent design consultancies.

Methodology

Design and Engineering Relationships

Due to the high importance of mechanical components or even exposed engines to motorcycle styling, almost always designers will have a greater sensitivity and awareness to engineering than will typical car designers. In OEM situations, large teams of professional engineers and specialists will collaborate on each project development, allowing the designer to focus on the more intangible or subjective aspects of design, such as styling, human-machine interface psychology, and market and cultural relationships. In other matters such as pure mechanical ergonomics (such as seat height, handlebar placement, etc.), or basic layout (the location of major components, storage, etc.) there is usually considerable overlap between the designer and engineer. The designer will nominally approach each problem from a human interface, or "feel" or "irrational" point of view (example : "Does this material feel cold or warm, and is this feeling appropriate to this vehicle's target consumer?"), while the engineer will attack each problem with the "rational" or clinical approach of empirically weighing the cause and effect of each design decision against the project's technical and economic design targets (example : "Can this material be moulded into the designer's desired shape? Will that be too expensive to produce?")

Research and Concept Design

In OEM motorcycle design, the normal procedure of developing a new motorcycle involves the same steps in other professional design disciplines : identifying a target consumer, researching them to identify benchmarks and project targets, then proposing concept directions in a written form known as a Design Brief or QFD. From this point, artwork is developed to visually communicate the designer's ideas. These are presented in 2Db drawing or illustrated form, from which a winning direction is down selected for further development. Once a satisfactory design is established on paper (the term paper is a generalization that can include traditional hand renderings, digital artwork or CAD drawings), then full scale modeling begins to realise the design in tangible 3D form.

Styling

Often used as an interchangeable term with "design", styling is in fact just one component of the design process. Typically, styling is developed through sketches, renderings and illustrations then realised in 3D form using automotive styling clay, specialised industrial modeling foams such as Sibatool, Renshape or Epiwood, or in increasingly limited cases plaster or body filler. As the most subjective part of the design process, the various members of the development team must depend heavily on the judgment, skill and experience of the appointed designer to create an appropriate look.

The most misunderstood element and the most dangerous to the success of a product, is the idea that team members should evaluate the design based on personal tastes or preferences. Industrial design is not an art form, but a focused creative expression using the scientific data and analysis in the Design Brief and QFD as ultimate guidelines. The target user, their needs and tastes should be reflected in the final design, not necessarily exclusively those of the design team. Of course, many complex variables such as the OEM brand identity, past successes and failures, and whimsical trends often skew or distort styling decisions. In instances where the factors are overwhelming, OEM's may err on the side of cautious conservative design.

Parallel Development

Because of the need to reduce development time and costs, the "styling" design model is usually developed in parallel with the engineering 3D design. While there is an increasing amount of digital design input in the modern OEM design process, nearly all major motorcycle manufacturers still rely on full scale clay models to render the master style model, then scan and import the styling surfaces into suitable 3D software packages (Alias, CATIA, ISEM Surf) for integration into the 3D engineering CAD platform (CATIA, ProEngineer, etc.). Once combined, the design team can virtually refine the motorcycle by optimising component assembly, checking for any undesirable interferences between parts, and predict and eliminate possible engineering problems. Typically, designers and engineers will have the greatest number of conflicts during this phase of development, as designers will fight to maintain the original styling and design of the clay model and artwork into the production vehicle, while the engineer will eliminate all problems in the most efficient manner possible. The success of the final product depends heavily on the level of cooperation between these often conflicting needs.

Amateur & Specialists

Custom Builders

In recent years, largely due to the popularity of television programs like *Orange County Chopper* and *Biker Build-off*, the building of one of a kind "chopper" or "cruiser" type motorcycles has become more mainstream, leading to a flourishing builder industry. As a whole, these vehicles are not designed in the professional sense, but rather crafted by hand by metal workers and artisans using traditional skills. The resulting vehicles tend to be very elaborate, expensive and difficult or impossible to reproduce in mass production, but are highly valued for the same reasons.

Among custom motorcycle culture, certain names have become famous for their creations and have led to mainstream acceptance of previously unacceptable design solutions such as extreme ergonomics, totally rigid rear wheels without the benefit of suspension, minimal lighting and limited ground clearance for cornering. These design characteristics are purely emotional in nature, being led by styling and image rather than technical or performance considerations.

"Specials"

Custom and Specials motorcycles are similar to the above but tend to be super sport type motorcycles, or at least high performance based, using as many special add on parts, one of a kind or limited series frames, racing wheels and parts or hand made components to maximise performance. While modifying motorcycles is an activity as old as the motorcycle itself, the "special" culture or "streetfighter" began to flourish in the mid 1970's as a response the myriad of high performance Japanese motorcycles then available, but whose power far exceeded their handling. Individuals would chose pre manufactured parts from catalogs or from other bikes and redesign their particular machine to suit their desires. In general this activity is limited to one of a kind vehicles and as with custom motorcycles, uses very little genuine engineering or design methodology, although some small scale manufacturers exist who make limited runs of a given model. In some cases, these tiny specialists were successful enough to grow into full scale OEM companies such as the Buell Motorcycle Company and Bimota of Italy.

References

- Cocco, G.; *Motorcycle Design and Technology*, 1999, Italy, ISBN 88-7911-189-2
- Heskett, J.; J. Heskett, 1980, Great Britain, ISBN 0-500-20181-1
- Royal College of Art, *Moving Objects*, Great Britain, ISBN 0-9536281-0-8

External links

- Motorcycle Design [1]
- UMEA Institute of Design [2]

Types of Motorcyles

Types of motorcycles

A Yamaha Zuma scooter, Kawasaki Vulcan cruiser, and Ducati 998 and Kawasaki Ninja sport bikes.

A vintage Yamaha sport bike and a Vespa scooter.

US Secret Service motor officer on a 250 cc (15 cu in) Honda Nighthawk standard at the Argentine embassy to the US.

There are many systems for classifying **types of motorcycles**, describing how the motorcycles are put to use, or the designer's intent, or some combination of the two. Six main categories are widely recognized: cruiser, sport, touring, standard, dual-purpose, and dirt bike. Sometimes sport touring motorcycles are recognized as a seventh category, and strong lines are sometimes drawn between motorcycles and their smaller cousins, mopeds, scooters and underbones. Other classification schemes include them as types of motorcycles. There is no universal system for classifying all types of motorcycles. There are strict classification systems enforced by competitive motorcycle sport sanctioning bodies, or by certain legal jurisdictions for motorcycle registration, emissions, road traffic safety rules or motorcyclist licensing. There are also informal classifications or nicknames used by manufacturers, riders, and the motorcycling media.

In India and Pakistan, motorcycles are more popular than cars as means of transport due to low operating and ownership cost. Typical displacements are small 50–450 cc (3.1–27 cu in), resulting in good fuel efficiency.

Street

Road motorcycles are motorcycles designed for being ridden on paved roads. They feature smooth tires with a light tread pattern and engines generally in the 125 cc (7.6 cu in) and over range. Most are capable of speeds up to 100 mph (160 km/h), and many of speeds in excess of 125 mph (201 km/h).

Cruiser

Main article: Cruiser (motorcycle)

Cruisers are styled after American machines from the 1930s to the early 1960s, such as those made by Harley-Davidson, Indian, and Excelsior-Henderson. Harley-Davidsons largely define the cruiser category, and large displacement V-twin engines are the norm, although other engine configurations and small to medium displacements also exist. Their engines are tuned for low end torque, making them less demanding to ride because it is not necessary to shift as frequently to accelerate or maintain control.

Harley-Davidson cruisers.

The riding position places the feet forward and the hands are up relatively high, so that the spine is erect or leaning back slightly. At low to moderate speeds cruisers are more comfortable than other styles, but riding for long periods at freeway speeds can lead to fatigue from pulling back on the handlebars to resist the force of the wind against the rider's chest. Cruisers have limited cornering ability due to a lack of ground clearance.

Choppers are a type of cruiser. Choppers are often custom projects that result in a bike modified to suit the owner's ideals, and as such are a source of pride and accomplishment. Cruisers are sometimes called custom even in the absence of aftermarket modifications (see Custom (motorcycle)). **Power cruiser** is a name used to distinguish bikes in this class that have significantly more engine output, around 80–100 hp (60–75 kW) as opposed to about 50–70 hp (37–52 kW). They often come with upgraded brakes and suspension, better ground clearance, and premium surface finishes, as well as more exotic or non-traditional styling.

Sport bike

Main article: Sport bike

A Suzuki GSX-R at Deals Gap.

Sport bikes emphasize speed, acceleration, braking, and cornering on paved roads, typically at the expense of comfort and fuel economy in comparison to less specialized motorcycles. Because of this, there are certain design elements that most motorcycles of this type will share. Sport bikes have comparatively high performance engines resting inside a lightweight frame. Inline-four engines dominate the sport bike category, with V-twins having a significant presence, and nearly every other engine configuration appearing in small numbers at one time or another. The combination of these elements helps maintain structural integrity and chassis rigidity. Braking systems combine higher performance brake pads and multi-piston calipers that clamp onto oversized vented rotors. Suspension systems are advanced in terms of adjustments and materials for increased stability and durability. Most sport bikes have fairings, often completely enclosing the engine, and having windscreens that effectively deflect the air at very high speeds, or at least reduce overall drag.

Sport bikes have high foot pegs, which position the legs closer to the body, to improve ground clearance when cornering, and a long reach to the hand controls, which positions the body and center of gravity forward, above the fuel tank. The rider leans forward into the wind, the force of which can comfortably support the rider's weight at speeds near 100 mph (160 km/h), but at lower speeds leaves too much weight on the arms and wrists, causing fatigue.

Streetfighters are derived from sport bikes, originally being customized sport bikes with the fairings removed and higher handlebars replacing the low clip on handlebars. Since the 1990s, factory streetfighters have been produced. As with naked bike and muscle bike (below), the name streetfigher is used to help clarify the middle ground occupied by designs that blend elements of both sport bikes and standards.

Touring

Main article: Touring motorcycle

Honda Gold Wing GL1800 touring motorcycle

Although any motorcycle can be equipped and used for touring, touring motorcycles are meant to excel at covering long-distances. They have large displacement engines, fairings and screens that offer a good weather and wind protection, large capacity fuel tanks for long ranges between fill-ups, and a relaxed, upright seating position. Passenger accommodation is excellent and expansive luggage space is the norm for this class. Large touring bikes are sometimes called **dressers**, especially those based on a cruiser platform. Such bikes can have wet weights of 850–900 lb (390–410 kg) and top 1300–1400 lb (590–640 kg) fully loaded with a rider, passenger, and gear.

A BMW R1100RS sport-touring motorcycle.

Sport touring motorcycles combine attributes of sport bikes and touring motorcycles. The rider posture is less extreme than a sport bike, giving greater long-distance comfort. Accommodation for a passenger is superior to a sport bike as well, along with luggage capacity. Being lighter, at 550–720 lb (250–330 kg) wet, than a pure touring bike and often having racier engines, suspensions and brakes, sport tourers corner better and are more at home being aggressively ridden on curvy canyon roads.

Standard

The Ducati Monster 696 naked bike

Standards are versatile, general purpose street motorcycles. They are recognized primarily by their upright riding position, partway between the reclining posture of the cruisers and the forward leaning sport bikes. Foot pegs are below the rider and handlebars are high enough to not force the rider to reach far forward, placing the shoulders above the hips in a natural position. Standards are often recommended to beginning motorcyclists due to their flexibility, relatively low cost, and moderate engines.

Standards usually do not come with fairings or windscreens, or if they have them, they are relatively small. Standard is often a synonym for **naked bike**, a term that became popular in the 1990s in response to the proliferation of fully-faired sport bikes. The standard seemed to have disappeared, fueling nostalgia for the return of the UJM, or Universal Japanese motorcycle. UJMs were admired for their simplicity, quality and versatility.

Muscle bike is a nickname for a type, derived from either a standard or sport bike design, that puts a disproportionately high priority on engine power.

Dual-sport

Main article: Dual-sport motorcycle

Dual-sports, sometimes written dual-purpose, are street legal machines that are also designed to enter off-road situations. Typically based on a dirt bike chassis, they have added lights, mirrors, signals, and instruments that allow them to be licensed for public roads. They are higher than other street bikes, with a high center of gravity and tall seat height, allowing good suspension travel for rough ground.

A BMW R1200GS dual-sport motorcycle.

Adventure-touring motorcycles are dual sports better adapted for long distance road travel with limited off-road excursions. Their weight and other features precludes them from tackling the extremes of off-road riding.

Supermoto motorcycles evolved from motocross and enduro machines. Supermoto competitions are usually held over a course that mixes tarmac (road racing) and off-road (motocross).sections. This increasingly popular type of motorcycle is often a dual-sport that has been fitted by the manufacturer with smaller rims and road tires. Supermotos are quickly gaining popularity as street bikes due to their combination of light weight, durability, relatively low cost, and sporty handling. A wide variety of supermoto machines have become available recently, such as the large Ducati Hypermotard and KTM 990SM, and smaller Honda CRF230M, Kawasaki KLX250SF, and Yamaha WR250X.

Scooters, underbones, and mopeds

Scooter engine sizes range smaller than motorcycles, 50–650 cc (3.1–40 cu in), and have all-enclosing bodywork that makes them cleaner and quieter than motorcycles, as well as having more built-in storage space. Automatic clutches and continuously variable transmissions (CVT) make them easier to learn and to ride. Scooters usually have smaller wheels than motorcycles. Scooters usually have the engine as part of the swingarm, so that their engines travel up and down with the suspension.

Underbones are small-displacement motorcycle with a step-through frame, descendants of the original Honda Super Cub. They are differentiated from scooters by their larger wheels and their use of footpegs instead of a floorboard. They often feature a gear shifter with an automatic clutch.

The moped used to be a hybrid of the bicycle and the motorcycle, equipped with a small engine (usually a small two-stroke engine up to 50 cc, but occasionally an electric motor) and a bicycle drivetrain, and motive power can be supplied by the engine, the rider, or both.

In many localities, mopeds are subject to less stringent licensing than bikes with larger engines and are popular as very cheap motorbikes, with the pedals seeing next to no use. Mopeds were very popular in the United States during the late 1970s and early 1980s, but their popularity has fallen off sharply since the mid 1980s. In response to rising fuel prices U.S. scooter and moped ridership saw a resurgence. Sales of motorcycles and scooters declined 43.2% in 2009, and continued to decrease in the first quarter of 2010, with scooter sales doing worst, down 13.3% compared to a 4.6% drop for all two wheelers.

Other types of small motorcycles include the monkey bike, welbike, and minibike.

Off-road

There are several different types of off-road motorcycles, also known as **dirt bikes**, designed and specialised for specific functions. For off-road use they typically, when compared to road going motorcycles, light weight, long suspension travel and high ground clearance, simple, rugged construction with little bodywork and no fairing for easy recovery after spills, and large wheels with knobby tires, often clamped to the rim with a rim lock.

A KTM dirt bike with a paddle tire.

There are specialized motorcycles are for a variety of off-road motorcycle sports:

- Motocross — A uniquely designed track of a variety of different obstacles where people compete to win the race. The motorcycles have a less than 2 gallon tank which makes them light. Their precise suspension travel allows riders to fly over jumps at high speeds. There are two different classifications of motocross classes. 250cc are usually two-stroke and 450cc are usually four-stroke. A rider chooses his/her bike depending on the preferences they prefer.
- Rally raid, or **Rallies** — long distance racing, typically through deserts for long distances. Road legal machine (like enduro) but with significantly more fuel. Capacities tend to be larger, around 450 cc to 660 cc (two or four stroke), an upper limit is often imposed for rider safety.

- Trials — An extremely specialized form of competition focused on balancing skills and precision rather than speed. Thus low weight and quick power is the priority leading to small (125 cc to 300 cc) engines, often two strokes being used. Seats are unnecessary and affect the center of gravity so they are not installed (sometime they are jokingly referred to as banana bikes due to the lack of a seat). Fuel is kept to a minimum so range is very limited.
- Track racing — High-speed oval racing, typically with no brakes, no suspension, at most two gears, fueled by methanol (not road legal machines).

Trials bikes have no seat.

Other types

There are specialty motorcycles adapted to job functions, like police motorcycles, motorcycle ambulances, dernys for use in track cycling events, and motorcycles used for towing cars. Feet forwards motorcycles are an experimental configuration. While motorcycles typically have two wheels, a tricycle or sidecar outfit with three wheels is usually called a motorcycle, or at least treated as one for purposes of registration or licensing. Early cyclecars, with four wheels, were constructed more like motorcycles than cars, and were sometimes treated as a kind of motorcycle.

See also

- Motorcycling
- Motorcycle racing
- Concept vehicle

Electric motorcycles and scooters

Electric motorcycles and scooters are vehicles with two or three wheels that use electric motors to attain locomotion.

Electric motorcycle of Zero Motorcycles

Increasingly accepted as capable, even appealing, forms of transportation, particularly in densely populated urban areas, electric two-wheel vehicles is a category that includes electric bicycles, electric kick scooters, electric motorcycles, and electric scooters. According to a recent report from Pike Research, worldwide sales of electric two-wheel vehicles (E2WVs) are expected to increase at a compound annual growth rate (CAGR) of 9.4% through 2016.

History

Detail: Electric motor and Lithium-Ion battery Z-Force

Main article: History of electric motorcycles and scooters

- **Late 1860s**: Earliest references to electric motorcycles can be found in patents.
- **1911**: Electric motorcycle available according to early Popular Mechanics article.
- **2007**: Li-Ion cell-powered Killacycle makes new quarter mile (400-metre) record of 7.824 seconds and 168 mph (270 km/h) in Phoenix, AZ, US at AHDRA 2007.

E-max electric scooter

Power source

Generally, the source of power for the electric motor has been batteries, but development in fuel cell technology has created several prototypes. Some examples are: the ENV from Intelligent Energy, Honda's scooter using the Honda FC Stack, and the Yamaha FC-AQEL. Also, petroleum hybrid-electric motorcycles are under development. Some examples are the Ecycle, and Yamaha's Gen-RYU.

Yamaha FC Aqel

Advantages and disadvantages

Electric motorcycles and scooters are rising in popularity because of higher gasoline prices. Battery technology is gradually improving making this form of transportation more practical.

Advantages of electric over gasoline power:

Stylish Eped City, Epeds Uk Ltd

1. The fuel costs for electric power are approximately 25% the cost of gasoline power (US, mid-2008; see Electric car, "Running costs" for the calculation)
2. Nearly silent
3. The Libert-E Xero has removable lithium ion batteries that can be charged using any 120v outlet
4. Environmental friendly (no exhausted gases at point of use)
5. Carbon tax and vehicle registration tax exemption in some countries
6. No parking/congestion charges in some countries
7. No road tax in some countries
8. Using grid power to charge batteries causes less pollution than gasoline scooters; (MIT wheel to well analysis of EVs [1]) the amount of emissions and residues caused depends on the sources of the electricity used
9. No trips needed to a gas station—can be recharged at home or in charging stations. But charging or battery swapping in service stations, when needed, are faster
10. It can be used in a V2G system
11. Lower maintenance costs and fewer maintenance activities
12. Can be ridden indoors
13. More affordable than electric cars
14. Many models dispense with a transmission or the need to shift gears, simplifying operation
15. Instant on / no warm-up time
16. Much lower amount of heat given off by motor than is typical for some internal combustion motorcycle engines

Disadvantages:

Electric scooters (and an electric bicycle) parked in Chengdu, China

1. Up front costs are higher than for a comparable gasoline powered motorcycle or scooter.[citation needed]
2. Shorter range before recharging.
3. Longer "fill up" or recharge time.
4. Lower maximum speed at similar price points.
5. Electric power outlets are often not conveniently located near streets or driveways. It is often difficult or impossible to bring the battery into an apartment, for example, for recharging.
6. Battery capacity can be as low as 20% on a cold winter day with -20 °C (lead battery)
7. As it is already difficult for motorcycles to be "noticed" by drivers of cars and trucks, the loss of characteristic engine noise might make riding these even more dangerous than their internal combustion engine powered counterparts.

Types

A scooter is a type of motorcycle with a step-through frame and usually with smaller wheels designed for urban transportation.

Various types of scooters

Scooters are divided into categories as per the particular niche that they are designed to operate in and speed requirements:

- Two-wheeled high speed seated scooters separated from motorcycles by swing through space in chassis 0-72 mph (0–116 km/h)
- Two-wheeled Stand-up scooters (like a kick scooter) 0-25 mph (0–40 km/h)
- Two-wheeled Seated scooters 0-25 mph (0–40 km/h)
- Two-wheeled, side-by-side stand-up scooters like manufactured by Segway PT 0-12 mph (0–20 km/h)
- Three-wheeled stand-up cambering scooter like Trikke Tribred (3CV 3-point carving vehicle) 18 mph (28 km/h) with dynamic suspension and front wheel drive
- Three-wheeled standup scooters 0-15 mph (0–25 km/h) (ie Easyglider X6)
- Three- and four-wheeled Mobility scooter (disability riders) 0-10 mph (0–15 km/h)
- Three- and four-wheeled Seated scooters/golf carts 0-25 mph (0–40 km/h)

Electric motorcycle or electric bicycle

Two-wheeled motorcycles are generally differentiated from electric bicycles and mopeds (motorized pedal cycles) by speed, with motorcycles having greater speeds—usually greater than 30 mph (about 50 km/h). This line for what constitutes a 2 wheeled motorcycle has blurred due to marketing, styling, and public opinion.

Electric motorcycle "Electrocat"

Certain models of electric bicycle take the form of scooters or small motorcycles, comprising of the standard features of common e-bikes, but with plastic or metal cladding, lighting systems; such as indicators and brake lights, and speedometers. They are however, classed as electric bicycles in most areas.

3-wheeled motorcycles

Due to vagueness in motor vehicle laws, any three-wheeled vehicle that can travel over 31 mph (50 km/h) may be classified as a motorcycle. This classification does not depend on whether the operator is fully enclosed by a "cage" or exposed to the elements. Several automotive startup companies made their initial designs three wheeled vehicles, because the motorcycle classification does not require the same costly battery of crash safety testing as a four wheeled vehicle. They may find a sales advantage because insurance and licensing requirements are simplified or non-existent if the local laws classify these types of vehicles as a bicycles.

For design purposes, three wheeled vehicles are divided into 2 categories:

- 1 wheel in front and 2 in back, known as a delta design or the traditional trike (tricycle) design
- 2 wheels in front and 1 in back, known as a tadpole design.

Some three wheeled motorcycles enclose the rider in a "cabin" or cockpit. These include the Twike, Myers Motors NmG.

Some three wheeled motorcycles have independent suspension allowing the vehicle to tilt or lean, such as the Carver one.

Self-balancing unicycle

The Uno dicycle is another type of electric vehicle that is sometimes described as an electric motorcycle.

Comparison of select production vehicles

See also: Hybrid_electric_motorcycle#Motorcycles

Name	Top Speed	Power	Cost	Vehicle type	Battery type	Battery life	Battery capacity	Range	Comments
Libert-E Xero R	30+ mph	1200w	$3,000	Scooter	LiPo Lithium Polymer	app.5 years, 1,200 cycles or 2 year warranty on battery	20Ah	65–80 miles	Libert-E Motor Models w/ removable batteries and 3-speed transmission [2]
Quantya Strada	55+ mph depending on final drive ratio	8.5 kW (11.4 hp) @ 4000 rpm	$10,700	Dual Sport	LiPo Lithium Polymer	app.5 years, 1,000 cycles or 2 year warranty on battery	2.3 kWh	25–30 miles	Quantya Motorcycles [3]
Brammo Enertia	60+ mph (96+ km/h)	13 kW (17 hp) @ 4500 rpm	$7,995	Motorcycle	6 Lithium iron phosphate by Valence	20,000 miles (32,000 km)	3.1 kWh	50+ miles (80+ kilometres)	Currently available at select Best Buy stores and online.
Xtreme Green Products [4]	65 mph (104 km/h)	4.5 kW Hub Motor	$8,495 [5]	Motorcycle	Lithium Ion Power Management System	7 years	60 A·h / 6 kWh	Over 100 miles (Over 160 km)	Review [6]
Vectrix VX-1	62 mph (100 km/h)	20 kW	$8,800 [7]	Scooter	Nickel metal hydride (NiMH) provided by GP Batteries	10 years or 50,000 miles / 80,000 km	30 A·h, 3.7 kW·h	68 miles @ 25 mph (110 km @ 40 km/h)	Review [8]

Tiger Ozone Electric [9]	1.14 HP/485 rpm	N/A	$1,000	Motorcycle	Lead acid	N/A	35 Ah.	N/A	More detail [10] Designed and manufactured in Thailand.
Eped Sport/City [11]	40 mph+	60 v 1,200 w	£1,495	Scooter	5 Crystal Technology Cells	400+ charge cycles	20 A·h	35 miles (55 km)	Epeds Wiki
E-Solex	21 mph	400W	E-solex [12]	Scooter				20 miles (without extra pedalling)	E-solex [12]
Yo Speed	(45 km/h)	750W	Rs.35000(~$815) [13]	Scooter				80 km @ 70 kg	
ZAP Xebra	40 mph (65 km/h)		$10,000	3 Wheel	Lead acid	3 years		25 miles at 30 mph (40 km at 50 km/h) [14]	review [15][*citation needed*]
ZAP Zapino [16]	30 mph (48 km/h)	3 kW	$3,500	Scooter	Lead acid (Lithium option)		38 A·h	30 miles	
EVT-4000e EVT-168 [17]	40 mph (60 km/h)	1,500 W	$2,900	Scooter	Lead acid, 4x12 or lithium ion	1.5 – 2 years, 1000+ charges for lithium	50 A·h	25 to 40 miles (40 to 60 km)	North American Distributor [18], Taiwanese Manufacturer [19]
Io-scooter [20]	30 mph (50 km/h)	1500W	€2,630	Scooter	Lead acid, 4x12	1.5 – 2 years	50 A·h	25 to 35 miles (40 to 55 km)	Io-scooter [20]
Trikke Tribred [21]	18 mph (28 km/h)	350W	$2,000	3CV 3-point cambering vehicle	Li-ion, 48V	3 years	12 A·h	16 to 30 miles (24 to 48 km)	Trikke [22]
Zero X	+ 50 mph (80 km/h)	17.4 kW 23 HP	High Power $9295 Standard $7495	Off-road Motorcycle	Patent-pending lithium ion array	?	2 kWh	40 miles (64 km) 2hrs	Zero Motorcycles
Zero MX	+ 50 mph (80 km/h)	17.4 kW 23 HP	High Power $9950 Standard $8295	Off-road Motorcycle	Patent-pending lithium ion array	?	2 kWh	40 miles (64 km) 2hrs	Zero Motorcycles

Zero S	+ 67 mph (108 km/h)	?	$9995	Supermoto	Patent-pending lithium ion array	?	4 kWh	60 miles (97 km)	Zero Motorcycles
Zero DS	+ 67 mph (108 km/h)	26 hp	$9995	Dual-Sport	Patent-pending lithium ion array	?	4 kWh	60 miles (97 km)	Zero Motorcycles
Native GPR-S [23]	70 mph (112 km/h)	14.2 kW	$8,500	Motorcycle	24 Lithium cells	2000+ charge cycles	3.3 kWh	60 miles (economy setting)	Native Cycles [23]
XM 5000Li [24]	60 mph (96 km/h)	5.000W	$6,499	Scooter	21 Lithium cells	2000+ charge cycles	60 A·h	85 miles (130 km)	Review [25]
ECPU scooter [26]	30 mph (50 km/h)	350~500W	$450(~Rs.22000)	Scooter	Lead acid 6 x 12 V 20 Ah	2 years	1.44 KWh	100 miles at 19 mph,70 miles at 30 mph (160 km at 32 km/h, 110 km at 45 km/h)	Review [26]
Z Electric Vehicle ZEV7000 [27]	74 mph (119 km/h)	7000 W	$7237	Scooter	Lithium max 60AH	10 years	3.36 KWh	62 miles at 50 mph -70 miles at 45 mph - 83 miles at 28 mph	Z Electric Vehicle [28]

Comparison of select upcoming vehicles

Name	Top Speed	Power	Cost	Vehicle type	Battery type	Battery life	Battery capacity	Range	Comments
VentureOne	75+ mph (120+ km/h)	40+ kW	$23,000	3 Wheel	Lithium-ion batteries by A123Systems	5000+ charge cycles		120 miles (about 200 km)	video [29] Available in 2010.
Aptera 2e	85 mph (135 km/h)	30 kW	$27,000	3 Wheel	Lithium Phosphate, unknown manufacturer	N/A	13 kWh	120 miles (190 km)	Production expected in Q4 2009.

List of electric motorcycles and scooters

See Category:Electric scooters and Category:Electric motorcycles

Promotion

Premier of the Republic of China (Taiwan) Liu Chao-shiuan said that the government-financed Industrial Technology Research Institute (ITRI) will help domestic manufacturers mass-produce 100,000 electric motorcycles in four years.

Charging an electric scooter's battery, using a small charger and a regular 250 V power outlet

See also

- Electric bicycle
- Electric dragbike
- Electric vehicle
- Electric kick scooter
- Electric vehicle conversion
- Mobility scooter
- Scooter (motorcycle)

External links

- Electric cycles and electric vehicles [30] at the Open Directory Project

Legality and Safety of Motorcycles

Legal definition of motorcycle

The **legal definition of a motorcycle** for the purposes of registration, taxation and rider licensing in most countries is a *powered two-wheel motor vehicle*. Most countries distinguish between mopeds up to 49 cc (scooters do not count as a separate category) and the more powerful, larger, vehicles known as motorcycles. Many jurisdictions include some forms of three-wheelers as motorcycles.

Australia and New Zealand

In New Zealand, "learner" and "restricted" motorcycles may only have a 250 cc engine capacity, restricting 15-year-old learner riders to speeds of around, or a bit more than, 160 km/h (99 mph).

A scooter and a motorcycle

- Note that on a learner licence on a motorcycle limits the rider to riding up to 70 km/h (maximum of 80 km/h in NSW, Australia), anything over this figure would be breaking the law.

The legal age to be eligible to apply for a New Zealand motorcycle licence is 15 years and over. New Zealand employs a three stage system for motor vehicle licensing. At age 15, an individual can gain their first licence known as their "learner licence". They must hold this for at least 6 months before they are able to move on to their "restricted licence". They must then hold this restricted licence for one and half years. After a period of 6–18 months, depending on age and additional training, a holder of a restricted licence may sit the third and final stage known as the "full licence". Until an individual has their full licence they are only able to ride a motorcycle which has an engine capacity of 250 cc or less.

A similar system is used in most states of Australia, with some variations. "Learners Permit" and "Provisional" licence holders must not have bikes that exceed a power to weight ratio of 150 kW/tonne or 660 cc, whichever comes first. All 250 cc bikes (with a few listed exceptions) are automatically included in this LAMS (Learner Approved Motorcycle Scheme) list.

Before getting a learners permit a pre-learner course is required, which issues a certificate of completion, valid for 3 months. Upon passing a computer test, the rider is granted a learners permit, which is valid for 12 months. Whilst on a learners permit, the rider may not carry a pillion or side car and may not exceed 80 kilometres per hour (50 mph) or the posted speed limit, whichever is lower, in certain jurisdictions.

To progress to a provisional licence, the rider must successfully complete a pre-provisional riders course, followed by a riding skills test called MOST (Motorcycle Operator Skill Test). The rider is then able to obtain a P1 provisional licence. These licences can be renewed and must be held without suspension for 12 months, after which time it can be upgraded to a P2 provisional licence, which is then to be held for 2 more years before the rider obtains their full licence, providing they have not breached any laws causing them to be suspended or disqualified in that period. P2 provisional riders are permitted to carry a pillion, P1 riders are not. There are exceptions to this rule for mature age licence holders, who may be eligible to bypass the P2 provisional period.

Canada and the US

In Canada and the United States three-wheeled motor vehicles fall under the auspices of motorcycle regulations. The laws and regulations for legal moped usage in the U.S. vary by state.

In many jurisdictions, the term "motorcycle" includes trikes

In the United States, licensing requirements vary widely among the states and territories, but generally riders are required to pass written and practical (on-cycle) competency tests. In about half the states, successful completion of a rider education course (such as those offered by the Motorcycle Safety Foundation) is accepted by state licensing agencies in lieu of examination. The specifics of the motorcycle and moped laws in the U.S. can be obtained from each individual state's Department of Motor Vehicles website.

United Kingdom

Motorcycle riders in the UK must normally take a one-day Compulsory Basic Training (CBT) course, regardless of which class of motorcycle they intend to ride. In addition a theory test must be taken prior to taking a practical test for any type of motorcycle licence.

Entry level to motorcycling at age 16 is the moped, a motorcycle of engine capacity no greater than 50 cc restricted to a maximum design speed of 50 km/h (31 mph).

At age 17 the rider may have a "light motorcycle" with an engine up to 125 cc and a power output not exceeding 11 kW (15 hp). Only a CBT certificate, obtained within the past two years, and a provisional licence is needed to ride a learner motorcycle with an L-plate. After passing a test on a 125 cc machine, riders will be restricted to ride a "large restricted motorcycle", which has a maximum power output of 25 kW (34 hp). After two years this restriction is lifted and any size or power of motorcycle may be ridden.

For riders over age 21 there is a direct access route to gaining a licence to ride a "large motorcycle" of any engine capacity or power, which allows somebody with no motorcycle experience to train and pass a test in around five days.

Three-wheeled vehicles weighing less than 8 cwt (896 lb / 406 kg) were long classified as motorcycles in the UK and could be driven with a full motorcycle licence. A requirement there be no reverse gear fitted was dropped in the 1960s. This exemption was linked to the enduring popularity of three-wheeled vehicles in the UK (such as the Reliant Regal van) but was abolished for new licence holders in October 2000. Mass-production of three-wheelers ceased in 1998 but the licensing exemption still benefits trikes and their riders.

Motorcycle safety

Motorcycle safety concerns many aspects of vehicle and equipment design as well as operator skill and training that are unique to motorcycle riding.

US Navy motorcycle training at Imperial Beach.

Accident rates

Motorcycles have a higher fatality rate per unit of distance travelled when compared with automobiles. According to the NHTSA, in 2006 18.06 cars out of 100,000 ended up in fatal crashes. The rate for motorcycles is 55.82 per 100,000. In 2004, figures from the UK Department for Transport indicated that motorcycles have 16 times the rate of serious injuries per 100 million vehicle kilometers compared to cars, and double the rate of bicycles.

A national study by the Australian Transport Safety Bureau (ATS) found that:

- Motorcycle rider death rates increased among all rider age groups between 1998 and 2000
- Motorcycle rider deaths were nearly 30 times more than drivers of other vehicles

- Motorcycle riders aged below 40 are 36 times more likely to be killed than other vehicle operators of the same age.
- Motorcycle riders aged 40 years and over are around 20 times more likely to be killed than other drivers of that same age.

According to 2005 data from the National Highway Traffic Safety Administration NHTSA, 4,008 motorcycle occupants were killed on United States roads in 2004, an 8% increase from 2003.

Some riders take an alternative approach to safety policy.

During that same period, drivers of automobiles showed a 10% increase in fatalities, and cyclists showed an 8% increase in fatalities. Pedestrians also showed a 10% increase in fatalities. A total of 37,304 automobile occupants were killed on U.S. roads in 2004.

Additional data from the United States reveals that there are over four million motorcycles registered in the United States. Motorcycle fatalities represent approximately five percent of all highway fatalities each year, yet motorcycles represent just two percent of all registered vehicles in the United States. One of the main reasons motorcyclists are killed in crashes is because the motorcycle itself provides virtually no protection in a crash. For example, approximately 80 percent of reported motorcycle crashes result in injury or death; a comparable figure for automobiles is about 20 percent.

Research

Two major scientific research studies into the causes of motorcycle accidents have been conducted in North America and Europe: the Hurt Report and the MAIDS report.

Hurt Report

Main article: Hurt Report

The only major work done on this subject in the USA is the Hurt Report, published in 1981 with data collected in Los Angeles and the surrounding rural areas. There have been longstanding calls for a new safety study in the US, and Congress has provided the seed money for such a project, but as yet the remainder of the funding has not all been pledged.

The Hurt Report concluded with a list of 55 findings, as well as several major recommendations for law enforcement and legislation. Among these, 75% of motorcycle accidents involved collision with another vehicle, usually a car. In the MAIDS report, the figure is 60%.

Other notable findings in the Hurt report (quoted below) were:

- 75% of accidents were found to involve a motorcycle and a passenger vehicle, while the remaining 25% of accidents were single motorcycle accidents.
- "In the single vehicle accidents, motorcycle rider error was present as the accident precipitating factor in about two-thirds of the cases, with the typical error being a slide-out and fall due to overbraking or running wide on a curve due to excess speed or under-cornering."
- "Almost half of the fatal accidents show alcohol involvement" and "injury severity increases with speed, alcohol involvement and motorcycle size."
- In the multiple vehicle accidents, the driver of the other vehicle violated the motorcycle right-of-way and caused the accident in two-thirds of those accidents.
- The report's additional findings show that the wearing of appropriate gear, specifically, helmets and durable garment, mitigates crash injuries substantially.
- "Vehicle failure accounted for less than 3% of these motorcycle accidents, and most of those were single vehicle accidents where control was lost due to a puncture flat" and "Weather is not a factor in 98% of motorcycle accidents."
- "The failure of motorists to detect and recognize motorcycles in traffic is the predominating cause of motorcycle accidents... Conspicuity of the motorcycle is a critical factor in the multiple vehicle accidents, and accident involvement is significantly reduced by the use of motorcycle headlamps-on In daylight and the wearing of high visibility yellow, orange or bright red jackets."

MAIDS report

Main article: MAIDS report

The most recent large-scale study of motorcycle accidents is the MAIDS report carried out in five European countries in 1999-2000, using the rigorous OECD standards, including a statistically significant sample size of over 900 crash incidents and over 900 control cases.

The MAIDS report tends to support most of the Hurt Report findings, for example that "69% of the OV [other vehicle] drivers attempted no collision avoidance manoeuvre," suggesting they did not see the motorcycle. And further that, "the largest number of PTW [powered two-wheeler] accidents is due to a perception failure on the part of the OV driver or the PTW rider." And "The data indicates that in 68.7% of all cases, the helmet was capable of preventing or reducing the head injury sustained by the rider (i.e., 33.2% + 35.5%). In 3.6% of all cases, the helmet was found to have no effect upon head injury" and "There were no reported cases in which the helmet was identified as the contact code for a serious or maximum neck injury."

Conflicting findings on conspicuity

A New Zealand study supported the Hurt Report's call for increased rider conspicuity, claiming fluorescent clothing, white or light colored helmets, and daytime headlights may reduce motorcycle injuries and death. The study found that wearing reflective or fluorescent clothing reduced the risk of a crash injury by 37%, a white helmet by 24%, and riding with headlights on by 27%.

However, the MAIDS report did not back up the claims that helmet color makes any difference in accident frequency, and that in fact motorcycles painted white were actually over-represented in the accident sample compared to the exposure data. While recognizing how much riders need to be seen, the MAIDS report documented that riders' clothing usually fails to do so, saying that "in 65.3% of all cases, the clothing made no contribution to the conspicuity of the rider or the PTW [powered two-wheeler, i.e. motorcycle]. There were very few cases found in which the bright clothing of the PTW rider enhanced the PTW's overall conspicuity (46 cases).There were more cases in which the use of dark clothing decreased the conspicuity of the rider and the PTW (120 cases)." The MAIDS report was unable to recommend specific items of clothing or colors to make riders better seen.

Controversy

Riders must be prepared for the unexpected.

In 2007, a report by the Insurance Institute for Highway Safety claimed that "supersport" motorcycles were four times more likely to be involved in highway crashes than other types. When reprinting this press release as a news report, USA Today omitted the word "insurance" from the "Insurance Institute for Highway Safety", giving a false impression the IIHS is a governmental agency, not a private corporation with a conflict of interest.

According to the American Motorcyclist Association (AMA), the IIHS report was an attempt to either ban entire categories of motorcycles, or a covert attempt to legislate requirement for speed governors in all vehicles. The IIHS report was not a new study, being an analysis of existing data from the national Fatal Accident Reporting System. The methodology consisted of a comparison of fatalities for different styles of motorcycles based on a rate per 10,000 registrations. The report did not incorporate key factors, such as the number of miles the bike was ridden, the traffic environment in which it was used, along with the age and experience of the rider, among others.

In an attempt to sort through this confusion, the AMA requested a copy of the classification system the IIHS used in its analysis and found several significant anomalies. For instance, although the IIHS report focused on speed and acceleration as the factors that make its "supersport" category so dangerous, the two most powerful motorcycles that were available at the time in the United States, the Kawasaki ZX-14 and Suzuki Hayabusa, are placed in the Sport category, which are rated considerably less dangerous. And they share that category with the Honda ST1300 and Yamaha FJR1300, two bikes that define the sport-touring class.

The AMA thought the timing of the IIHS report was unusual. The National Transportation Safety Board specifically asked the Federal Highway Administration to work with states to develop uniform data-collection procedures that will result in better information about the number of miles traveled by motorcycles, one of the most important factors in evaluating crash statistics. As a result, this could be one of the final reports to use registration data exclusively, which is less accurate in reflecting actual motorcycle use.

This new IIHS report is remarkably similar to a study the group financed 20 years ago that also purported to show higher fatality rates among sportbikes. At that time, the IIHS used its study as the springboard for a well-orchestrated campaign that included ready-made news footage it fed to TV news operations across the country. That campaign culminated in the introduction of a bill in the U.S. Senate to impose a horsepower limit on all motorcycles sold in the U.S.

In response to that previous attempt by the IIHS to ban sportbikes, the AMA conducted an analysis of the study and raised questions that the Association submitted to Harry Hurt, lead researcher on the most comprehensive study of motorcycle crashes ever conducted. Hurt reviewed the research and declared it "fatally flawed" for exactly the kind of methodology problems seen in the new IIHS report. The Association then coordinated a campaign among motorcyclists across the country that eventually led the senator to withdraw his proposed legislation.

The new IIHS report came out just as the AMA and the motorcycling community was successful in getting federal funding for the first comprehensive motorcycle safety study since the Hurt Report.

Consequences of accidents

Once the collision has occurred, or the rider has lost control through some other mishap, several common types of injury occur when the bike falls:

- Collision with less forgiving protective barriers, or badly placed roadside "furniture" (lampposts, signs, fences etc.) This is often simply a result of poor road design, and can be engineered out to a large degree. Note that when one falls off a motorcycle in the middle of a curve, lamps and signs create a "wall" of sorts with little chance to avoid slamming against a pole.
- Concussion and brain damage, as the head violently contacts other vehicles or objects. Riders wearing an approved helmet reduce the risk of death by 37 percent.
- Breakage of joints (elbows, shoulders, hips, knees and wrists), fingers, spine and neck, for the same reason. The most common breakages are the shoulder and the pelvis.
- Soft tissue (skin and muscle) damage (road rash) as the body slides across the surface. This can be prevented entirely with the proper use of motorcycle-specific protective apparel such as a leather jacket or reinforced denim and textile pants.

- There is also a condition known as biker's arm, where the nerves in the upper arm are damaged during the fall, causing a permanent paralysis of arm movement.
- Facial disfigurement, if in the absence of a full-face helmet, the unprotected face slides across the ground or smashes into an object. Thirty-five percent of all crashes show major impact on the chin-bar area.

The Hurt Report also commented on injuries after an accident stating that the likelihood of injury is extremely high in these motorcycle accidents - 98% of the multiple vehicle collisions and 96% of the single vehicle accidents resulted in some kind of injury to the motorcycle rider; 45% resulted in more than a minor injury.<ref name=

Personal protective equipment

Main article: Motorcycle personal protective equipment

To address the risks of motorcycling, before and after a fall, motorcyclists use personal protective equipment (PPE, or more commonly "motorcycle gear"). Many developed countries now require certain articles of PPE, and manufacturers and governments recommend its extensive use.

A motorcyclist wearing helmet, gloves, boots, and armored, reflective textile jacket and pants.

Functions of PPE

- Improved Visibility — Although for decades the popular image of the motorcycle rider has been of someone clad head-to-toe in black leather, in the light of the Hurt Report findings, and the day-to-day experiences of motorcyclists themselves, many riders choose higher-visibility gear. Bright colors and retroreflective strips are common on quality equipment.
- Abrasion Resistance — Thick, tough leather provides the most abrasion resistance in a crash, but fabrics such as cordura, kevlar and ballistic nylon provide significant protection too. In addition, fabrics are generally cheaper, easier to maintain, waterproof, and more comfortable in hot weather. Thick leather, which affords the most abrasion resistance, can be uncomfortable in temperatures exceeding 85 °F (29 °C) and above 100 °F (38 °C) may cause heat stress & loss of control with insufficient fluid replacement. Some PPE may be constructed of fabrics made into a 'mesh' that provides cooling and a stable surface for the attachment of padding (see below).
- Impact protection — Quality jackets and pants provide significant extra padding in the vulnerable joint regions described above. This can take the form of simple foam padding, or dual-density foam that stiffens when compressed, sometimes with plastic or carbon fiber outer-shells that distribute the impact across the pad. Integrated pieces can be found in some jackets.

- Weather Protection — One important aspect of PPE not mentioned above is protection from the elements. Extreme weather can make a long ride unbearable or dangerous. PPE provides protection from wind, rain and cold.

Items of PPE

- Helmet — A full-face helmet provides the most protection. Thirty-five percent of all crashes show major impact on the chin-bar area. However, 3/4- and 1/2-helmets also are available. Some motorcycle training sitesWikipedia:Avoid weasel words have banned the use of half-helmets because of avoidable injuries sustained by riders wearing them.
- Gloves — Commonly made of leather, cordura, or Kevlar, or some combination. Some include carbon fiber knuckle protection or other forms of rigid padding. Gloves designed specifically for motorcycle use have slightly curved fingers and the seams are on the outer surfaces to allow the motorcyclist to maintain his grip and control on the handlebars and clutch/brake levers. Some gloves also provide protection to the wrist.
- Jackets — Generally made from leather, ballistic nylon, cordura, Kevlar or other synthetics. Most jackets include special padding on elbows, spine and shoulders. Airbag system technology is now available fitted to jackets and vests for accident protection and impact protection for both riders and pillions. Competition-approved hard armor is superior to soft padding. Competition-approved back and chest protectors can be worn underneath jackets. Inflatable airbag jackets can offer an additional airbag for neck support.

A full-face helmet credited for saving its user.

Half helmets or "skid lids" are worn to meet minimum legal requirements, without much crash protection.

- Pants — Made of the same material as jackets, usually including special protection for the knees and hips.
- Boots — Especially those for sport riding, include reinforcement and plastic caps on the ankles, and toe area. Boots designed for cruiser-style riders often have steel-reinforced toes (However this reduces sensitivity of the foot when changing gear). Boots should always have a rubber sole (as opposed to leather or other less-flexible materials). Despite their toughness and protection, most boots are very lightweight. Some even include titanium plating.

- Goggles or Helmet Visor — Eye protection is of utmost importance - an insect or a kicked-up pebble in the eye at speed has enough momentum to cause significant damage. Such an event could easily cause the rider to lose control and crash. Besides this danger, squinting into the wind is unpleasant at best and watering eyes are quite distracting.
- Ear plugs — Most riders experience substantial wind noise at speeds above 40 to 50 mph (64 to 80 km/h); at speeds of 65 to 70 mph (105 to 110 km/h), hearing damage can occur in as little as 15 minutes.[citation needed] Ear plugs help protect against hearing damage, and reduce fatigue during long rides.
- Vests — Made with high-visibility colors and retroreflective materials, vests can be worn over jackets to increase the chance of being seen and allow drivers to better judge the speed and position of riders, especially in adverse conditions of dark and wet.
- Other PPE — Dirt bike riders wear a range of plastic armor to protect against injury from falling and hitting other riders and bikes, running into track barriers, and being hit by flying debris kicked up by the tires of other riders' bikes. This type of armor typically covers the back, chest, and sometimes the extremities.

It is increasingly common for gloves, jackets, pants, and boots to be outfitted with hard plastics on probable contact areas in an effort to ensure that when a motorcyclist contacts the ground, his clothing will permit him to slide relatively easily as opposed to "crumpling", risking injury to body parts being stressed in abnormal directions.

Since the first line of protection in crash contact is the outer shell of clothing, designers have moved that further from the body. The ultimate protective shell so far is an airbag that stays with the driver as he flies off the bike. However, increasing use of "exoskeleton" plastic shields attached to clothing points toward design of a complete roll bar belted to the driver. A near-stage design is a plastic or light alloy double "wheel" perimeter rim around the driver, over his head and in front and behind him. When the driver unbelts himself and gets off the bike, he leaves the wheel roll bar with the bike. But when the driver flies off the bike, the roll bar flies with him and makes contact with hard surfaces. The driver is relatively safe from contact, belted within a contact rim extending out around him.

Riders sometimes use the acronyms MOTGMOTT and ATGATT, which stand for "Most Of The Gear Most Of The Time" and "All The Gear All The Time", when describing their personal gear preferences.

Training

Main article: Motorcycle training

Novice motorcyclists being trained

In many developed countries riders are now either required or encouraged to attend safety classes in order to obtain a separate motorcycle driving license.

Training can help to bridge the gap between a novice and experienced rider as well as improving the skills of a more experienced rider. Skills training would seem to be the answer to reducing the KSI ("killed or seriously injured") rate among motorcycle riders. However, research shows that some who undergo advanced skills training are more likely to be at a higher risk while using the roads (Rutter & Quine, 1996). This risk compensation effect was commented on in the findings of the evaluation of the "Bikesafe Scotland," scheme where a number of those who undertook training said they rode faster in non-built-up areas after the course (Ormston et al., 2003). This is not to say that training in not important, but that more advanced training should be tempered with psychological training (Broughton 2005).

In the United States, the Motorcycle Safety Foundation (MSF) provides a standardized curriculum to the states that, in turn, provide low cost safety training for new and current riders. Two states, Oregon and Idaho, eschew MSF's curriculum in favor of their own. Even with over 1,500 locations in USA, and over 120,000 annual students, MSF only trains about 3% of the owners of 4,000,000 new motorcycles sold for highway use. Motorcycle injuries and fatalities among U.S. military personnel has continually risen since the early 2000s. Among other DoD-initiated programs, the Air National Guard seeks to understand why national safety programs haven't sufficiently reduced mishaps, and how those programs might be modified to cause productive behaviorial change.

In the United Kingdom, for example, organizations such as the IAM and RoSPA offer advanced motorcycle rider training with the aim of reducing accident rates. There is often an added incentive to riders in the form of reduced insurance premiums.

In Canada, the Canada Safety Council (CSC), a non-profit organization, provides motorcycle safety training courses for beginner and novice riders through its Gearing Up training program. Again, as in the USA and UK, the focus is on improved rider skills to reduce accident rates. Insurance premiums may be reduced upon successful completion as this program is recognised and supported nationally by the Motorcycle and Moped Industry Council (MMIC).

Countersteering

Main article: Countersteering

According to the Hurt Report, the path between straight-line motion and free equilibrium turn requires an initial steering motion opposite that of the steady turn. In accidents, most riders would over brake and skid the rear wheel, and under brake the front when greatly reducing collision avoidance deceleration. The ability to countersteer and swerve was essentially absent. Because of this, the Motorcycle Safety Foundation teaches countersteering to all students in all of its schools, as do all motorcycle racing schools. Countersteering is included in the US State motorcycle operator manuals and tests, such as Washington, New Jersey, California, and Missouri. These rider's manuals typically simplify countersteering using some version of the standard verbiage "PRESS — To turn, the motorcycle must lean. To lean the motorcycle, press on the handgrip in the direction of the turn. Press left — lean left — go left. Press right — lean right — go right. Higher speeds and/or tighter turns require the motorcycle to lean more." This text, and often the entire manual, is copied verbatim from the manual published by the MSF.

Confusion results from the shortness of the initial countersteering input required to get the bike to lean, which is only 0.5 seconds in average curves. Gentle turns might require only 0.125 seconds, while sharp turns might require 1.0 seconds of countersteering at corner entry.

Motorcycle equipment

On most new motorcycles, the headlights turn on as soon as the bike is started as a legal requirement. Some bikes have modulated headlights. This is accomplished using headlight modulators. This is still a subjective issue in some European countries. The argument is that the forced use of the headlight will lose all safety benefits if cars are also required to have their lights "hardwired." There is also an argument that the forced use of the headlight is seen as "aggressive" by other road users and so reinforces negative stereotypes of bike riders held by some. Modulators are legal in the US and Canada. It has been suggested that bright yellow front turn signals would be more practical and more effective than headlights in the daytime.

Crash bars (also called "safety bars," or "roll bars") are common equipment on cruiser-type bikes. They are designed to protect a rider's legs (and the motor) from injury in a rollover and in a glancing contact with other vehicles. The Hurt Report concluded that crash bars are not an effective injury countermeasure; the reduction of injury to the ankle-foot is balanced by increase of injury to the thigh-upper leg, knee, and lower leg.

Airbag devices

Fuel tank mounted airbags as well as wearable jacket airbag devices change the way we think about the risks involved with motorcycles. Accidents occur within a very short time and a rider may not be able to instinctively protect him or herself when a crash takes place. This is where an airbag device becomes useful and potentially lifesaving.

The first motorcycle crash tests with an airbag were performed in 1973 and proved that airbag systems could be advantageous to a rider. These tests were followed up by tests in the 1990s that showed airbag devices could not fully restrain a rider when traveling more than 30 mph (48 km/h), but it still reduced a rider's velocity and his/her trajectory. Honda has recently developed a fuel tank mounted airbag for the Goldwing model that takes just 0.15 seconds to deploy. Crash sensors in the front wheel send data to the airbag ECU (electronic control unit) which in turn activates the airbag inflater. The airbag then takes the force of the rider.

Fuel tank mounted airbags can aid in saving many lives. It has been proven with crash test dummies that this type of airbag technology is very beneficial during a frontal collision. This is important because statistically, 62% of motorcycle accidents in the U.S. are frontal collisions. Additional tests were performed to show that when a motorcycle rider impacts a car during a frontal collision, the fuel tank mounted airbag averts the person from traveling into the vehicle. This significantly reduced the head trauma by 83% that otherwise would have occurred according to the data from the crash test dummy. A rider would have lived with an airbag, whereas the fatality rate would be higher without the airbag. It has also been pointed out that this can only work if the accident is at low speed and follows the same dynamics as a car accident. It should be viewed as passenger vehicle airbags - a worthwhile supplement, but not as a replacement for any other safety devices including a change in the basic design of road going motorcycles.

The second airbag device which is now available is an inflatable airbag jacket. A rider can wear an airbag jacket that is tethered to the motorcycle, so if he or she is thrown from the bike during a collision, the jacket will automatically inflate for a 20 second period to provide a cushion for the rider. This will lessen the upper body and internal injuries to a rider that may often be fatal. Mugen Denko pioneered the development of airbag jackets in 1985 and conducted many tests, although the idea was initially patented in Hungary in 1976. Full inflation of these jackets can now be achieved in 25ms.[citation needed] The majority of the airbag jackets on the market are tethered to the motorcycle, but Dainese has a technology called D-Air which has a built-in computer chip. This computer chip constantly detects the rider's environment and if it detects a collision, the jacket will then self-inflate. This jacket is currently aimed specifically at the racing environment and undergoing testing by Dainese-sponsored riders. Hit Air, the maker of another airbag jacket, performed tests on its jacket which showed that its safety effectiveness surpassed that of a normal riding jacket or a jacket with extra padding protection. Little independent testing has been done to date on the effectiveness of these devices. The airbag jackets provide reusable airbag protection to the neck, chest, back, shoulders, hips, bottom and spine. Cost of airbag jackets are approx $US500.

As demand for safety measures increases, so the need for motorcycle airbags may grow in popularity over the coming years. Yamaha and Suzuki are currently testing airbag systems, so they will be available on additional motorcycles and so that more people will request airbag devices more often. According to Honda's web site, the Goldwing model motorcycle currently retails for US$23,099 and the airbag is only an additional US$1,250 option.

With the advances in this technology, it may be possible to apply this knowledge to produce airbags for jet-skis, ATVs, and go-karts.

See also

- Driver visibility
- Highsider
- Lane splitting
- List of motorcycle deaths in U.S. by year
- Lowsider
- Motorcycle training

Further reading

- Bayly, M., Regan, M., & Hosking, S. (2006). Intelligent transport systems and motorcycle safety. [Report No. 260]. Melbourne, Australia: Monash University, Accident Research Centre.
- Berg, F. A., & Rucker, P. (2002). Airbag prototype for a mid-sized touring motorcycle. International Research Council on Biomechanics of Injury Conference. Stuttgart, Germany: DEKRA Automobil.
- Blanchard, H. T., & Tabloski, P. A. (2006). Motorcycle safety: Educating riders at the teachable moment. Journal of Emergency Nursing, 32(4), 330-332.
- Broughton, P.S. and Walker, L. (2009), Motorcycling and Leisure: Understanding the Recreational PTW Rider: Ashgate Publishing: Aldershot.
- Elliott, M. A., Baughan, C. J., Broughton, J., Chinn, B., Grayson, G. B., Knowles, J., et al. (2003). Motorcycle safety: A scoping study. [Report No. TRL581]. Transport Research Laboratory.
- Huang, B., & Preston, J. (2004). A literature review on motorcycle collisions: Final report. Oxford University, Transport Studies Unit.
- Pierce, A. (2002). The personal airbag. Tech Directions, 61(7), 10.
- "Fatal Single Vehicle Motorcycle Crashes, report by the US [[National Highway Traffic Safety Administration [1]]"]. October 2001.
- "Casualty rates: by road user type and severity: 1994 to 2004" [2] (PDF). Department of Transport, UK.
- "In-Depth Study of Motorcycle Accidents" [3]. Department of Transport, UK. November 2004.

External links

- US Dept of Transportation [4] - Statistics on Motorcycle Fatalities
- Daytime running lights for motorcycles [5] Proceedings of 19th Conference on the Enhanced Safety of Vehicles, Washington 2005
- MAIDS Motorcycle Accident Study: Lessons From 921 Crashes [6]

Characterisitcs and Dynamics of Motorcycles

Single-track vehicle

A **single-track vehicle** is a vehicle that leaves a single ground track as it moves forward. Single-track vehicles usually have little or no lateral stability when stationary but develop it when moving forward or controlled. In the case of wheeled vehicles, the track of the front and rear wheel usually follow slightly different paths when turning or when out of alignment.

Single-track vehicles have unique dynamics that, in the case of wheeled vehicles, are discussed at length in bicycle and motorcycle dynamics, that usually require leaning into a turn, and that usually include countersteering. Single-track vehicles can roll on wheels, slide, float, or hydroplane.

Wheeled

- the bicycle and all its varieties, such as tandem, tall, and recumbent
- the motorcycle and all its varieties, such as scooter and feet-forwards
- the kick scooter and all its varieties
- the unicycle and monowheel
- the inline skate and roller ski when only one is in contact with the ground or when the second follows behind the first

Sliding

- the snowboard and monoski
- the skirider
- the ice skate when only one is in contact with the ice or when the second follows behind the first

Intermittent contact

- the pogo stick
- the bipedal robot

Hydroplaning

- the slalom water ski
- the wakeboard

Approximately single-track

A vehicle is approximately single-track when the axle track is small enough with respect to the center of mass height to require leaning into a turn. Countersteering may or may not be required.

- the skateboard and all its varieties, such as the snakeboard
- the surfboard
- the caster board when the rear wheel closely follows the front wheel track
- the Uno dicycle

See also

- Dicycle

Bicycle and motorcycle dynamics

Bicycle and motorcycle dynamics is the science of the motion of bicycles and motorcycles and their components, due to the forces acting on them. Dynamics is a branch of classical mechanics, which in turn is a branch of physics. Bike motions of interest include balancing, steering, braking, accelerating, suspension activation, and vibration. The study of these motions began in the late 19th century and continues today.

A computer-generated, simplified model of bike and rider demonstrating an uncontrolled right turn.

Bicycles and motorcycles are both single-track vehicles and so their motions have many fundamental attributes in common and are fundamentally different from and more difficult to study than other wheeled vehicles such as dicycles, tricycles, and quadracycles. As with unicycles, bikes lack lateral stability when stationary, and under most circumstances can only remain upright when moving forward. Experimentation and mathematical analysis have shown that a bike stays upright when it is steered to keep its center of mass over its wheels. This steering is usually supplied by a rider, or in certain circumstances, by the bike itself. Several factors, including geometry, mass distribution, and gyroscopic effect all contribute to varying degrees to this self-stability, but long-standing hypotheses and claims that gyroscopic effect is the main stabilizing force have been discredited.

While remaining upright may be the primary goal of beginning riders, a bike must lean in order to maintain balance in a turn: the higher the speed or smaller the turn radius, the more lean is required. This balances the roll torque about the wheel contact patches generated by centrifugal force due to the turn with that of the gravitational force. This lean is usually produced by a momentary steering in the opposite direction, a maneuver often referred to as countersteering. Unlike other wheeled vehicles, the primary control input on bikes is steering torque, not position.

Although longitudinally stable when stationary, bikes often have a high enough center of mass and a short enough wheelbase to lift a wheel off the ground under sufficient acceleration or deceleration. When braking, depending on the location of the combined center of mass of the bike and rider with respect to the point where the front wheel contacts the ground, bikes can either skid the front wheel or flip the bike and rider over the front wheel. A similar situation is possible while accelerating, but with respect to the rear wheel.

History

The history of the study of bike dynamics is nearly as old as the bicycle itself. It includes contributions from famous scientists such as Rankine, Appell, and Whipple. In the early 19th century Karl von Drais, credited with inventing the two-wheeled vehicle variously called the laufmaschine, velocipede, draisine, and dandy horse, showed that a rider could balance his device by steering the front wheel. By the end of the 19th century, Emmanuel Carvallo and Francis Whipple showed with rigid-body dynamics that some safety bicycles could actually balance themselves if moving at the right speed. It is not clear to whom should go the credit for tilting the steering axis from the vertical which helps make this possible.

Draisine.

In 1970, David Jones published an article in *Physics Today* showing that gyroscopic effects are not necessary to balance a bicycle. Since 1971, when he named the weave and capsize modes, Robin Sharp has written about the mathematical behavior of motorcycles and bicycles, and his work has continued to the present day with David Limebeer. Both men were at Imperial College, London. In 2007, Meijaard, Papadopoulos, Ruina, and Schwab published the canonical linearized equations of motion, in the *Proceedings of the Royal Society A*, along with verification by two different methods.

Forces

If the bike and rider are considered to be a single system, the forces that act on that system and its components can be roughly divided into two groups: internal and external. The external forces are due to gravity, inertia, contact with the ground, and contact with the atmosphere. The internal forces are caused by the rider and by interaction between components.

External forces

As with all masses, gravity pulls the rider and all the bike components toward the earth. At each tire contact patch there are ground reaction forces with both horizontal and vertical components. The vertical components mostly counteract the force of gravity, but also vary with braking and accelerating. For details, see the section on *longitudinal stability* below. The horizontal components, due to friction between the wheels and the ground, including rolling resistance, are in response to propulsive forces, braking forces, and turning forces. Aerodynamic forces due to the atmosphere are mostly in the form of drag, but can also be from crosswinds. At normal bicycling speeds on level ground, aerodynamic drag is the largest force resisting forward motion. At faster speed, aerodynamic drag becomes overwhelmingly the largest force resisting forward motion.

Turning forces are generated during maneuvers for balancing in addition to just changing direction of travel. These may be interpreted as centrifugal forces in the accelerating reference frame of the bike and rider; or simply as inertia in a stationary, inertial reference frame and not forces at all. *Gyroscopic* forces acting on rotating parts such as wheels, engine, transmission, etc., are also due to the inertia of those rotating parts. They are discussed further in the section on gyroscopic effects below.

Internal forces

Internal forces are mostly caused by the rider or by friction. The rider can apply torques between the steering mechanism (front fork, handlebars, front wheel, etc.) and rear frame, and between the rider and the rear frame. Friction exists between any parts that move against each other: in the drive train, between the steering mechanism and the rear frame, etc. Many bikes have front and rear suspensions, and some motorcycles have a steering damper to dissipate undesirable kinetic energy. On bikes with rear suspensions, feedback between the drive train and the suspension is an issue designers attempt to handle with various linkage configurations and dampers.

Motions

Motions of a bike can be roughly grouped into those out of the central plane of symmetry: lateral; and those in the central plane of symmetry: longitudinal or vertical. Lateral motions include balancing, leaning, steering, and turning. Motions in the central plane of symmetry include rolling forward, of course, but also stoppies, wheelies, brake diving, and most suspension activation. Motions in these two groups are linearly decoupled, that is they do not interact with each other to the first order. An uncontrolled bike is laterally unstable when stationary and can be laterally self-stable when moving under the right conditions or when controlled by a rider. Conversely, a bike is longitudinally stable when stationary and can be longitudinally unstable when undergoing sufficient acceleration or deceleration.

Lateral dynamics

Of the two, lateral dynamics has proven to be the more complicated, requiring three-dimensional, multibody dynamic analysis with at least two generalized coordinates to analyze. At a minimum, two coupled, second-order differential equations are required to capture the principal motions. Exact solutions are not possible, and numerical methods must be used instead. Competing theories of how bikes balance can still be found in print and online. On the other hand, as shown in later sections, much longitudinal dynamic analysis can be accomplished simply with planar kinetics and just one coordinate.

Balance

A bike remains upright when it is steered so that the ground reaction forces exactly balance all the other internal and external forces it experiences, such as gravitational if leaning, inertial or centrifugal if in a turn, gyroscopic if being steered, and aerodynamic if in a crosswind. Steering may be supplied by a rider or, under certain circumstances, by the bike itself. This self-stability is generated by a combination of several effects that depend on the geometry, mass distribution, and forward speed of the bike. Tires, suspension, steering damping, and frame flex can also influence it, especially in motorcycles.

Even when staying relatively motionless, a rider can balance a bike by the same principle. While performing a track stand, the rider can keep the line between the two contact patches under the combined center of mass by steering the front wheel to one side or the other and then moving forward and backward slightly to move the front contact patch from side to side as necessary. Forward motion can be generated simply by pedaling. Backwards motion can be generated the same way on a fixed-gear bicycle. Otherwise, the rider can take advantage of an opportune slope of the pavement or lurch the upper body backwards while the brakes are momentarily engaged.

If the steering of a bike is locked, it becomes virtually impossible to balance while riding. On the other hand, if the gyroscopic effect of rotating bike wheels is cancelled by adding counter-rotating wheels, it is still easy to balance while riding.

Forward speed

The rider applies torque to the handlebars in order to turn the front wheel and so to control lean and maintain balance. At high speeds, small steering angles quickly move the ground contact points laterally; at low speeds, larger steering angles are required to achieve the same results in the same amount of time. Because of this, it is usually easier to maintain balance at high speeds.

Center of mass location

The farther forward (closer to front wheel) the center of mass of the combined bike and rider, the less the front wheel has to move laterally in order to maintain balance. Conversely, the further back (closer to the rear wheel) the center of mass is located, the more front wheel lateral movement or bike forward motion will be required to regain balance. This can be noticeable on long-wheelbase recumbents and choppers. It can also be an issue for touring bikes with a heavy load of gear over or even behind the rear wheel. Mass over the rear wheel can be more easily controlled if it is lower than mass over the front wheel.

A bike is also an example of an inverted pendulum. Just as a broomstick is easier to balance than a pencil, a tall bike (with a high center of mass) can be easier to balance when ridden than a low one because its lean rate will be slower. However, a rider can have the opposite impression of a bike when it is stationary. A top-heavy bike can require more effort to keep upright, when stopped in traffic for example, than a bike which is just as tall but with a lower center of mass. This is an example of a vertical second-class lever. A small force at the end of the lever, the seat or handlebars at the top of the bike, more easily moves a large mass if the mass is closer to the fulcrum, where the tires touch the ground. This is why touring cyclists are advised to carry loads low on a bike, and panniers hang down on either side of front and rear racks.

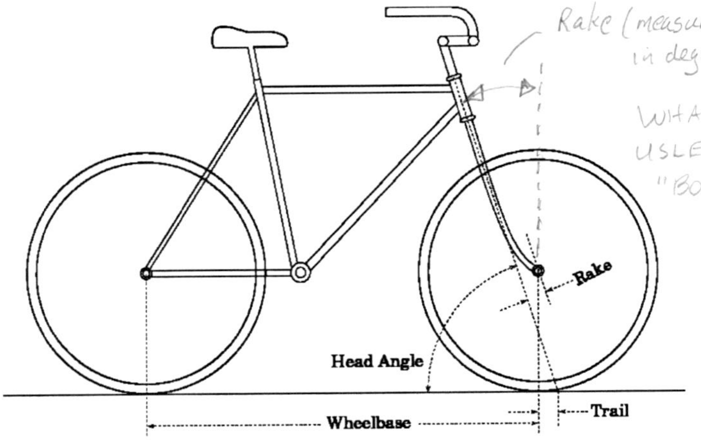

Bicycle head angle, rake, and trail

hat influences how easy or difficult a bike will be to ride is **trail**, the distance that the front wheel ground contact point trails behind the steering axis ground contact point. The steering axis is the axis about which the entire steering mechanism (fork, handlebars, front wheel, etc.) pivots. In traditional bike designs, with a steering axis tilted back from the vertical, trail causes the front wheel to steer into the direction of a lean, independent of forward speed. This can be seen by pushing a stationary bike to one side. The front wheel will usually also steer to that side. In a lean, gravity provides this force.

Trail is a function of head angle, fork offset or rake, and wheel size. Their relationship can be described by this formula:

$$\text{Trail} = \frac{(R_w \cos(A_h) - O_f)}{\sin(A_h)}$$

where R_w is wheel radius, A_h is the head angle measured clock-wise from the horizontal and O_f is the fork offset or rake. Trail can be increased by increasing the wheel size, decreasing or slackening the head angle, or decreasing the fork rake.

The more trail a bike has, the more stable it feels. Bikes with negative trail (where the contact patch is actually in front of where the steering axis intersects the ground), while still ridable, feel very unstable. Bikes with too much trail feel difficult to steer. Normally, road racing bicycles have more trail than mountain bikes or touring bikes. In the case of mountain bikes, less trail allows more accurate path selection off-road, and also allows the rider to recover from obstacles on the trail which might knock the front wheel off course. Touring bikes are built with small trail to allow the rider to control a bike weighed down with baggage. As a consequence, an unloaded touring bike can feel unstable. In bicycles, fork rake, often a curve in the fork blades forward of the steering axis, is used to diminish trail. In motorcycles, rake refers to the head angle instead, and offset created by the triple tree is used to diminish trail.

A small survey by Whitt and Wilson found:

- touring bicycles with head angles between 72° and 73° and trail between 43 mm and 60 mm
- racing bicycles with head angles between 73° and 74° and trail between 28 mm and 45 mm

- track bicycles with head angles of 75° and trail between 23.5 mm and 37 mm.

However, these ranges are not hard and fast. For example, LeMond Racing Cycles offers both with forks that have 45 mm of offset or rake and the same size wheels:

- a 2006 Tete de Course, designed for road racing, with a head angle that varies from 71¼° to 74°, depending on frame size, and thus trail that varies from 69 mm to 51.5 mm.
- a 2007 Filmore, designed for the track, with a head angle that varies from 72½° to 74°, depending on frame size, and thus trail that varies from 61 mm to 51.5 mm.

The amount of trail a particular bike has may vary with time for several reasons. On bikes with front suspension, especially telescopic forks, compressing the front suspension, due to heavy braking for example, can steepen the steering axis angle and reduce trail. Trail also varies with lean angle, and steering angle, usually decreasing from a maximum when the bike is straight upright and steered straight ahead. Finally, even the profile of the front tire can influence how trail varies as the bike is leaned and steered.

A measurement similar to trail, called either **mechanical trail**, **normal trail**, or **true trail**, is the *perpendicular* distance from the steering axis to the centroid of the front wheel contact patch.

Steering mechanism mass distribution

Another factor that can also contribute to the self-stability of traditional bike designs is the distribution of mass in the steering mechanism, which includes the front wheel, the fork, and the handlebar. If the center of mass for the steering mechanism is in front of the steering axis, then the pull of gravity will also cause the front wheel to steer in the direction of a lean. This can be seen by leaning a stationary bike to one side. The front wheel will usually also steer to that side independent of any interaction with the ground. Additional parameters, such as the fore-to-aft position of the center of mass and the elevation of the center of mass also contribute to the dynamic behavior of a bike.

Gyroscopic effects

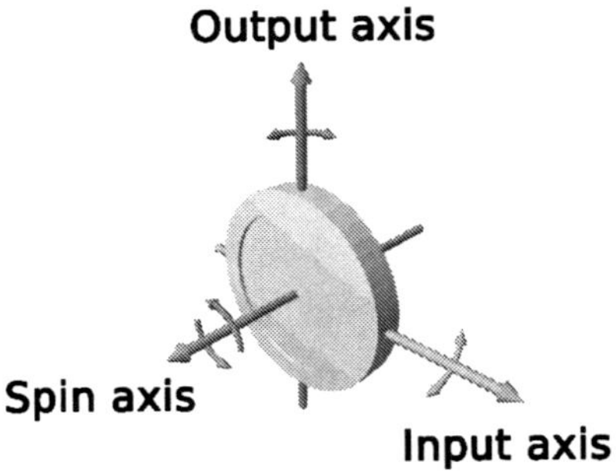

Gyroscopic effect on front wheel of a bike. Appling a torque (in green) about the lean axis results in a reaction torque (in blue) about the steer axis.

The role of the gyroscopic effect in most bike designs is to help steer the front wheel into the direction of a lean. This phenomenon is called *precession* and the rate at which an object precesses is inversely proportional to its rate of spin. The slower a front wheel spins, the faster it will precess when the bike leans, and vice-versa. The rear wheel is prevented from precessing as the front wheel does by friction of the tires on the ground, and so continues to lean as though it were not spinning at all. Hence gyroscopic forces do not provide any resistance to tipping.

At low forward speeds, the precession of the front wheel is too quick, contributing to an uncontrolled bike's tendency to oversteer, start to lean the other way and eventually oscillate and fall over. At high forward speeds, the precession is usually too slow, contributing to an uncontrolled bike's tendency to understeer and eventually fall over without ever having reached the upright position. This instability is very slow, on the order of seconds, and is easy for most riders to counteract. Thus a fast bike may feel stable even though it is actually not self-stable and would fall over if it were uncontrolled. A bicycle wheel with an internal flywheel for enhanced gyroscopic effect is under development as a commercial product, the Gyrobike, for making it easier to learn to ride bicycles.

Another contribution of gyroscopic effects is a roll moment generated by the front wheel during countersteering. For example, steering left causes a moment to the right. The moment is small compared to the moment generated by the out-tracking front wheel, but begins as soon as the rider applies torque to the handlebars and so can be helpful in motorcycle racing. For more detail, see the countersteering article.

Self-stability

Between the two unstable regimes mentioned in the previous section, and influenced by all the factors described above that contribute to balance (trail, mass distribution, gyroscopic effects, etc.), there may be a range of forward speeds for a given bike design at which these effects steer an uncontrolled bike upright.

However, even without self-stability a bike may be ridden by steering it to keep it over its wheels. Note that the effects mentioned above that would combine to produce self-stability may be overwhelmed by additional factors such as headset friction and stiff control cables. This video [1] shows a riderless bicycle exhibiting self-stability.

Turning

In order to turn a bike, that is, change its direction of forward travel, the front wheel is turned approximately in the desired direction, as with any front-wheel steered vehicle. Friction between the wheels and the ground then generates the centripetal acceleration necessary to alter the course from straight ahead as a combination of cornering force and camber thrust. The radius of the turn of an upright (not leaning) bike can be roughly approximated, for small steering angles, by:

$$r = \frac{w}{\delta \cos(\phi)}$$

where r is the approximate radius, w is the wheelbase, δ is the steer angle, and ϕ is the caster angle of the steering axis.

Leaning

However, unlike other wheeled vehicles, bikes must also lean during a turn to balance the relevant forces: gravitational, inertial, frictional, and ground support. The angle of lean, θ , can easily be calculated using the laws of circular motion:

$$\theta = \arctan\left(\frac{v^2}{gr}\right)$$

where v is the forward speed, r is the radius of the turn and g is the acceleration of gravity. This is in the idealized case. A slight increase in the lean angle may be required on motorcycles to compensate for the width of modern tires at the same forward speed and turn radius.

For example, a bike in a 10 m (33 ft) radius steady-state turn at 10 m/s (22 mph) must be at an angle of 45°. A rider can lean with respect to the bike in order to keep either the torso or the bike more or less upright if desired. The angle that matters is the one between the horizontal plane and the plane defined by the tire contacts and the location of the center of mass of bike and rider.

This lean of the bike decreases the actual radius of the turn proportionally to the cosine of the lean angle. The resulting radius can be roughly approximated (within 2% of exact value) by:

$$r = \frac{w \cos(\theta)}{\delta \cos(\phi)}$$

where r is the approximate radius, w is the wheelbase, θ is the lean angle, δ is the steer angle, and ϕ is the caster angle of the steering axis. As a bike leans, the tires' contact patches move farther to the side causing wear. The portions at either edge of a motorcycle tire that remain unworn by leaning into turns is sometimes referred to as chicken strips.

Countersteering

Main article: Countersteering

In order to initiate a turn and the necessary lean in the direction of that turn, a bike must momentarily steer in the opposite direction. This is often referred to as countersteering. With the front wheel now at an angle to the direction of motion, a lateral force is developed at the contact patch of the tire. This force creates a torque around the longitudinal (roll) axis of the bike. This torque causes the bike to roll in the opposite direction of the turn. Where there is no external influence, such as an opportune side wind to create the force necessary to lean the bike, countersteering happens in every turn.

As the lean approaches the desired angle, the front wheel must be steered in the direction of the turn, depending on the forward speed, the turn radius, and the need to maintain the lean angle. Once in a turn, the radius can only be changed with an appropriate change in lean angle. This can only be accomplished by additional countersteering out of the turn to increase lean and decrease radius, then into the turn to decrease lean and increase radius. To exit the turn, the bike must again countersteer, momentarily steering more into the turn in order to decrease the radius, thus increasing inertial forces, and thereby decreasing the angle of lean.

Steady-state turning

Once a turn is established, the torque that must be applied to the steering mechanism in order to maintain a constant radius at a constant forward speed depends on the forward speed and the geometry and mass distribution of the bike. At speeds below the capsize speed, described below in the section on *Eigenvalues* and also called the *inversion* speed, the self-stability of the bike will cause it to tend to steer into the turn, righting itself and exiting the turn, unless a torque is applied in the opposite direction of the turn. At speeds above the capsize speed, the capsize instability will cause it to tend to steer out of the turn, increasing the lean, unless a torque is applied in the direction of the turn. At the capsize speed no input steering torque is necessary to maintain the steady-state turn.

Steering angle

Several effects influence the steering angle, the angle at which the front assembly is rotated about the steering axis, necessary to maintain a steady-state turn. Some of these are unique to single-track vehicles, while others are also experienced by automobiles. Some of these may be mentioned elsewhere in this article, and they are repeated here, though not necessarily in order of importance, so that they may be found in one place.

First, the actual kinematic steering angle, the angle projected onto the road plane to which the front assembly is rotated is a function of the steering angle and the steering axis angle:

$$\Delta = \delta \cos(\phi)$$

where Δ is the kinematic steering angle, δ is the steering angle, and ϕ is the caster angle of the steering axis.

Second, the lean of the bike decreases the actual radius of the turn proportionally to the cosine of the lean angle. The resulting radius can be roughly approximated (within 2% of exact value) by:

$$r = \frac{w \cos(\theta)}{\delta \cos(\phi)}$$

where r is the approximate radius, w is the wheelbase, θ is the lean angle, δ is the steering angle, and ϕ is the caster angle of the steering axis.

Third, because the front and rear tires can have different slip angles due to weight distribution, tire properties, etc., bikes can experience understeer or oversteer. When understeering, the steering angle must be greater, and when oversteering, the steering angle must be less than it would be if the slip angles were equal to maintain a given turn radius. Some authors even use the term *counter-steering* to refer to the need on some bikes under some conditions to steer in the opposite direction of the turn (negative steering angle) to maintain control in response to significant rear wheel slippage.

Fourth, camber thrust contributes to the centripetal force necessary to cause the bike to deviate from a straight path, along with cornering force due to the slip angle, and can be the largest contributor. Camber thrust contributes to the ability of bikes to negotiate a turn with the same radius as automobiles but with a smaller steering angle. When a bike is steered and leaned in the same direction, the camber angle of the front tire is greater than that of the rear and so can generate more camber thrust, all else being equal.

No hands

While countersteering is usually initiated by applying torque directly to the handlebars, on lighter vehicles such as bicycles, it can also be accomplished by shifting the rider's weight. If the rider leans to the right relative to the bike, the bike will lean to the left to conserve angular momentum, and the combined center of mass will remain in the same vertical plane. This leftward lean of the bike, called **counter lean** by some authors, will cause it to steer to the left and initiate a right-hand turn as if the rider had countersteered to the left by applying a torque directly to the handlebars. Note that this technique may be complicated by additional factors such as headset friction and stiff control cables.

Gyroscopic effects

As mentioned above in the section on balance, one effect of turning the front wheel is a roll moment caused by gyroscopic precession. The magnitude of this moment is proportional to the moment of inertia of the front wheel, its spin rate (forward motion), the rate that the rider turns the front wheel by applying a torque to the handlebars, and the cosine of the angle between the steering axis and the vertical.

For a sample motorcycle moving at 22 m/s (50 mph) that has a front wheel with a moment of inertia of 0.6 kg·m^2, turning the front wheel one degree in half a second generates a roll moment of 3.5 N·m. In comparison, the lateral force on the front tire as it tracks out from under the motorcycle reaches a maximum of 50 N. This, acting on the 0.6 m (2 ft) height of the center of mass, generates a roll moment of 30 N·m.

While the moment from gyroscopic forces is only 12% of this, it can play a significant part because it begins to act as soon as the rider applies the torque, instead of building up more slowly as the wheel out-tracks. This can be especially helpful in motorcycle racing.

Two-wheel steering

Because of theoretical benefits, such as a tighter turning radius at low speed, attempts have been made to construct motorcycles with two-wheel steering. One working prototype by Ian Drysdale in Australia is reported to "work very well." Issues in the design include whether to provide active control of the rear wheel or let it swing freely. In the case of active control, the control algorithm needs to decide between steering with or in the opposite direction of the front wheel, when, and how much. One implementation of two-wheel steering, the Sideways bike, lets the rider control the steering of both wheels directly.

Milton W. Raymond built a long low two-wheel steering bicycle, called "X-2", with various steering mechanisms to control the two wheels independently. Steering motions included "balance", in which both wheels move together to steer the tire contact under the center of gravity; and "true circle", in which the wheels steer equally in opposite directions and thus steering the bicycle without substantially changing the lateral position of the tire contacts relative to the center of mass. X-2 was also able to go "crabwise" with the wheels parallel but out of line with the frame, for instance with the front wheel near the roadway center line and rear wheel near the curb. "Balance" steering allowed easy balancing despite long wheelbase and low center of mass, but no self-balancing ("no hands") configuration was discovered. True circle, as expected, was essentially impossible to balance, as steering does not correct for misalignment of the tire patch and center of mass. Crabwise cycling at angles tested up to about 45° did not show a tendency to fall over, even under braking.[citation needed] X-2 is mentioned in passing in Whitt and Wilson's *Bicycling Science* 2nd edition.

Rear-wheel steering

Because of the theoretical benefits, especially a simplified front-wheel drive mechanism, attempts have been made to construct a ridable rear-wheel steering bike. The Bendix Company built a rear-wheel steering bicycle, and the U.S. Department of Transportation commissioned the construction of a rear-wheel steering motorcycle: both proved to be unridable. Rainbow Trainers, Inc. in Alton, IL, offered US$5,000 to the first person "who can successfully ride the rear-steered bicycle, Rear Steered Bicycle I". One documented example of someone successfully riding a rear-wheel steering bicycle is that of L. H. Laiterman at MIT, on a specially designed recumbent bike. The difficulty is that turning left, accomplished by turning the rear wheel to the right, initially moves the center of mass to the right, and vice versa. This complicates the task of compensating for leans induced by the environment. Examination of the eigenvalues shows that the rear-wheel steering configuration is inherently unstable.

Center steering

Between the extremes of bicycles with classical front-wheel steering and those with strictly rear-wheel steering is a class of bikes with a pivot point somewhere between the two referred to as center-steering, similar to articulated steering. An early implementation of the concept was the Phantom bicycle in the early 1870s promoted as a safer alternative to the penny-farthing. This design allows for simple front-wheel drive and current implementations appear to be quite stable, even ridable no-hands, as many photographs illustrate. These designs, such as the Python Lowracer, usually have very lax head angles (40° to 65°) and positive or even negative trail. The builder of a bike with negative trail states that steering the bike from straight ahead forces the seat (and thus the rider) to rise slightly and this offsets the destabilizing effect of the negative trail.

Tiller effect

Tiller effect is the expression used to describe how handlebars that extend far behind the steering axis (head tube) act like a tiller on a boat, in that one moves the bars to the right in order to turn the front wheel to the left, and vice versa. This situation is commonly found on cruiser bicycles, some recumbents, and even some cruiser motorcycles. It can be troublesome when it limits the ability to steer because of interference or the limits of arm reach.

Tires

Tires have a large influence over bike handling, especially on motorcycles. Tire inflation pressures have also been found to be important variables in the behavior of a motorcycle at high speeds. Because the front and rear tires can have different slip angles due to weight distribution, tire properties, etc., bikes can experience understeer or oversteer. Of the two, understeer, in which the front wheel slides more than the rear wheel, is more dangerous since front wheel steering is critical for maintaining balance. Also, because real tires have a finite contact patch with the road surface that can generate a scrub torque, and when in a turn, can experience some side slipping as they roll, they can generate torques about an axis normal to the plane of the contact patch.

One torque generated by tires is due to asymmetries in the side-slip along the length of the contact patch. The resultant force of this side-slip occurs behind the geometric center of the contact patch, a distance described as the pneumatic trail, and so creates a torque on the tire. Since the direction of the side-slip is towards the outside of the turn, the force on the tire is towards the center of the turn. Therefore, this torque tends to turn the front wheel in the direction of the side-slip, away from the direction of the turn, and therefore tends to *increase* the radius of the turn.

Another torque is produced by the finite width of the contact patch and the lean of the tire in a turn. The portion of the contact patch towards the outside of the turn is actually moving rearward, with respect to the wheel's hub, faster than the rest of the contact patch, because of its greater radius from the hub. By the same reasoning, the inner portion is moving rearward more slowly. So the outer and inner portions of the contact patch slip on the pavement in opposite directions, generating a torque that tends to turn the front wheel in the direction of the turn, and therefore tends to *decrease* the turn radius.

The combination of these two opposite torques creates a resulting yaw torque on the front wheel, and its direction is a function of the side-slip angle of the tire, the angle between the actual path of the tire and the direction it is pointing, and the camber angle of the tire (the angle that the tire leans from the vertical). The result of this torque is often the suppression of the inversion speed predicted by rigid wheel models described above in the section on steady-state turning.

High side

Main article: Highsider

A **highsider**, **highside**, or **high side** is a type of bike motion which is caused by a rear wheel gaining traction when it is not facing in the direction of travel, usually after slipping sideways in a curve. This can occur under heavy braking, acceleration, a varying road surface, or suspension activation, especially due to interaction with the drivetrain. It can take the form of a single slip-then-flip or a series of violent oscillations.

Maneuverability and handling

Bike maneuverability and handling is difficult to quantify for several reasons. The geometry of a bike, especially the steering axis angle makes kinematic analysis complicated. Under many conditions, bikes are inherently unstable and must always be under rider control. Finally, the rider's skill has a large influence on the bike's performance in any maneuver. Bike designs tend to consist of a trade-off between maneuverability and stability.

Rider control inputs

The primary control input that the rider can make is to apply a torque directly to the steering mechanism via the handlebars. Because of the bike's own dynamics, due to steering geometry and gyroscopic effects, direct position control over steering angle has been found to be problematic.

A secondary control input that the rider can make is to lean the upper torso relative to the bike. As mentioned above, the effectiveness of rider lean varies inversely with the mass of the bike. On heavy bikes, such as motorcycles, rider lean mostly alters the ground clearance requirements in a turn, improves the view of the road, and improves the bike system dynamics in a very low-frequency passive manner.

Differences from automobiles

The need to keep a bike upright to avoid injury to the rider and damage to the vehicle even limits the type of maneuverability testing that is commonly performed. For example, while automobile enthusiast publications often perform and quote skidpad results, motorcycle publications do not. The need to "set up" for a turn, lean the bike to the appropriate angle, means that the rider must see further ahead than is necessary for a typical car at the same speed, and this need increases more than in proportion to the speed.

Rating schemes

Several schemes have been devised to rate the handling of bikes, particularly motorcycles.

- The **roll index** is the ratio between steering torque and roll or lean angle.
- The **acceleration index** is the ratio between steering torque and lateral or centripetal acceleration.
- The **steering ratio** is the ratio between the theoretical turning radius based on ideal tire behavior and the actual turning radius. Values less than one, where the front wheel side slip is greater than the rear wheel side slip, are described as under-steering; equal to one as neutral steering; and greater than one as over-steering. Values less than zero, in which the front wheel must be turned opposite the direction of the curve due to much greater rear wheel side slip than front wheel have been described as counter-steering. Riders tend to prefer neutral or slight over-steering. Car drivers tend to prefer under-steering.
- The **Koch index** is the ratio between peak steering torque and the product of peak lean rate and forward speed. Large, touring motorcycles tend to have a high Koch index, sport motorcycles tend to have a medium Koch index, and scooters tend to have a low Koch index. It is easier to maneuver light scooters than heavy motorcycles.

Lateral motion theory

Although its equations of motion can be linearized, a bike is a nonlinear system. The variable(s) to be solved for cannot be written as a linear sum of independent components, i.e. its behavior is not expressible as a sum of the behaviors of its descriptors. Generally, nonlinear systems are difficult to solve and are much less understandable than linear systems. In the idealized case, in which friction and any flexing is ignored, a bike is a conservative system. Damping, however, can still be demonstrated: side-to-side oscillations will decrease with time. Energy added with a sideways jolt to a bike running straight and upright (demonstrating self-stability) is converted into increased forward speed, not lost, as the oscillations die out.

A bike is a nonholonomic system because its outcome is path-dependent. In order to know its exact configuration, especially location, it is necessary to know not only the configuration of its parts, but also their histories: how they have moved over time. This complicates mathematical analysis. Finally, in the language of control theory, a bike exhibits non-minimum phase behavior. It turns in the direction opposite of how it is initially steered, as described above in the section on countersteering

Degrees of freedom

The number of degrees of freedom of a bike depends on the particular model being used. The simplest model that captures the key dynamic features, four rigid bodies with knife edge wheels rolling on a flat smooth surface, has 7 degrees of freedom (configuration variables required to completely describe the location and orientation of all 4 bodies):

1. x coordinate of rear wheel contact point
2. y coordinate of rear wheel contact point
3. orientation angle of rear frame (yaw)
4. rotation angle of rear wheel
5. rotation angle of front wheel
6. lean angle of rear frame (roll)
7. steering angle between rear frame and front end

Adding complexity to the model, such as suspension, tire compliance, frame flex, or rider movement, adds degrees of freedom. While the rear frame does pitch with leaning and steering, the pitch angle is completely constrained by the requirement for both wheels to remain on the ground, and so can be calculated geometrically from the other seven variables. If the location of the bike and the rotation of the wheels are ignored, the first five degrees of freedom can also be ignored, and the bike can be described by just two variables: lean angle and steer angle.

Equations of motion

The equations of motion of an idealized bike, consisting of

- a rigid frame,
- a rigid fork,
- two knife-edged, rigid wheels,
- all connected with frictionless bearings and rolling without friction or slip on a smooth horizontal surface and
- operating at or near the upright and straight-ahead, unstable equilibrium

can be represented by a single fourth-order linearized ordinary differential equation or two coupled second-order differential equations, the lean equation

$$M_{\theta\theta}\ddot{\theta}_r + K_{\theta\theta}\theta_r + M_{\theta\psi}\ddot{\psi} + C_{\theta\psi}\dot{\psi} + K_{\theta\psi}\psi = M_\theta$$

and the steer equation

$$M_{\psi\psi}\ddot{\psi} + C_{\psi\psi}\dot{\psi} + K_{\psi\psi}\psi + M_{\psi\theta}\ddot{\theta}_r + C_{\psi\theta}\dot{\theta}_r + K_{\psi\theta}\theta_r = M_\psi,$$

where

- θ_r is the lean angle of the rear assembly,

- ψ is the steer angle of the front assembly relative to the rear assembly and
- M_θ and M_ψ are the moments (torques) applied at the rear assembly and the steering axis, respectively. For the analysis of an uncontrolled bike, both are taken to be zero.

These can be represented in matrix form as

$$M\ddot{\mathbf{q}} + C\dot{\mathbf{q}} + K\mathbf{q} = \mathbf{f}$$

where

- M is the symmetrical mass matrix which contains terms that include only the mass and geometry of the bike,
- C is the so-called damping matrix, even though an idealized bike has no dissipation, which contains terms that include the forward speed v and is asymmetric,
- K is the so-called stiffness matrix which contains terms that include the gravitational constant g and $v^2$and is symmetric in g and asymmetric in v^2,
- $\mathbf{q}$ is a vector of lean angle and steer angle, and
- $\mathbf{f}$ is a vector of external forces, the moments mentioned above.

In this idealized and linearized model, there are many geometric parameters (wheelbase, head angle, mass of each body, wheel radius, etc.), but only four significant variables: lean angle, lean rate, steer angle, and steer rate. These equations have been verified by comparison with multiple numeric models derived completely independently.

Eigenvalues

It is possible to calculate eigenvalues, one for each of the four state variables (lean angle, lean rate, steer angle, and steer rate), from the linearized equations in order to analyze the normal modes and self-stability of a particular bike design. In the plot to the right, eigenvalues of one particular bicycle are calculated for forward speeds of 0–10 m/s (22 mph). When the real parts of all eigenvalues (shown in dark blue) are negative, the bike is self-stable. When the imaginary parts of any eigenvalues (shown in cyan) are non-zero, the bike exhibits oscillation. The eigenvalues are point symmetric about the origin and so any bike design with a self-stable region in forward speeds will not be self-stable going backwards at the same speed.

There are three forward speeds that can be identified in the plot to the right at which the motion of the bike changes qualitatively:

1. The forward speed at which oscillations begin, at about 1 m/s (2.2 mph) in this example, sometimes called the *double root* speed due to there being a repeated root to the characteristic polynomial (two of the four eigenvalues have exactly the same value). Below this speed, the bike simply falls over as an inverted pendulum does.
2. The forward speed at which oscillations do not increase, where the weave mode eigenvalues switch from positive to negative in a Hopf bifurcation at about 5.3 m/s (12 mph) in this example, is called the *weave speed*. Below this speed, oscillations increase until the uncontrolled bike falls over.

Above this speed, oscillations eventually die out.

3. The forward speed at which non-oscillatory leaning increases, where the capsize mode eigenvalues switch from negative to positive in a pitchfork bifurcation at about 8 m/s (18 mph) in this example, is called the *capsize speed*. Above this speed, this non-oscillating lean eventually causes the uncontrolled bike to fall over.

Between these last two speeds, if they both exist, is a range of forward speeds at which the particular bike design is self-stable. In the case of the bike whose eigenvalues are shown here, the self-stable range is 5.3–8.0 m/s (12–18 mph). The fourth eigenvalue, which is usually stable (very negative), represents the castoring behavior of the front wheel, as it tends to turn towards the direction in which the bike is traveling. Note that this idealized model does not exhibit the *wobble or shimmy* and *rear wobble* instabilities described above. They are seen in models that incorporate tire interaction with the ground or other degrees of freedom.

Experimentation with real bikes has so far confirmed the weave mode predicted by the eigenvalues. It was found that tire slip and frame flex are *not important for the lateral dynamics of the bicycle in the speed range up to 6* m/s. The idealized bike model used to calculate the eigenvalues shown here does not incorporate any of the torques that real tires can generate, and so tire interaction with the pavement cannot prevent the capsize mode from becoming unstable at high speeds, as Wilson and Cossalter suggest happens in the real world.

Modes

Bikes, as complex mechanisms, have a variety of modes: fundamental ways that they can move. These modes can be stable or unstable, depending on the bike parameters and its forward speed. In this context, "stable" means that an uncontrolled bike will continue rolling forward without falling over as long as forward speed is maintained. Conversely, "unstable" means that an uncontrolled bike will eventually fall over, even if forward speed is maintained. The modes can be differentiated by the speed at which they switch stability and the relative phases of leaning and steering as the bike experiences that mode. Any bike motion consists of a combination of various amounts of the possible modes, and there are three main modes that a bike can experience: capsize, weave, and wobble. A lesser known mode is rear wobble, and it is usually stable.

Capsize

Capsize is the word used to describe a bike falling over without oscillation. During capsize, an uncontrolled front wheel usually steers in the direction of lean, but never enough to stop the increasing lean, until a very high lean angle is reached, at which point the steering may turn in the opposite direction. A capsize can happen very slowly if the bike is moving forward rapidly. Because the capsize instability is so slow, on the order of seconds, it is easy for the rider to control, and is actually used by the rider to initiate the lean necessary for a turn.

For most bikes, depending on geometry and mass distribution, capsize is stable at low speeds, and becomes less stable as speed increases until it is no longer stable. However, on many bikes, tire interaction with the pavement is sufficient to prevent capsize from becoming unstable at high speeds.

Weave

Weave is the word used to describe a slow (0–4 Hz) oscillation between leaning left and steering right, and vice-versa. The entire bike is affected with significant changes in steering angle, lean angle (roll), and heading angle (yaw). The steering is 180° out of phase with the heading and 90° out of phase with the leaning. This AVI movie [2] shows weave.

For most bikes, depending on geometry and mass distribution, weave is unstable at low speeds, and becomes less pronounced as speed increases until it is no longer unstable. While the amplitude may decrease, the frequency actually increases with speed.

Wobble or shimmy

Wobble, *shimmy*, *tank-slapper*, *speed wobble*, and *death wobble* are all words and phrases used to describe a rapid (4–10 Hz) oscillation of primarily just the front end (front wheel, fork, and handlebars). The rest of the bike remains essentially unaffected. This instability occurs mostly at high speed and is similar to that experienced by shopping cart wheels, airplane landing gear, and automobile front wheels. While wobble or shimmy can be easily remedied by adjusting speed, position, or grip on the handlebar, it can be fatal if left uncontrolled. This AVI movie [3] shows wobble.

Wobble or shimmy begins when some otherwise minor irregularity, such as fork asymmetry, accelerates the wheel to one side. The restoring force is applied in phase with the progress of the irregularity, and the wheel turns to the other side where the process is repeated. If there is insufficient damping in the steering the oscillation will increase until system failure occurs. The oscillation frequency can be changed by changing the forward speed, making the bike stiffer or lighter, or increasing the stiffness of the steering, of which the rider is a main component.

Rear wobble

The term *rear wobble* is used to describe a mode of oscillation in which lean angle (roll) and heading angle (yaw) are almost in phase and both 180° out of phase with steer angle. The rate of this oscillation is moderate with a maximum of about 6.5 Hz. Rear wobble is heavily damped and falls off quickly as bike speed increases.

Design criteria

The effect that the design parameters of a bike have on these modes can be investigated by examining the eigenvalues of the linearized equations of motion. For more details on the equations of motion and eigenvalues, see the section on the equations of motion above. Some general conclusions that have been drawn are described here.

The lateral and torsional stiffness of the rear frame and the wheel spindle affects wobble-mode damping substantially. Long wheelbase and trail and a flat steering-head angle have been found to increase weave-mode damping. Lateral distortion can be countered by locating the front fork torsional axis as low as possible.

Cornering weave tendencies are amplified by degraded damping of the rear suspension. Cornering, camber stiffnesses and relaxation length of the rear tire make the largest contribution to weave damping. The same parameters of the front tire have a lesser effect. Rear loading also amplifies cornering weave tendencies. Rear load assemblies with appropriate stiffness and damping, however, were successful in damping out weave and wobble oscillations.

One study has shown theoretically that, while a bike leaned in a turn, road undulations can excite the weave mode at high speed or the wobble mode at low speed if either of their frequencies match the vehicle speed and other parameters. Excitation of the wobble mode can be mitigated by an effective steering damper and excitation of the weave mode is worse for light riders than for heavy riders.

Other hypotheses

Although bicycles and motorcycles can appear to be simple mechanisms with only four major moving parts (frame, fork, and two wheels), these parts are arranged in a way that makes them complicated to analyze. While it is an observable fact that bikes can be ridden even when the gyroscopic effects of their wheels are canceled out, the hypothesis that the gyroscopic effects of the wheels are what keep a bike upright is common in print and online.

Examples in print:

- "Angular momentum and motorcycle counter-steering: A discussion and demonstration", A. J. Cox, *Am. J. Phys.* 66, 1018–1021 ~1998
- "The motorcycle as a gyroscope", J. Higbie, *Am. J. Phys.* 42, 701–702
- *The Physics of Everyday Phenomena*, W. T. Griffith, McGraw–Hill, New York, 1998, pp. 149–150.
- *The Way Things Work.*, Macaulay, Houghton-Mifflin, New York, NY, 1989

And online:

- www.physlink.com [4]
- www.straightdope.com [5]
- www.everything2.com [6]
- library.thinkquest.org [7]

- www.rider-ed.com [8]
- The Third Gyroscope [9]

Longitudinal dynamics

Bikes may experience a variety of longitudinal forces and motions. On most bikes, when the front wheel is turned to one side or the other, the entire rear frame pitches forward slightly, depending on the steering axis angle and the amount of trail. On bikes with suspensions, either front, rear, or both, **trim** is used to describe the geometric configuration of the bike, especially in response to forces of braking, accelerating, turning, drive train, and aerodynamic drag.

The load borne by the two wheels varies not only with center of mass location, which in turn varies with the amount and location of passengers and luggage, but also with acceleration and deceleration. This phenomenon is known as load transfer or weight transfer, depending on the author, and provides challenges and opportunities to both riders and designers. For example, motorcycle racers can use it to increase the friction available to the front tire when cornering, and attempts to reduce front suspension compression during heavy braking has spawned several motorcycle fork designs.

The net aerodynamic drag forces may be considered to act at a single point, called the center of pressure. At high speeds, this will create a net moment about the rear driving wheel and result in a net transfer of load from the front wheel to the rear wheel. Also, depending on the shape of the bike and the shape of any fairing that might be installed, aerodynamic lift may be present that either increases or further reduces the load on the front wheel.

Stability

Though longitudinally stable when stationary, a bike may become longitudinally unstable under sufficient acceleration or deceleration, and Euler's second law can be used to analyze the ground reaction forces generated. For example, the normal (vertical) ground reaction forces at the wheels for a bike with a wheelbase L and a center of mass at height h and at a distance b in front of the rear wheel hub, and for simplicity, with both wheels locked, can be expressed as:

$N_r = mg\left(\frac{L-b}{L} - \mu\frac{h}{L}\right)$ for the rear wheel and $N_f = mg\left(\frac{b}{L} + \mu\frac{h}{L}\right)$ for the front wheel.

The frictional (horizontal) forces are simply

$F_r = \mu N_r$ for the rear wheel and $F_f = \mu N_f$ for the front wheel,

where μ is the coefficient of friction, m is the total mass of the bike and rider, and g is the acceleration of gravity. Therefore, if

$$\mu \geq \frac{L-b}{h},$$

which occurs if the center of mass is anywhere above or in front of a line extending back from the front wheel contact patch and inclined at the angle

$$\theta = \tan^{-1}\left(\frac{1}{\mu}\right)$$

above the horizontal, then the normal force of the rear wheel will be zero (at which point the equation no longer applies) and the bike will begin to flip or loop forward over the front wheel.

On the other hand, if the center of mass height is behind or below the line, as is true, for example on most tandem bicycles or long-wheel-base recumbent bicycles, then, even if the coefficient of friction is 1.0, it is impossible for the front wheel to generate enough braking force to flip the bike. It will skid unless it hits some fixed obstacle, such as a curb.

Similarly, powerful motorcycles can generate enough torque at the rear wheel to lift the front wheel off the ground in a maneuver called a wheelie. A line similar to the one described above to analyze braking performance can be drawn from the rear wheel contact patch to predict if a wheelie is possible given the available friction, the center of mass location, and sufficient power. This can also happen on bicycles, although there is much less power available, if the center of mass is back or up far enough or the rider lurches back when applying power to the pedals.

Of course, the angle of the terrain can influence all of the calculations above. All else remaining equal, the risk of pitching over the front end is reduced when riding up hill and increased when riding down hill. The possibility of performing a wheelie increases when riding up hill, and is a major factor in motorcycle hillclimbing competitions.

Braking

Most of the braking force of standard upright bikes comes from the front wheel. As the analysis above shows, if the brakes themselves are strong enough, the rear wheel is easy to skid, while the front wheel often can generate enough stopping force to flip the rider and bike over the front wheel. This is called a *stoppie* if the rear wheel is lifted but the bike does not flip, or an *endo* (abbreviated form of *end-over-end*) if the bike flips. On long or low bikes, however, such as cruiser motorcycles and recumbent bicycles, the front tire will skid instead, possibly causing a loss of balance.

In the case of a front suspension, especially telescoping fork tubes, the increase in downward force on the front wheel during braking may cause the suspension to compress and the front end to lower. This is known as *brake diving*. A riding technique that takes advantage of how braking increases the downward force on the front wheel is known as *trail braking*.

Front wheel braking

The limiting factors on the maximum deceleration in front wheel braking are:

- the maximum, limiting value of static friction between the tire and the ground, often between 0.5 and 0.8 for rubber on dry asphalt,
- the kinetic friction between the brake pads and the rim or disk, and
- pitching or looping (of bike and rider) over the front wheel.

For an upright bicycle on dry asphalt with excellent brakes, pitching will probably be the limiting factor. The combined center of mass of a typical upright bicycle and rider will be about 60 cm (24 in) back from the front wheel contact patch and 120 cm (47 in) above, allowing a maximum deceleration of 0.5 g (5 m/s^2 or 16 ft/s^2). If the rider modulates the brakes properly, however, pitching can be avoided. If the rider moves his weight back and down, even larger decelerations are possible.

Front brakes on many inexpensive bikes are not strong enough so, on the road, they are the limiting factor. Cheap cantilever brakes, especially with "power modulators", and Raleigh-style side-pull brakes severely restrict the stopping force. In wet conditions they are even less effective. Front wheel slides are more common off-road. Mud, water, and loose stones reduce the friction between the tire and trail, although knobby tires can mitigate this effect by grabbing the surface irregularities. Front wheel slides are also common on corners, whether on road or off. Centripetal acceleration adds to the forces on the tire-ground contact, and when the friction force is exceeded the wheel slides.

Rear wheel braking

The rear brake of an upright bicycle can only produce about 0.1 g (1 m/s^2) deceleration at best, because of the decrease in normal force at the rear wheel as described above. All bikes with only rear braking are subject to this limitation: for example, bikes with only a coaster brake, and fixed-gear bikes with no other braking mechanism. There are, however, situations that may warrant rear wheel braking

- Slippery surfaces. Under front wheel braking, the lower coefficient of friction may cause the front wheel to skid which often results in a loss of balance.
- Front flat tire. Braking a wheel with a flat tire can cause the tire to come off the rim which greatly reduces friction and, in the case of a front wheel, result in a loss of balance.
- Long mountain descents. Alternating between front and rear brakes can help reduce heat buildup which can cause a blowout when using rim brakes.

Suspension

Main article: Bicycle suspension

Main article: Suspension (motorcycle)

Bikes may have only front, only rear, full suspension or no suspension that operate primarily in the central plane of symmetry; though with some consideration given to lateral compliance. The goals of a bike suspension are to reduce vibration experienced by the rider, maintain wheel contact with the ground, and maintain vehicle trim. The primary suspension parameters are stiffness, damping, sprung and unsprung mass, and tire characteristics. Besides irregularities in the terrain, braking and acceleration forces can also activate the suspension as described above.

Vibration

The study of vibration in bikes includes its causes, such as engine balance, wheel balance, ground surface, and aerodynamics; its transmission and absorption; and its effects on the bike, the rider, and safety. An important factor in any vibration analysis is a comparison of the natural frequencies of the system with the possible driving frequencies of the vibration sources. A close match means mechanical resonance that can result in large amplitudes. A challenge in vibration damping is to create compliance in certain directions (vertically) without sacrificing frame rigidity needed for power transmission and handling (torsionally). Another issue with vibration for the bike is the possibility of failure due to material fatigue Effects of vibration on riders include discomfort, loss of efficiency, Hand-Arm Vibration Syndrome, a secondary form Raynaud's disease, and whole body vibration. Vibrating instruments may be inaccurate or difficult to read.

In bicycles

The primary cause of vibrations in a properly functioning bicycle is the surface over which it rolls. In addition to pneumatic tires and traditional bicycle suspensions, a variety of techniques have been developed to damp vibrations before they reach the rider. These include materials, such as carbon fiber, either in the whole frame or just key components such as the front fork, seatpost, or handlebars; tube shapes, such as curved seat stays; and special inserts, such as Zertz by Specialized, and Buzzkills by Bontrager.

In motorcycles

In addition to the road surface, vibrations in a motorcycle can be caused by the engine and wheels, if unbalanced. Manufacturers employ a variety of technologies to reduce or damp these vibrations, such as engine balance shafts, rubber engine mounts, and tire weights. The problems that vibration causes have also spawned an industry of after-market parts and systems designed to reduce it. Add-ons include handlebar weights, isolated foot pegs, and engine counterweights. At high speeds, motorcycles and their riders may also experience aerodynamic flutter or buffeting. This can be abated by changing the air flow over key parts, such as the windshield.

Experimentation

A variety of experiments have been performed in order to verify or disprove various hypotheses about bike dynamics.

- David Jones built several bikes in a search for an unridable configuration.
- Richard Klein built several bikes to confirm Jones's findings.
- Richard Klein also built a "Torque Wrench Bike" and a "Rocket Bike" to investigate steering torques and their effects.
- Keith Code built a motorcycle with fixed handlebars to investigate the effects of rider motion and position on steering.
- Schwab and Kooijman have performed measurements with an instrumented bike.

See also

- Bicycle and motorcycle geometry
- Bicycle fork
- Bicycle tire
- Camber angle
- Camber thrust
- Caster angle
- Cornering force
- Countersteering
- Highsider
- Lowsider
- Motorcycle fork
- Slip angle
- Speed wobble
- Stoppie
- Trail braking
- Wheelie

Further reading

- 'An Introduction to Bicycle Geometry and Handling' [10], Karl Anderson
- 'What keeps the bicycle upright?' [11] by Jobst Brandt
- 'Report on Stability of the Dahon Bicycle' [12] by John Forester

External links

Videos:

- Video of riderless bicycle demonstrating self-stability [13]
- Wobble movie (AVI) [3]
- Weave movie (AVI) [2]
- Wobble Crash (Flash) [14]

Research centers:

- Bicycle Dynamics at Delft University of Technology [15]
- Bicycle Mechanics at Cornell University [13]
- Bicycle Science at the University of Illinois [16]
- Motorcycle Dynamics at Padua University [17]
- Control and Power Research Group at Imperial College [18]

Conferences:

- Bicycle and Motorcycle Dynamics 2010 [19]: Symposium on Dynamics and Control of Single Track Vehicles, Delft University of Technology, Oct 20-22, 2010

Purposes of Motorcycles

Touring motorcycle

A **touring motorcycle** is a type of motorcycle designed for long-distance touring and heavy commuting. Although any motorcycle can be used to tour with, manufacturers have brought specific models designed to address the particular needs of these riders. Common to the touring motorcycle models is usually large displacement fairings and windshields (to offer a high degree of weather and wind protection), large capacity fuel tanks (for long ranges between fill-ups), engines offering lots of low-end horsepower, and a more relaxed, more upright seating position than sport bikes. These motorcycles can be further subdivided into multiple sub-categories, which are commonly used terms within the motorcycle industry.

Full-dress tourers

BMW K 1200 LT at Glacier National Park

Full-Dress touring motorcycles are generally characterized by extremely large fairings and ample bodywork compared to other forms of tourers, the integration of hard luggage into the design of the motorcycle (often including both saddlebags and a top-mounted box), very large displacement, torque-rich engines, and a very upright, comfortable riding position. Additionally, standard and optional amenities on full-dress tourers often include equipment not normally offered on other motorcycles, such as complete stereos (AM/FM radios with CD players or MP3 connections are standard, and satellite radio is becoming increasingly common), heated seats and hand-grips, GPS navigation systems, selective venting, power windshields, and, for certain models in certain model-years, such oddities as integrated air compressors and air bags. Full-dress tourers are designed specifically for riding on pavement, although they may be taken onto hard, compacted dirt roads; they are specifically not designed for off-road duties. Common current examples of full-dress tourers include the Yamaha Royal Star Venture, the Honda Goldwing, the BMW K1200LT, and the Harley-Davidson Electra Glide, all of which have become quite popular. Also, Victory Motorcycles recently introduced its new, controversially styled model, the Vision Tour.

Global on- and off-road tourers

This category encompasses dual-sport motorcycles designed specifically to provide global touring capabilities on both pavement and off-road with the intent of making virtually any destination reachable. Motorcycles in this category share a unique combination of traits that provide them very high ground clearance (for off-road purposes); particularly large fuel reserves; large displacement understressed engines for high reliability and heavy torque output; large size; and good high-speed highway behavior and handling. This combination of traits (along with their weight) is also what separates them from traditional off-road, Enduro, and MX class motorcycles.

BMW R1200GS dual-purpose motorcycle

It is common for a large selection of purpose-driven options to be available for global tourers, including skid plates (to protect the engine and transmission during off-road use), larger and additional fuel tanks than stock, metal-formed hard luggage for extreme condition use, hardened GPS navigation systems designed to handle off-road abuse, etc. These bikes do not necessarily ship with hard luggage, but usually offer them as optional extras either from the manufacturer or via third-party suppliers. These motorcycles are often used as the basis for competitions in extreme rally events, including the grueling Dakar Rally.

Noteworthy current examples include the BMW F800GS and F650GS and R1200GS; the KTM 950 and 990 Adventure series; the Suzuki DL1000 and DL650 V-Strom; and the Kawasaki KLR650. In recent years, other manufacturers have also introduced models with some off-road ability like the Buell Ulysses and the Triumph Tiger, although from 2007 the Tiger is much more road oriented.

Sport-tourers

Main article: Sport touring

Sport tourers are a hybrid form between sport bikes and tourers, allowing long-distance riding at higher speeds but with more emphasis on sport-like performance (in both handling and speed) than standard tourers. These bikes offer a middle ground between both segments. The paradigm arguably originated with the 1976 BMW R 100 RS, which combined BMW's traditional strengths in touring with a full-coverage racing fairing that surrounded clip on-like handlebars, and featured a semi-crouched riding position. The sport touring category includes such motorcycles as the Honda VFR (Interceptor) and ST series; the Yamaha FJR1300; the Triumph Sprint and Sprint ST; Ducati ST series; the Moto Guzzi Norge; the Suzuki Katana; the Kawasaki Concours 14 (1400GTR); as well as many BMW GT, ST, and RT models. These bikes sometimes ship with hard luggage, but some manufacturers offer them as optional extras, either from the manufacturers themselves or via third-party suppliers.

Cruiser (motorcycle)

Main article: Types of motorcycles

Cruiser is the term for motorcycles that mimic the design style of American machines from the 1930s to the early 1960s, including those made by Harley-Davidson, Indian, Excelsior and Henderson. The market for models evocative of the early cruisers has grown to embrace 60% of the U.S. market, such that all major motorcycle manufacturers—from Honda to Suzuki to Moto Guzzi to BMW have currently or have had important models evocative of the American cruiser.

BMW R1200C Cruiser

Moto Guzzi California Jackal

The riding position on a cruiser usually but not always places the feet forward and the hands up, with the spine erect or leaning back slightly. Many "power cruisers" and Japanese cruisers of the 1980s have featured more neutral riding positions.

Chopper-style motorcycles are considered cruisers.

Many cruising motorcycles have limited performance and turning ability due to a low-slung design. Riders who enjoy cornering at higher speeds may need to customize to enhance lean angle, or start with a performance or sport-cruiser.

Cruisers are often custom projects that result in a bike modified to suit the owner's ideals, and as such are a source of pride and accomplishment. Cruisers are sometimes called custom even in the absence of aftermarket modifications.

Motorcycle sport

Motorcycle sport is a broad field that encompasses all sporting aspects of motorcycling. The disciplines are not all "races" or timed-speed events, as several disciplines test a competitor's various riding skills.

Motorcycle racing

Main article: Motorcycle racing

Motorcycle racing (also known as Moto racing and Bike racing) is a motorcycle sport involving racing motorcycles. Motorcycle racing can be divided into two categories, tarmac-based road disciplines and off road.

Track racing

Main article: Track racing

Track racing is a motorcycle sport where teams or individuals race opponents around an oval track. There are differing variants, with each variant racing on a different surface type.

Rally

A **road rally** is a navigation event on public roads whereby competiors must visit a number of checkpoints in diverse geographical locations while still obeying road traffic laws (not to be confused with car rallies such as WRC).

Other Motorcycle sports

Land speed

Main article: Motorcycle land speed record

Land Speed is where a single rider accelerates over a 1 to 3-mile (4.8 km) long straight track (usually on dry lake beds) and is timed for top speed through a trap at the end of the run. The rider must exceed the previous top speed record for that class or type of bike for their name to be placed on the record books. See—[1] for an example.

Enduro

Main article: Enduro

Enduro isn't exactly racing, because the main objective is to traverse a series of checkpoints, arriving exactly "on time" in accordance with your beginning time and the time it is supposed to take to arrive at each checkpoint. The courses are usually run over thick wooded terrain, sometimes with large obstacles such as logs, ditches, and sudden drops.

Freestyle Motocross

Main article: Freestyle Motocross

A competition based upon points for acrobatic ability on an MX bike over jumps.

Trials

Main article: Motorcycle Trials

Known in the US as "Observed Trials", it is not racing, but a sport nevertheless. Trials is a test of skill on a motorcycle whereby the rider attempts to traverse an observed **section** without placing a foot on the ground (and traditionally, although not always, without ceasing forward motion). The winner is the rider with the least penalty points.

Trials commonly take place on rocky terrain

Time and Observation

Time and observation trials are trials with a time limit. The person who completes the route the quickest sets the "standard time" and all other competitors must finish within a certain amount of time of the standard time to be counted as a finisher (they received penalty points for every minute after the quickest finisher). This is combined with the penalty points accrued from the observed sections to arrive at a winner, who is not alway the quickest rider or the rider who lost the less marks on observation but the rider who balanced these competing demands the best. One of the most famous time and observation trials is the "Scott" trial held annually in North Yorkshire.

Indoor Trials

Indoor Trials are trials held in stadiums (not necessarily with a roof) which by their very nature use man made artificial sections in contrast to outdoor trials with rely heavily on the natural terrain.

Long Distance Trials (non-competitive)

Main article: Trail riding

Motoball (Motorcycle Polo)

Similar to football, but all players (except goalkeepers) are riding motorcycles, and the ball is much bigger.

External links

Sanctioning bodies

A Supersport bike at Phillip Island.

- Fédération Internationale de Motocyclismo [2] (FIM) - World governing body
- Motorcycling Australia (MA) [3]- Australian Governing Body
- Auto Cycle Union [4] - UK governing body
- American Motorcyclist Association [5] (AMA) - US governing body
- Motosport South Africa [6] (MSA) - South African governing body
- Federation Francaise de moto [7] (FFM) - French governing body
- MCUI Southern Centre [8] - "governing body of motor cycle sport in Leinster, Munster and Connacht" (i.e., Republic of Ireland)
- Championship Cup Series [9] - Sanctioning body for Sportman Level motorcycle road racing in the United States

Primary Manufacturers

Honda

HONDA The Power of Dreams	
Type	Public (TYO: 7267 [1]) & (NYSE: HMC [2])
Industry	• Automotive • Aviation
Founded	24 September 1948
Founder(s)	• Soichiro Honda • Takeo Fujisawa
Headquarters	Minato, Tokyo, Japan
Area served	Worldwide
Key people	• Satoshi Aoki (Chairman) • Takanobu Ito (CEO)
Products	• Automobiles • Motorcycles • Scooters • ATVs • Electrical Generators • Water pumps • Lawn and Garden Equipments • Tillers • Outboard motors • Robotics • Jets • Jet Engines
Revenue	▲ US$ 120.27 Billion (*FY 2009*)
Operating income	▲ US$ 2.34 Billion (*FY 2009*)
Net income	▲ US$ 1.39 Billion (*FY 2009*)
Total assets	▲ US$ 124.98 Billion (*FY 2009*)

Total equity	▲ US$ 40.6 Billion (*FY 2009*)
Employees	181,876
Subsidiaries	• Acura • Honda Aircraft Company
Website	Honda Worldwide [3]

Honda Motor Company, Ltd. (Japanese: 本田技研工業株式会社 *Honda Giken Kōgyō Kabushiki-gaisha*, Honda Technology Research Institute Company, Limited) listen (TYO: 7267 [1]) is a Japanese multinational corporation primarily known as a manufacturer of automobiles and motorcycles.

Honda is the world's largest manufacturer of motorcycles as well as the world's largest manufacturer of internal combustion engines measured by volume, producing more than 14 million internal combustion engines each year. Honda surpassed Nissan in 2001 to become the second-largest Japanese automobile manufacturer. As of August 2008, Honda surpassed Chrysler as the fourth largest automobile manufacturer in the United States. Honda is the sixth largest automobile manufacturer in the world.

Honda was the first Japanese automobile manufacturer to release a dedicated luxury brand, Acura, in 1986. Aside from their core automobile and motorcycle businesses, Honda also manufactures garden equipment, marine engines, personal watercraft and power generators, amongst others. Since 1986, Honda has been involved with artificial intelligence/robotics research and released their ASIMO robot in 2000. They have also ventured into aerospace with the establishment of GE Honda Aero Engines in 2004 and the Honda HA-420 HondaJet, scheduled to be released in 2011. Honda spends about 5% of its revenues into R&D.

History

From a young age, Honda's founder, Soichiro Honda (本田 宗一郎, *Honda Sōichirō*) had a great interest in automobiles. He worked as a mechanic at a Japanese tuning shop, Art Shokai, where he tuned cars and entered them in races. A self-taught engineer, he later worked on a piston design which he hoped to sell to Toyota. The first drafts of his design were rejected, and Soichiro worked painstakingly to perfect the design, even going back to school and pawning his wife's jewelry for collateral. Eventually, he won a contract with Toyota and built a factory to construct pistons for them, which was destroyed in an earthquake. Due to a gasoline shortage during World War II, Honda was unable to use his car, and his novel idea of attaching a small engine to his bicycle attracted much curiosity. He then established the Honda Technical Research Institute in Hamamatsu, Japan, to develop and produce small 2-cycle motorbike engines. Calling upon 18,000 bicycle shop owners across Japan to take part in revitalizing a nation torn apart by war, Soichiro received enough capital to engineer his first motorcycle, the Honda Cub. This marked the beginning of Honda Motor Company, which would grow a short time later to be the world's largest manufacturer of motorcycles by 1964.

The first production automobile from Honda was the T360 mini pick-up truck, which went on sale in August 1963. Powered by a small 356 cc straight-4 gasoline engine, it was classified under the cheaper Kei car tax bracket.[citation needed] The first production car from Honda was the S500 sports car, which followed the T360 into production in October 1963. Its chain driven rear wheels point to Honda's motorcycle origins.[citation needed]

"Honda" in Japanese is 本田, which literally means "root field" or "original field".

Corporate profile and divisions

Honda is headquartered in Minato, Tokyo, Japan. Their shares trade on the Tokyo Stock Exchange and the New York Stock Exchange, as well as exchanges in Osaka, Nagoya, Sapporo, Kyoto, Fukuoka, London, Paris and Switzerland.

Honda headquarters building in Japan

The company has assembly plants around the globe. These plants are located at China, United States, Pakistan, Canada, England, Japan, Belgium, Brazil, New Zealand, Indonesia, India, Thailand, Turkey and Perú.

Honda's Net Sales and Other Operating Revenue by Geographical Regions in 2007

Geographic Region	Total revenue (in millions of ¥)
Japan	1,681,190
North America	5,980,876
Europe	1,236,757
Asia	1,283,154
Others	905,163

American Honda Motor Company is based in Torrance, California. Honda Canada Inc. is headquartered in the Scarborough district of Toronto, Ontario, and is building new corporate headquarters in Markham, Ontario, scheduled to relocate in 2008; their manufacturing division, Honda of Canada Manufacturing, is based in Alliston, Ontario. Honda has also created joint ventures around the world, such as Honda Siel Cars and Hero Honda Motorcycles in India, Guangzhou Honda and Dongfeng Honda in China, and Honda Atlas in Pakistan.

Current market position

With high fuel prices and a weak U.S. economy in June 2008, Honda reported a 1% sales increase while its rivals, including the Detroit Big Three and Toyota, have reported double-digit losses. Honda's sales were up almost 20 percent from the same month last year. The Civic and the Accord were in the top five list of sales. Analysts have attributed this to two main factors. First, Honda's product lineup consists of mostly small to mid-size, highly fuel-efficient vehicles. Secondly, over the last ten years, Honda has designed its factories to be flexible, in that they can be easily retooled to produce any Honda model that may be in-demand at the moment.

Nonetheless, Honda, Nissan, and Toyota, were still not immune to the global financial crisis of 2008, as these companies reduced their profitability forecasts. The economic crisis has been spreading to other important players in the vehicle related industries as well. In November 2009 the Nihon Keizai Shinbun reported that Honda Motor exports have fallen 64.1%.

At the 2008 Beijing Auto Show, Honda presented the Li Nian ("concept" or "idea") 5-door hatchback and announced that they were looking to develop an entry-level brand exclusively for the Chinese market similar to Toyota's Scion brand in the USA. The brand would be developed by a 50-50 joint-venture established in 2007 with Guangzhou Automobile Industry Group.

Leadership

- 1948–1973 — Soichiro Honda
- 1973–1983 — Kiyoshi Kawashima
- 1983–1990 — Tadashi Kume
- 1990–1998 — Nobuhiko Kawamoto
- 1998–2004 — Hiroyuki Yoshino
- 2004–2009 — Takeo Fukui
- since 2009 — Takanobu Ito

Products

Automobiles

Honda's global lineup consists of the Fit, Civic, Accord, Insight, CR-V, and Odyssey. An early proponent of developing vehicles to cater to different needs and markets worldwide, Honda's lineup varies by country and may feature vehicles exclusive to that region. A few examples are the latest Acura TL luxury sedan and the Ridgeline, Honda's first light-duty pickup truck. Both were engineered primarily in North America and are exclusively produced and sold there.

The **Honda Civic** is a line of compact cars developed and manufactured by Honda. In North America, the Civic is the second-longest continuously running nameplate from a Japanese manufacturer; only its perennial rival, the Toyota Corolla, introduced in 1968, has been in production longer. The Civic, along with the Accord and Prelude, comprised Honda's vehicles sold in North America until the 1990s, when the model lineup was expanded. Having gone through several generational changes, the Civic has become larger and more upmarket, and it currently slots between the Fit and Accord.

The 2006 Ridgeline was a reintroduction of the concept of a Uni-Body truck. Earlier examples of this concept are the Subaru Brat and Baja, Volkswagen Rabbit pick-up, and Dodge Rampage/Plymouth Scamp.

2008 Honda Accord (USA spec)

Honda increased global production in September 2008 to meet demand for small cars in the U.S. and emerging markets. The company is shuffling U.S. production to keep factories busy and boost car output, while building fewer minivans and sport utility vehicles as light truck sales fall.

Honda produces the Insight, a hybrid electric vehicle that competes with the Toyota Prius

Eight Generation Honda Civic (Philippine Version)

Its first entrance into the pickup segment, the lightduty Ridgeline, won Truck of the Year from *Motor Trend* magazine in 2006 (also in 2006, the redesigned Civic won Car of the Year from the magazine, giving Honda a rare double win of Motor Trend honors).

In the U.S., five of EPA's top ten most fuel-efficient cars from 1984 to 2010 comes from Honda, more than any other automakers. The five models are: 2000-2006 Honda Insight(53 mpg combined), 1986-87 Honda Civic Coupe HF (46 mpg combined), 1994-95 Honda Civic hatchback VX (43 mpg combined), 2006- Honda Civic Hybrid (42 mpg combined), and 2010- Honda Insight (41 mpg combined).(mpg revised in accordance with 2008 regulation change)

Motorcycles

Honda is the largest motorcycle manufacturer in Japan and has been since it started production in 1955. At its peak in 1982, Honda manufactured almost 3 million motorcycles. By 2006 this figure had reduced to around 550,000 but was still higher than its three domestic competitors.

During the 1960s, when it was a small manufacturer, Honda broke out of the Japanese motorcycle market and began exporting to the U.S. Taking Honda's story as an archetype of the smaller manufacturer entering a new market already occupied by highly dominant competitors, the story of their market entry, and their subsequent huge success in the U.S. and around the world, has been the subject of some academic controversy. Competing explanations have been advanced to explain Honda's strategy and the reasons for their success.

The first of these explanations was put forward when, in 1975, Boston Consulting Group (BCG) was commissioned by the UK government to write a report explaining why and how the British motorcycle industry had been out-competed by its Japanese competitors. The report concluded that the Japanese firms, including Honda, had sought a very high scale of production (they had made a large number of motorbikes) in order to benefit from economies of scale and learning curve effects. It blamed the decline of the British motorcycle industry on the failure of British managers to invest enough in their businesses to profit from economies of scale and scope.

2004 Honda Super Cub

The second explanation was offered in 1984 by Richard Pascale, who had interviewed the Honda executives responsible for the firm's entry into the U.S. market. As opposed to the tightly focused strategy of low cost and high scale that BCG accredited to Honda, Pascale found that their entry into the U.S. market was a story of "miscalculation, serendipity, and organizational learning" – in other words, Honda's success was due to the adaptability and hard work of its staff, rather than any long term strategy. For example, Honda's initial plan on entering the U.S. was to compete in large motorcycles, around 300 cc. It was only when the team found that the scooters they were using to get themselves around their U.S. base of San Francisco attracted positive interest from consumers that they came up with the idea of selling the Super Cub.

The most recent school of thought on Honda's strategy was put forward by Gary Hamel and C. K. Prahalad in 1989. Creating the concept of core competencies with Honda as an example, they argued that Honda's success was due to its focus on leadership in the technology of internal combustion engines. For example, the high power-to-weight ratio engines Honda produced for its racing bikes provided technology and expertise which was transferable into mopeds. Honda's entry into the U.S. motorcycle market during the 1960s is used as a case study for teaching introductory strategy at business schools worldwide.

It created the first luxury Japanese car (1985 Legend) and motorcycle (2006 Gold Wing bikes) equipped with an airbag, as well as the first mid-size pickup truck with independent rear suspension (2006 Ridgeline).

Power Equipment

Production started in 1953 with H-type engine (prior to motorcycle).

Honda power equipements reached record sales in 2007 with 6,4 million units. By 2010 (Fiscal year ended March 31) this figure had decreased to 4,7 million units. Cumulative production of power products has exceeded 85 million units (as of September, 2008).

Honda power equipement include:

Engine

Tiller

Lawn mower

Riding mower

Trimmer

Mower

Blower

Sprayer

Hedge trimmer

Snowthrower

Generator, welder

Water-pump

Power-carrier

Outboard engine

Inflatable boat

Electric 4-wheel Scooter

Compact Household Cogeneration Unit

Engines

Honda engines powered the entire 33-car starting field of the 2010 Indianapolis 500 and for the fifth consecutive race, there were no engine-related retirements during the running of the Memorial Day Classic.

Honda, despite being known as an engine company, has never built a V8 for passenger vehicles. In the late 1990s, the company resisted considerable pressure from its American dealers for a V8 engine (which would have seen use in top-of-the-line Honda SUVs and Acuras), with American Honda reportedly sending one dealer a shipment of V8 beverages to silence them.

Robots

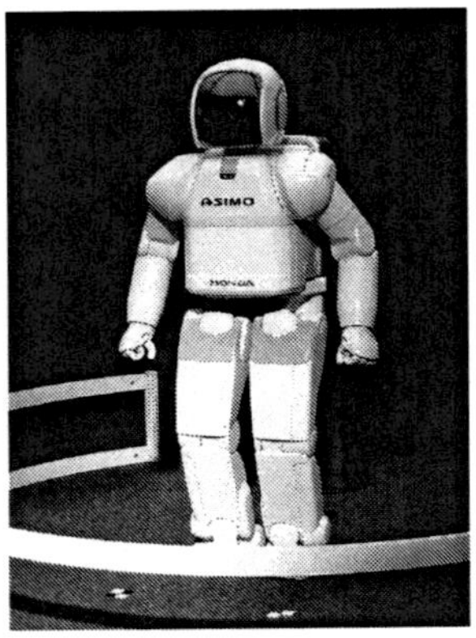

ASIMO at Expo 2005

ASIMO is the part of Honda's Research & Development robotics program [4]. It is the eleventh in a line of successive builds starting in 1986 with Honda E0 moving through the ensuing Honda E series and the Honda P series. Weighing 54 kilograms and standing 130 centimeters tall, ASIMO resembles a small astronaut wearing a backpack, and can walk on two feet in a manner resembling human locomotion, at up to 6 km/h (3.7 mph). ASIMO is the world's only humanoid robot able to ascend and descend stairs independently. However, human motions such as climbing stairs are difficult to mimic with a machine, which ASIMO has demonstrated by taking two plunges off a staircase.

Honda's robot ASIMO (see below) as an R&D project brings together expertise to create a robot that walks, dances and navigates steps. 2010 marks the year Honda has developed a machine capable of reading a users brainwaves to move ASIMO. The system uses a helmet covered with electroencephalography and near-infrared spectroscopy sensors that monitor electrical brainwaves and cerebral blood flow—signals that alter slightly during the human thought process. The user thinks of one of a limited number of gestures it wants from the robot, which has been fitted with a Brain Machine Interface.

Aircraft

Main article: Honda HA-420 HondaJet

Honda has also pioneered new technology in its HA-420 HondaJet that allows new levels of reduced drag, increased aerodynamics and fuel efficiency thus reducing operating costs.[*citation needed*]

Mountain bikes

See also: Honda RN-01 G-cross

Honda has also built a Downhill racing bike, known as the Honda RN-01. Honda has taken on several people to pilot the bike, among them is Greg Minnaar. The team is known as Team G Cross Honda. The key feature of this bike is the gearbox, which replaces the standard Derailleur found on most bikes.

Motorsports

Honda has been active in motorsports, like Motorcycle Grand Prix, Superbike racing and others.

Automobile

See also: Honda Racing F1

Honda entered Formula One as a constructor for the first time in the 1964 season at the German Grand Prix with Ronnie Bucknum at the wheel. 1965 saw the addition of Richie Ginther to the team, who scored Honda's first point at the Belgian Grand Prix, and Honda's first win at the Mexican Grand Prix. 1967 saw their next win at the Italian Grand Prix with John Surtees as their driver. In 1968, Jo Schlesser was killed in a Honda RA302 at the French Grand Prix. This racing tragedy, coupled with their commercial difficulties selling automobiles in the United States, prompted Honda to withdraw from all international motorsport that year.

After a learning year in 1965, Honda-powered Brabhams dominated the 1966 French Formula Two championship in the hands of Jack Brabham and Denny Hulme. As there was no European Championship that season, this was the top F2 championship that year. In the early 1980s Honda returned to F2, supplying engines to Ron Tauranac's Ralt team. Tauranac had designed the Brabham cars for their earlier involvement. They were again extremely successful. In a related exercise, John Judd's Engine Developments company produced a turbo "Brabham-Honda" engine for use in IndyCar racing. It won only one race, in 1988 for Bobby Rahal at Pocono.

Honda returned to Formula One in 1983, initially with another Formula Two partner, the Spirit team, before switching abruptly to Williams in 1984. In the late 1980s and early 1990s, Honda powered cars won six consecutive Formula One Constructors Championships. WilliamsF1 won the crown in 1986 and 1987. Honda switched allegiance again in 1988. New partners Team McLaren won the title in 1988, 1989, 1990 and 1991. Honda withdrew from Formula One at the end of 1992, although the related Mugen-Honda company maintained a presence up to the end of 1999, winning four races with Ligier and Jordan Grand Prix.

Honda debuted in the CART IndyCar World Series as a works supplier in 1994. The engines were far from competitive at first, but after development, the company powered six consecutive drivers championships. In 2003, Honda transferred its effort to the rival IRL IndyCar Series. In 2004, Honda-powered cars overwhelmingly dominated the IndyCar Series, winning 14 of 16 IndyCar races, including the Indianapolis 500, and claimed the IndyCar Series Manufacturers' Championship, Drivers' Championship and Rookie of the Year titles. In 2006, Honda became the sole engine supplier for the IndyCar Series, including the Indianapolis 500. In the 2006 Indianapolis 500, for the first time in Indianapolis 500 history, the race was run without a single engine problem.

During 1998, Honda considered returning to Formula One with their own team. The project was aborted after the death of its technical director, Harvey Postlethwaite. Honda instead came back as an official engine supplier to British American Racing (BAR) and Jordan Grand Prix. Honda bought a stake in the BAR team in 2004 before buying the team outright at the end of 2005, becoming a constructor for the first time since the 1960s. Honda won the 2006 Hungarian Grand Prix with driver Jenson Button.

It was announced on 5 December 2008, that Honda would be exiting Formula One with immediate effect due to the 2008 global economic crisis. The team was sold to former team principal Ross Brawn, renamed Brawn GP and subsequently Mercedes GP.

Honda became an official works team in the British Touring Car Championship in 2010.

Motorcycles

Main article: Honda Racing Corporation

Honda Racing Corporation (HRC) was formed in 1982. The company combines participation in motorcycle races throughout the world with the development of high potential racing machines. Its racing activities are an important source for the creation of leading edge technologies used in the development of Honda motorcycles. HRC also contributes to the advancement of motorcycle sports through a range of activities that include sales of production racing motorcycles, support for satellite teams, and rider education programs.

Soichiro Honda, being a race driver himself, could not stay out of international motorsport. In 1959, Honda entered five motorcycles into the Isle of Man TT race, the most prestigious motorcycle race in the world. While always having powerful engines, it took until 1961 for Honda to tune their chassis well enough to allow Mike Hailwood to claim their first Grand Prix victories in the 125 and 250 cc classes. Hailwood would later pick up their first senior TT wins in 1966 and 1967. Honda's race bikes were known for their "sleek & stylish design" and exotic engine configurations, such as the 5-cylinder, 22,000 rpm, 125 cc bike and their 6-cylinder 250 cc and 380 cc bikes.

In 1979, Honda returned to Grand Prix motorcycle racing with their exotic, monocoque-framed, four-stroke NR500. The NR500 featured elongated cylinders each with 8 valves and with connecting rods in pairs, in an attempt to comply with the FIM rules which limited engines to four cylinders. Honda engineered the elongated cylinders in an effort to provide the valveinant two-stroke racers. Unfortunately, it seemed Honda tried to accomplish too much at one time and the experiment failed. For the 1982 season, Honda debuted their first two stroke race bike, the NS500 and in 1983, Honda won their first 500 cc Grand Prix World Championship with Freddie Spencer. Since then, Honda has become a dominant marque in motorcycle Grand Prix racing, winning a plethora of top level titles with riders such as Valentino Rossi and Mick Doohan.

In motocross, Honda has claimed six motocross world championships. In the World Enduro Championship, Honda has captured six titles, most recently with Stefan Merriman in 2003 and with Mika Ahola in 2007 and 2008.

In observed trials, Honda has claimed three world championships with Belgian rider Eddy Lejeune.

Electric and alternative fuel vehicles

Compressed natural gas

2009 Honda Civic GX hooked up to Phill refueling system

The Honda Civic GX is the only purpose-built natural gas vehicle (NGV) commercially available in some parts of the U.S. The Honda Civic GX first appeared in 1998 as a factory-modified Civic LX that had been designed to run exclusively on compressed natural gas. The car looks and drives just like a contemporary Honda Civic LX, but does not run on gasoline. In 2001, the Civic GX was rated the cleanest-burning internal combustion engine in the world by the U.S. Environmental Protection Agency (EPA).

First leased to the City of Los Angeles, in 2005, Honda started offering the GX directly to the public through factory trained dealers certified to service the GX. Before that, only fleets were eligible to purchase a new Civic GX. In 2006, the Civic GX was released in New York, making it the second state where the consumer is able to buy the car. Home refueling is available for the GX with the addition of the Phill Home Refueling Appliance.

Top: Brazilian flexible-fuel Honda Civic. Below: U.S. Honda Civic Hybrid.

Flexible-fuel

Honda's Brazilian subsidiary launched flexible-fuel versions for the Honda Civic and Honda Fit in late 2006. As others Brazilian flex-fuel vehicles, these models run on any blend of hydrous ethanol (E100) and E20-E25 gasoline. Initially, and in order to test the market preferences, the carmaker decided to produce a limited share of the vehicles with flex-fuel engines, 33 percent of the Civic production and 28 percent of the Fit models. Also, the sale price for the flex-fuel version was higher than the respective gasoline versions, around US$1,000 premium for the Civic, and US$650 for the Fit, despite the fact that all other flex-fuel vehicles sold in Brazil had the same tag price as their gasoline versions. In July 2009, Honda launched in the Brazilian market its third flexible-fuel car, the Honda City.

2010 Honda Insight hybrid electric vehicle (Second generation).

During the last two months of 2006, both flex-fuel models sold 2,427 cars against 8,546 gasoline-powered automobiles, jumping to 41,990 flex-fuel cars in 2007, and reaching 93,361 in 2008. Due to the success of the flex versions, by early 2009 a hundred percent of Honda's automobile production for the Brazilian market is now flexible-fuel, and only a small percentage of gasoline version is produced in Brazil for exports.

Honda FCX Clarity hydrogen fuel cell vehicle

In March 2009, Honda launched in the Brazilian market the first flex-fuel motorcycle in the world. Produced by its Brazilian subsidiary Moto Honda da Amazônia, the CG 150 Titan Mix is sold for around US$2,700.

Hybrid electric

In late 1999, Honda launched the first commercial hybrid electric car sold in the U.S. market , the Honda Insight, just one month before the introduction of the Toyota Prius, and initially sold for US$20,000. The first-generation Insight was produced from 2000 to 2006 and had a fuel economy of 70 miles per US gallon (3.4 L/100 km; 84 mpg$_{\text{-imp}}$) for the EPA's highway rating, the most fuel-efficient mass-produced car at the time. Total global sales for the Insight amounted to only around 18,000 vehicles.

Honda introduced the second-generation Insight in its home nation of Japan in February 2009, and released it in other markets through 2009 and in the U.S. market in April 2009. At $19,800 as a five-door hatchback it will be the least expensive hybrid available in the U.S. Honda expects to sell 200,000 of the vehicles each year, with half of those sales in the United States.

Since 2002, Honda has also been selling the Honda Civic Hybrid (2003 model) in the U.S. market,. It was followed by the Honda Accord Hybrid, offered in model years 2005 through 2007. Sales of the Honda CR-Z began in Japan in February 2010, becoming Honda's third hybrid electric car in the market.

Hydrogen fuel cell

In Takanezawa, Japan, on 16 June 2008, Honda Motors produced the first assembly-line FCX Clarity, a hybrid hydrogen fuel cell vehicle. More efficient than a gas-electric hybrid vehicle, the FCX Clarity combines hydrogen and oxygen from ordinary air to generate electricity for an electric motor.

The vehicle itself does not emit any pollutants and its only by products are heat and water. The FCX Clarity also has an advantage over gas-electric hybrids in that it does not use an internal combustion engine to propel itself. Like a gas-electric hybrid, it uses a lithium ion battery to assist the fuel cell during acceleration and capture energy through regenerative braking, thus improving fuel efficiency. The lack of hydrogen filling stations throughout developed countries will keep production volumes low. Honda will release the vehicle in groups of 150. California is the only U.S. market with infrastructure for fueling such vehicle, though the number of stations is still limited. Building more stations is expensive, as the California Air Resources Board (CARB) granted $6.8 million for four H2 fueling stations, costing $1.7 million USD each.

Marketing

Honda's official slogan is "The Power of Dreams". They have never used this slogan to sell their products. Mr. Honda's belief is that well built products will sell themselves.

In 2003, Honda released its Cog advertisement in the UK and on the Internet. To make the ad, the engineers at Honda constructed a Rube Goldberg Machine made entirely out of car parts from a Europe Domestic Market Honda Accord (upon which the USDM Acura TSX is based). To the chagrin of the engineers at Honda, all the parts were taken from two of only six hand-assembled pre-production models of the Accord. The advertisement depicted a single cog which sets off a chain of events that ends with the Honda Accord moving and Garrison Keillor speaking the tagline, "Isn't it nice when things just... work?" It took 606 takes to get it perfect.

In 2004, they produced the Hate Something advert [5], usually immediately followed by a shortened version of the 2005/2006 Impossible Dream [6] advert.

In 2006, Honda released its Choir advertisement, for the UK and the internet. This featured a 60-person choir who sang the car noises as film of the Honda Civic are shown.

In December 2005, Honda released The Impossible Dream a two-minute panoramic advertisement filmed in New Zealand, Japan and Argentina which illustrates the founder's dream to build performance vehicles. While singing The Impossible Dream (The Quest), a man reaches for his racing helmet, leaves his trailer on a minibike, then rides a succession of vintage Honda vehicles: a motorcycle, then a car, then a powerboat, then goes over a waterfall only to reappear piloting a hot air balloon, with Garrison Keillor saying "I couldn't have put it better myself" as the song ends. The song is from the 1960s musical "Man Of La Mancha", sung by Andy Williams.

For the last several years in the United States, during model close-out sales for the current year before the start of the new model year, Honda's advertising has featured an animated character known simply as Mr. Opportunity, voiced by Rob Paulsen. The casual looking man talks about various deals offered by Honda and ends with the phrase "I'm Mr. Opportunity, and I'm knockin'", followed by him "knocking" on the television screen or "thumping" the speaker at the end of radio ads. Also, commercials for Honda's international hatchback, the Jazz, are parodies of well-known pop culture images such as Tetris and Thomas The Tank Engine.

In late 2006, Honda released an ad with ASIMO exploring a museum, looking at the exhibits with almost child-like wonderment (spreading out its arms in the aerospace exhibit, waving hello to an astronaut suit that resembles him, etc.), while Garrison Keillor ruminates on progress. It concludes with the tagline: "More forwards please".

Honda also sponsored ITV's coverage of Formula One in the UK for 2007. However they had announced that they would not continue in 2008 due to the sponsorship price requested by ITV being too high.

In May 2007, focuses on their strengths in racing and the use of the Red H badge — a symbol of what is termed as "Hondamentalism". The campaign highlights the lengths that Honda engineers go to in order to get the most out of an engine, whether it is for bikes, cars, powerboats — even lawnmowers. Honda released its Hondamentalism [7] campaign. In the TV spot, Garrison Keillor says, "An engineer once said to build something great is like swimming in honey", while Honda engineers in white suits walk and run towards a great light, battling strong winds and flying debris, holding on to anything that will keep them from being blown away. Finally one of the engineers walks towards a red light, his hand outstretched. A web address is shown for the Hondamentalism website. The digital campaign aims to show how visitors to the site share many of the Hondamentalist characteristics.

At the beginning of 2008, Honda released - the Problem Playground. The advert outlines Honda's environmental responsibility, demonstrating a hybrid engine, more efficient solar panels and the FCX Clarity, a hydrogen powered car. The 90 second advert features large scale puzzles, involving Rubik's cubes, large shapes and a 3-dimensional puzzle.

On 29 May 2008, Honda, in partnership with Channel 4, broadcast a live advertisement. It showed skydivers jumping from an aeroplane over Spain and forming the letters H, O, N, D and A in mid-air. This live advertisement is generally agreed to be the first of its kind on British television. The advert lasted three minutes. The next flight of one of the two planes involved resulted in a fatal crash as the plane broke apart in mid-air.

In 2009, American Honda released the "Dream the Impossible Documentary Series," a collection of 5-8 minute web vignettes that focus on the core philosophies of Honda. Current short films include Failure: The Secret to Success, Kick Out the Ladder and Mobility 2088. They feature Honda employees as well as Danica Patrick, Christopher Guest, Ben Bova, Chee Pearlman, Joe Johnston and Orson Scott Card. The film series plays at dreams.honda.com.

Sports

In Australia, Honda advertised heavily during most motor racing telecasts, and was the official sponsor of the 2006 FIA Formula 1 telecast on broadcaster channel "Ten". In fact, it was the only manufacturer involved in the 2006 Indy Racing League season. In a series of adverts promoting the history of Honda's racing heritage, Honda claimed it "built" cars that won 72 Formula 1 Grand Prix. ScepticsWikipedia:Avoid weasel words have accused Honda of interpreting its racing history rather liberally, saying that virtually all of the 72 victories were achieved by Honda *powered* (engined) machines, whereas the cars themselves were designed and built by Lotus F1, Williams F1, and McLaren F1 teams, respectively. However, former and current staff of the McLaren F1 team have reiterated that Honda contributed more than just engines and provided various chassis, tooling, and aerodynamic parts as well as funding. Ayrton Senna, arguably the greatest F1 driver of all time, repeatedly stated that Honda probably played the most significant role in his three world championships. He had immense respect for founder, Soichiro Honda, and had a good relationship with Nobuhiko Kawamoto, the chairman of Honda at that time. Senna once called Honda "the greatest company in the world".

As part of its marketing campaign, Honda is an official partner and sponsor of the National Hockey League, the Anaheim Ducks of the NHL, and the arena named after it: Honda Center. Honda is also a sponsor of Major League Soccer. The "Honda Player of the Year" award is presented in United States soccer. The "Honda Sports Award" is given to the best female athlete in each of twelve college sports in the United States. One of the twelve Honda Sports Award winners is chosen to receive the Honda-Broderick Cup, as "Collegiate Woman Athlete of the Year."

Facilities (partial list)

Main article: List of Honda facilities

U.S. Honda models

Cars	Accord	Civic	Fit	
Energy/Hybrid/Other	Civic Hybrid	FCX Clarity	Insight	CR-Z
SUVs	Pilot	Element		
Trucks	Ridgeline			
Crossovers	CR-V	Crosstour		
Vans	Odyssey			

Sales

Calendar Year	Total U.S. sales
1999	1,076,893
2000	1,158,860
2001	1,207,639
2002	1,247,834
2003	1,349,847
2004	1,394,398
2005	1,462,472
2006	1,509,358
2007	1,551,542
2008	1,284,261
2009	1,150,784

See also

- Acura
- Dongfeng Honda Automobile Company — joint venture
- Honda advanced technology
- Honda Aircraft Company
- Honda Airport
- Honda Atlas Cars Pakistan
- Honda Automobile (China) Company — importer of cars into China
- Honda Battle of the Bands
- Honda Canada Inc.
- Honda F.C. (Football (soccer) club)
- Honda Heat (Rugby union club)
- Honda Type R
- List of Honda assembly plants
- List of Honda engines
- List of Honda motorcycles
- List of Honda transmissions
- List of Honda vehicles
- RPA (Rubin Postaer and Associates)

References

- "Move Over, Volvo: Honda Sets New Safety Standard for Itself", an article in the "News" section of the March, 2004 issue of *Motor Trend*, on page 32
- 2004 Annual Corporate Report [8]
- The story of Honda's entry and growth in the American market is documented in Terry Sanders' film The Japan Project: Made in Japan. Honda [9]
- Honda's Midlife Crisis: Honda's slipping market position and views of Fukui Takeo (Chief Executive magazine, December 2005 issue) [10]
- Honda's Corporate History [11]

External links

- Honda Worldwide site [3]
- Honda Press Library [12] (Japanese, but with graphical timelines of car and bike models)
- Honda Automobiles [13] at the Open Directory Project
- Honda Motorcycles [14] at the Open Directory Project

pnb:□ن□ا

Kawasaki Heavy Industries

Type	Public
Industry	Rolling stock, Aerospace, Shipbuilding, Construction, Automobiles
Founded	15 October 1896
Headquarters	Chūō-ku, Kobe, Japan Minato, Tokyo Japan
Key people	Satoshi Hasegawa, President
Revenue	US$15.08 billion (As of March 31, 2008)
Employees	30,563 (As of 31 March 2008)
Website	http://www.khi.co.jp

Kawasaki Heavy Industries, Ltd. (川崎重工業株式会社 *Kawasaki Jūkōgyō Kabushiki-gaisha*) (English pronunciation: /kaʊ.əˈsɑːki/; TYO: 7012 [1]) is an international corporation based in Japan. It has headquarters in both Chūō-ku, Kobe and Minato, Tokyo.

The company is named after its founder Shozo Kawasaki and has no connection with the city of Kawasaki, Kanagawa.

Even though it originally started out as a ship-building company, its most visible consumer product lines are its motorcycles and all-terrain vehicles, although the company and its subsidiaries also manufacture personal water craft, ships, industrial plants, tractors, trains, small engines, and aerospace equipment (including military aircraft). Subcontract work on jet aircraft (including jumbo jets) has been done for Boeing, Embraer, and Bombardier.

Products

Aerospace

Main article: Kawasaki Heavy Industries Aerospace Company

Japanese Experiment Module *"Kibō"*

Kawasaki is active in a diverse range of the aerospace industry. The Company is a contractor for the Japanese Ministry of Defense and has built aircraft such as the T-4 intermediate jet trainer and the P-3C antisubmarine warfare patrol airplane. It is currently developing two large, next-generation aircraft, the XP-1 maritime patrol airplane and the C-X transport aircraft. Kawasaki also builds helicopters, including the BK117, jointly developed and manufactured with Eurocopter. It also produces the CH-47J / JA helicopter.

In the commercial aviation business, the company is involved in the joint international development and production of large passenger aircraft. It is involved in joint development and production of the Boeing 767, Boeing 777 and Boeing 787 with The Boeing Company, and the 170, 175, 190 and 195 jets with Empresa Brasileira de Aeronáutica. It is also involved in the joint international development and production of turbofan engines for passenger aircraft such as the V2500, the RB211/Trent, the PW4000 and the CF34.

Kawasaki also work for the Japan Aerospace Exploration Agency. The Company was responsible for the development and production of the payload fairings, payload attach fittings (PAF) and the construction of the launch complex for the H-II rocket. It continues to provide services for the H-IIA rocket.

Kawasaki has also participated in projects such as the development of reusable launch vehicles for spacecraft that will handle future space transport, space robotics projects such as the Japanese Experiment Module for the International Space Station, the HOPE-X experimental orbiting plane and the docking mechanism for the ETS-VII.

Main products

- Aircraft
- Space systems
- Helicopters
- Simulators
- Jet engines
- Missiles
- Electronic equipment

Rolling stock

Main article: Kawasaki Heavy Industries Rolling Stock Company

Lineup of JR East Shinkansen trains, October 2009

Kawasaki is Japan's largest manufacturer of rolling stock. It began operations in the industry in 1906. It manufactures express and commuter trains, subway cars, freight trains, locomotives, monorails and new transit systems. Kawasaki is also involved in the development and design of high-speed trains such as Japan's Shinkansen.

Main Products

- Electric cars (including Shinkansen trains)
- Monorails
- Passenger coaches and freight cars
- Diesel locomotives
- Electric locomotives
- Platform screen door systems
- Passenger coaches and freight cars integrated transit systems

A train of Kawasaki *MARC III* bi-levels at BWI Rail Station on the Penn Line headed towards Baltimore.

Shipbuilding

Main article: Kawasaki Shipbuilding Corporation

Kawasaki Shipbuilding Corp – Kobe Works

Kawasaki Shipbuilding Corporation is a wholly-owned subsidiary of Kawasaki Heavy Industries. Its product range include high-performance LNG and LPG carriers, container ships, bulk carriers and VLCCs, as well as submarines. The Company is also involved in the development of offshore structures and research vessels.

Kawasaki also produces marine machinery and equipment, including main engines, propulsion systems, steering gears, deck and fishing machinery.

Main products

- LNG carriers
- LPG carriers
- Container ships
- High speed vessels

- Submarines
- VLCCs (Very Large Crude Carriers)
- Bulk carriers
- Offshore structures
- Marine machinery and equipment

Energy plants and facilities

Kawasaki's key offering are high-performance gas turbines. The company is also involved in development of new energy sources as an alternative to fossil fuels such as wind power generation, biomass power generation, photovoltaic systems and rechargeable batteries.

Main products

- Small and medium-sized gas turbine generators
- Gas turbine cogeneration systems
- Wind turbine generators
- Ash handling systems
- Combined cycle power plants
- Nuclear power plant equipment
- Boilers

Industrial equipment

Kawasaki develops and builds a vast array of industrial plants and equipment, including large cement, chemical and nonferrous metal plants, prime movers, and compact precision machinery. It also offers industrial plant engineering from design to sales.

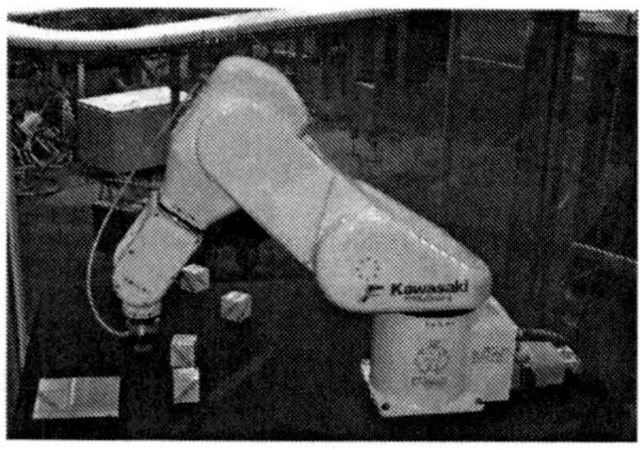

Kawasaki FS-03N industrial robot

Kawasaki also develops automation systems. Industrial robots for processes such as assembly, handling, welding, painting and sealing, as well as automation systems for distribution and logistics such as automated product- and cargo-handling systems for plants and airports.

Main products

- Industrial plants
- Industrial robots
- Aerodynamic machinery
- Hydraulic equipment

Environment and recycling

Kawasaki is involved in the development of equipment that prevents pollution in a wide range of industries. Among the leading products are fuel gas desulfurization and denitrification systems, and ash handling systems. The Company also supplies municipal refuse incineration plants, gasification and melting systems, sewage treatment and sludge incineration plants.

Kawasaki has also been developing systems that enable a wide range of municipal and industrial waste to be recovered, recycled and put to new use. Such systems include refuse paper and plastic fuel production facilities that convert wastepaper/plastics into an easy-to-handle solid fuel, equipment that converts old tires into highway paving materials and tiles, and machinery that sorts glass bottles by size and color.

Main products

- Municipal refuse incineration plans
- Water treatment systems
- Industrial waste recycling equipment
- Flue gas desulfurization equipment

Infrastructure

Kawasaki's history of building steel structures spans more than a century, with bridge-building among its first businesses. The company offers of storage solutions for LNG,

Kawasaki's portfolio also includes retractable roofs, floors and other giant structures, the Sapporo Dome's retractable surface is one example.

For construction, Kawasaki produces products such as wheel loaders, tunnel machines, rollers, snowplows and purpose specific loaders. The tunnel boring machines used to excavate the Channel Tunnel and the 14.14 m diameter shield machines used in the Tokyo Bay Aqua-Line construction are two well-known examples.

Main products

- Wheel loaders
- Construction machinery
- Shield Machines
- tunnel boring machines
- Steel bridges
- LNG and LPG tanks
- Airport and port-related products
- Snowplows

Transportation

Main article: Kawasaki Heavy Industries Consumer Products and Machinery Company

Kawasaki produces motorcycles, jet skis, ATVs and cars. Kawasaki's motorcycle include the Ninja sport bikes, and cruisers, dual-purpose and motocross motorcycles, as well as utility vehicles, ATVs and general-purpose gasoline engines. Kawasaki's "Jet Ski" has become a genericized trademark for any type of personal watercraft.

Kawasaki Ninja ZX-RR

Affiliates and subsidiaries

Japan

- Akashi Ship Model Basin Co., Ltd.
- Alna Yusoki-Yohin Co., Ltd.
- Benic Solution Corp.
- EarthTechnica Co., Ltd.
- Enetec Co., Ltd.
- Fukae Powtec Corp.
- JP Steel Plantech Co.
- Kawaju Akashi Service Co., Ltd.
- Kawasaki Engineering Co., Ltd.
- Kawasaki Oita Manufacturing Co., Ltd.
- Kawasaki Metal Industries, Ltd.
- Kawasaki Setsubi Kogyo Co., Ltd.
- Kawasaki Shipbuilding Corporation
- Kawasaki Plant Systems, Ltd.
- Kawasaki Precision Machinery Ltd.

Kawasaki Heavy Industries' Kobe head offices are located in the Kobe Crystal Tower

- Kawasaki Machine Systems, Ltd.
- Kawasaki Motors Corporation Japan
- Kawasaki Hydromechanics Corp.
- Kawasaki Life Corporation
- Kawasaki Naval Engine Service, Ltd.
- Kawaju Akashi Engineering Co., Ltd.

- KEE Environmental Construction, Co. Ltd.
- KEE Environmental Service, Ltd.
- Kawaju Gifu Service Co., Ltd.
- Kawaju Gifu Engineering Co., Ltd.
- Kawasaki Prime Mover Engineering Co., Ltd.
- Kawasaki Construction Co., Ltd.
- Kawasaki Rolling Stock Technology Co., Ltd.
- Kawasaki Rolling Stock Component Co., Ltd.
- Kawaju Shoji Co., Ltd.
- Kawaju Techno Service Corp.
- Kawaju Tokyo Service Corp.
- Kawaju Facilitech Co., Ltd.
- Kawasaki Thermal Engineering Co., Ltd.
- K Career Partners Corp.
- K-GES Co., Ltd.
- K-Tec Corp.
- KGM (Kawaju Gifu Manufacturing) Co., Ltd.
- Kawasaki Setsubi Kogyo Co., Ltd.
- Kawasaki Construction Machinery, Hokkaido Ltd.
- Kawaju Sakaide Service Co., Ltd.
- Kawaju Kobe Support Co., Ltd.
- Kawaju Marine Engineering Co., Ltd.
- KHI JPS Co., Ltd.
- Kawasaki Shipbuilding Inspection Co., Ltd.
- Kawasaki Gas Turbine Research Center Ltd.
- Nichijo Manufacturing Co., Ltd.
- NIPPI Corporation
- Sapporo Kawasaki Rolling Stock Engineering Co., Ltd.
- Technica Corp.
- Union Precision Die Co., Ltd.

International

North America

- Canadian Kawasaki Motors Inc.
- Kawasaki Construction Machinery Corp. of America
- Kawasaki Heavy Industries (U.S.A.), Inc.
- Kawasaki Motors Corp., U.S.A.
- Kawasaki Motors Manufacturing Corp., U.S.A.
- Kawasaki Precision Machinery (U.S.A.), Inc.
- Kawasaki Rail Car, Inc.
- Kawasaki Robotics (U.S.A.), Inc.

South America

- Kawasaki do Brasil Industria e Comercio Ltda.
- Kawasaki Motores do Brasil Ltda.
- Autotecnica Colombiana S.A

Asia

- Kawasaki Marine Machinery Co. Ltd. (Wuhan)
- Kawasaki Heavy Industries Ship Engineering Co. Ltd. (Nantong, China; COSCO)
- Kawasaki Heavy Industries Machinery Trading Co. Ltd. (Shanghai, China)
- Kawasaki Heavy Industries Technology Co. Ltd. (Dalian, China)
- Kawasaki Precision Machinery (China) Ltd.
- Kawasaki Robotics Co. Ltd. (Tianjin, China)
- Kawasaki Heavy Industries Ltd. (Hong Kong)
- Kawasaki Machine Systems Ltd. (Korea)
- Kawasaki Gas Turbine Asia Sdn. Bhd. (Malaysia)
- Kawasaki Bajaj Motor Ltd. (India)
- P.T. Kawasaki Motor (Indonesia)
- Kawasaki Heavy Industries Pte. Ltd. (Singapore)
- Kawasaki Motors Enterprise Co. Ltd. (Thailand)
- Kawasaki Heavy Industries Design & Technical Service Inc. (Makati, Philippines)
- Kawasaki Motors Corporation (Philippines)

Oceania

- Kawasaki Motors Pty. Ltd.

Europe

- Kawasaki
- Kawasaki Precision Machinery (U.K.) Limited
- Kawasaki Robotics (U.K.) Ltd.
- Kawasaki Robotics G.m.b.H.
- Kawasaki Gas Turbine Europe GmbH
- Kawasaki Motors Europe N.V.
- Kawasaki Heavy Industries Europe Finance B.V.
- Kawasaki Heavy Industries (Europe) B.V.

External links

- Official website [2]
- Kawasaki motorcycles [3] at the Open Directory Project

Suzuki

Type	Public (TYO: 7269 [1])
Industry	Automobile
Founded	1909 (as Suzuki Loom Works)
Founder(s)	Michio Suzuki
Headquarters	Hamamatsu, Shizuoka, Japan
Key people	Osamu Suzuki, Chairman of the Board, President, CEO, COO and Representative Director
Products	• Automobiles • Engines • Motorcycles • ATVs • Outboard Motors
Revenue	▼$33.46 billion (2008)
Operating income	▼$856.6 million (2008)
Net income	▼$305.43 million (2008)
Employees	14,266 (2009)
Subsidiaries	• Magyar Suzuki • Maruti Suzuki • Pak Suzuki Motor
Website	GlobalSuzuki.com [2]

Suzuki Motor Corporation (スズキ株式会社 *Suzuki Kabushiki-Kaisha*) is a Japanese multinational corporation headquartered in Hamamatsu, Japan that specializes in manufacturing compact automobiles and 4x4 vehicles, a full range of motorcycles, all-terrain vehicles (ATVs), outboard marine engines, wheelchairs and a variety of other small internal combustion engines. **Suzuki** is the 9th largest automobile manufacturer in the world by production volume, employs over 45,000 people, has 35 main production facilities in 23 countries and 133 distributors in 192 countries.[*citation needed*] According to statistics from the Japan Automobile Manufacturers Association (JAMA), Suzuki is Japan's second-largest manufacturer of small cars and trucks.

"Suzuki" is pronounced Japanese pronunciation: [suzuki] in Japanese, with a high tone on the [ki]. It is pronounced English pronunciation: /səˈzuːki/ *sə-ZOO-kee* in English, with a stressed *zu.* This pronunciation is used by the Suzuki company in marketing campaigns directed towards English-speakers.

History

In 1909, Michio Suzuki (1887–1982) founded the Suzuki Loom Works in the small seacoast village of Hamamatsu, Japan. Business boomed as Suzuki built weaving looms for Japan's giant silk industry. In 1929, Michio Suzuki invented a new type of weaving machine, which was exported overseas. Suzuki filed as many as 120 patents and utility model rights.[citation needed] The company's first 30 years focused on the development and production of these exceptionally complex machines.[citation needed]

Despite the success of his looms, Suzuki realized his company had to diversify and he began to look at other products. Based on consumer demand, he decided that building a small car would be the most practical new venture. The project began in 1937, and within two years Suzuki had completed several compact prototype cars. These first Suzuki motor vehicles were powered by a then-innovative, liquid-cooled, four-stroke, four-cylinder engine. It featured a cast aluminum crankcase and gearbox and generated 13 horsepower (9.7 kW) from a displacement of less than 800cc.

With the onset of World War II, production plans for Suzuki's new vehicles were halted when the government declared civilian passenger cars a "non-essential commodity." At the conclusion of the war, Suzuki went back to producing looms. Loom production was given a boost when the U.S. government approved the shipping of cotton to Japan. Suzuki's fortunes brightened as orders began to increase from domestic textile manufacturers. But the joy was short-lived as the cotton market collapsed in 1951.

Faced with this colossal challenge, Suzuki's thoughts went back to motor vehicles. After the war, the Japanese had a great need for affordable, reliable personal transportation. A number of firms began offering "clip-on" gas-powered engines that could be attached to the typical bicycle. Suzuki's first two-wheel ingenuity came in the form of a motorized bicycle called, the "Power Free." Designed to be inexpensive and simple to build and maintain, the 1952 Power Free featured a 36 cc, one horsepower, two-stroke engine. An unprecedented feature was the double-sprocket gear system, enabling the rider to either pedal with the engine assisting, pedal without engine assist, or simply disconnect the pedals and run on engine power alone. The system was so ingenious that the patent office of the new democratic government granted Suzuki a financial subsidy to continue research in motorcycle engineering, and so was born Suzuki Motor Corporation.

In 1953, Suzuki scored the first of many racing victories when the tiny 60 cc "Diamond Free" won its class in the Mount Fuji Hill Climb.

By 1954, Suzuki was producing 6,000 motorcycles per month and had officially changed its name to Suzuki Motor Co., Ltd. Following the success of its first motorcycles, Suzuki created an even more successful automobile: the 1955 Suzuki Suzulight. Suzuki showcased its penchant for innovation from the beginning. The Suzulight included front-wheel drive, four-wheel independent suspension and rack-and-pinion steering—features common on cars half a century later.

1955 Suzulight

Historical timeline

- 1909 – Suzuki Loom Works founded in Hamamatsu, Shizuoka Prefecture, by Mr. Michio Suzuki.
- 1920 – Reorganized, incorporated, and capitalized at 500,000 yen as Suzuki Loom Manufacturing Co. with Michio Suzuki as president.
- 1952 – 'Power Free' motorized bicycle marketed.
- 1954 – Company name changed to Suzuki Motor Co.,Ltd.
- 1955 – Lightweight car Suzuki Suzulight (360 cc, 2-stroke) front wheel drive, marketed helping to usher in Japan's light-weight car age.
- 1961 – Suzuki Loom Manufacturing Co. established by separating the loom machine division from the motor works and lightweight truck 'Suzulight Carry' marketed.
- 1962 – Suzuki won the 50 cc class championship at the Isle of Man TT
- 1963 – U.S. Suzuki Motor Corp., a direct sales subsidiary, opened in Los Angeles.
- 1965 – 'D55'(5.5 hp, 2-stroke) outboard motor marketed and makes early inroads and Fronte 800 marketed.
- 1967 – Thai Suzuki Motor Co., Ltd. established as a local assembly plant.
- 1968 – Carry full-cab van marketed.
- 1970 – LJ-Series (Jimny) 4X4 marketed.
- 1971 – Ts185 Enduro marketed.
- 1971 – GT750 motorcycle marketed.
- 1973 – Suzuki Canada Ltd., opened in Ontario, Canada.
- 1974 – P.T. Suzuki Indonesia Manufacturing established in Jakarta, Indonesia, entry into medical equipment field by marketing the Suzuki Motor Chair Z600 motorized wheelchair, expansion into the housing field initiated with Suzuki Home marketing two models of prefab 'Mini-House' and three types of storage sheds.
- 1975 – Antonio Suzuki Corp., a joint venture for knockdown production and sales, established in Manila, the Philippines.

- 1976 – GS-Series motorcycles marketed.
- 1977 – LJ80 4x4 vehicle marketed and exports of GS1000H motorcycle began.
- 1979 – Alto marketed.
- 1979 – SC100 marketed in the UK.
- 1980 – Suzuki Australia Pty. Ltd. established in Sydney, Australia and entry into general purpose engine field by marketing three electric power generator models.
- 1981 – Business ties with General Motors (U.S.) and Isuzu Motors, Ltd.(Japan) signed.
- 1982 – 4X4 production began at PAK Suzuki Motor Co., Ltd. in Karachi, Pakistan and won maker championship for 7th consecutive year at the World Road Race Grand Prix 500.
- 1982 – SC100 Discontinued in favour of Alto.
- 1983 – Enters into a partnership with Maruti Udyog Ltd. to produce cars in India.
- 1983 – Cultus/Swift 1.0-liter passenger car marketed and 4X4 production started at Maruti Udyog Ltd. in New Delhi, India.
- 1984 – Suzuki New Zealand Ltd. established in Wanganui, New Zealand and began export of Chevrolet Sprint to the United States. Car production technical assistance contract signed with China National Aerotechnology Import & Export Beijing Corporation. Operation of Suzuki Motor GmbH Deutschland began in Heppenheim, Germany.
- 1985 – SUZUKI of AMERICA AUTOMOTIVE CORP. established with the introduction of the Samurai, and the GSX-R750 motorcycle with an oil-cooled engine marketed and scooter production started at Avello S.A. of Spain. Agreement with Santana Motors to produce Suzuki cars in their Linares factory in Andalusia, Spain.
- 1986 – American Suzuki Motor Corp. is formed merging U.S. Suzuki Motor Corp and Suzuki of America Automotive Corp.
- 1987 – Cultus/Swift production began in Colombia and total aggregate car exports reached 2 million units.
- 1988 – Escudo/Vitara 4x4 marketed and total aggregate car production reached 10 million units..
- 1989 – CAMI Automotive Inc. established and began operation in Ontario, Canada. Swift GT/GLX and Sidekick sales begin in the United States.
- 1990 – Corporate name changed to Suzuki Motor Corporation.
- 1991 – Car production started in Korea through technical ties with Daewoo Shipbuilding & Heavy Machinery Ltd and Cappuccino 2-seater marketed.

The Suzuki plant in Esztergom, Hungary has over 6000 employees. (As of 2007)

- 1993 – Passenger car production/sales began at Suzuki Egypt S.A.E., opening ceremony for new car production plant held at Magyar Suzuki Corp. in Esztergom, Hungary and Wagon R passenger car marketed.
- 1994 – Maruti Udyog Ltd. of India total aggregate car production reached 1 million units.
- 1995 – Total aggregate motorcycle export reached 20 million units
- 1996 – Start of production in Vietnam (Motorcycles and automobiles)
- 1997 – Achieved 10 million cumulative automobile sales for overseas market and 4-stroke outboard motors win the Innovation Award at The International Marine Trade Exhibit and Conference (IMTEC) in Chicago.
- 1998 – Suzuki and General Motors form strategic alliance and Chongqing Chang'an Suzuki Automobile Co., Ltd. received official approval from the Chinese government for production of passenger cars.
- 1999 – Aggregate motorcycle production reaches 40 million units and Jiangxi Changhe Suzuki Automobile Co., Ltd. receives official approval from the Chinese government for production of commercial vehicles.
- 2000 – The company commemorates the 80th anniversary, aggregate car production at Kosai Plant reaches 10 million units and Suzuki production starts at General Motors de Argentina S.A.
- 2001 – Aggregate Launch of Suzuki Liana/Aerio. worldwide sales of Jimny/SJ reaches 2 million units, production of Alto reaches 4 million units and Suzuki achieves "Zero-Level" target of landfill waste
- 2002 – Achieved 30 million cumulative automobile sales for worldwide market and America's #1 warranty: 100,000/7-year powertrain limited warranty.
- 2003 – Suzuki is #1 in Kei car sales for the 30th consecutive year and Twin, the first hybrid Kei car in Japan, marketed.
- 2004 – Aggregate domestic automobile sales reach 15 million units.
- 2005 – Swift was awarded the 2006 RJC Car of the Year.
- 2006 – New XL7 is marketed particularly to the North American market; and GM divested, selling 92.36 million shares and reducing their stake to 3%.
- 2008 – Suzuki introduces its first production fuel-injected motocross bike; and GM divested its remaining 3% stake in Suzuki.
- 2009 – Suzuki introduces its first production pickup truck called the Equator. Volkswagen AG and Suzuki reach a common understanding to establish a close long-term strategic partnership.
- 2010 – Volkswagen AG completed the purchase of 19.9% of Suzuki's outstanding shares.

Maruti Suzuki

Main article: Maruti Suzuki

Maruti Suzuki Swift

Based in Gurgaon, India, Maruti Suzuki India Limited is Suzuki's largest and most valuable subsidiary with an annual production of 1,018,365 units in the fiscal 2009-2010. Suzuki has a 54.2% stake in the Indian auto giant and the rest is owned by the various Indian public and financial institutions. The company was incorporated in 1981 and is listed on the Bombay Stock Exchange and National Stock Exchange of India. In 2005-2006, the company had a 54% market share of the passenger car market in India. Nearly 75,000 people are employed directly by Maruti and its partners.

Maruti Suzuki was born as a Government of India company, with Suzuki as a minor partner, to make a people's car for middle class India. Over the years, the product range has widened, ownership has changed hands and the customer has evolved.

Maruti Suzuki offers 14 models, ranging from India's one-time best selling car, Maruti 800, for less than INR 200,000 (US$ 5000) to the premium sedan Maruti Suzuki SX4 and luxury SUV, Maruti Suzuki Grand Vitara. Maruti 800 was the first model launched by the company in 1983 followed by mini-van Maruti Omni in 1984. Both models were huge success in their respective categories because of the use of high-end technology and good fuel efficiency. Maruti Gypsy, launched in 1985, came into widespread use with the Indian Army and Indian Police Service becoming its primary customers. The short-lived Maruti 1000 too achieved moderate success until it was replaced by Maruti Esteem in 1994, to counter increasing competition in the medium-sedan category.

Maruti Zen, launched in 1993, was the company's second compact car model and also became extremely popular in India because of its high performance. The company went on to launch another compact car Maruti Wagon-R followed by Maruti Baleno in 1999. However, with increasing competition from Tata, Hyundai, Honda and Daewoo Motors, Maruti was not able to achieve the same success with Baleno as it had with its earlier models. So it replaced Maruti Suzuki Baleno with the Suzuki SX4. Currently Suzuki SX4 is facing stiff competition from the Honda City.

In 2000, Maruti Alto was launched. The launch of Tata Indica and Hyundai Santro had affected Maruti's sales but Alto helped secure the company's position as the auto leader in India. It is currently the largest selling car in India. The Maruti models include Maruti Suzuki Grand Vitara, launched in 2003, Maruti Versa, launched in 2004, Maruti Suzuki Swift, launched in 2005, Maruti Zen Estilo and Maruti Suzuki SX4, launched in 2007. The Alto, Swift and SX4 are leaders in their respective segments in the Indian Market.

On 14 February, Maruti Suzuki India, a Suzuki subsidiary in India, announced that it achieved one million total accumulated production volume of the Alto. The Alto has reached the million units mark in just seven years and five months since its launch on September 2000. The last half of the million has come in a record 25 months. The Alto has been India's largest volume-selling car, every month, for the past 37 consecutive months. Its popularity has continued to grow since its launch, with customers attracted to its combination of fuel efficiency, contemporary design and looks and features including Electronic Power Steering and air-conditioning. With this the Alto became the third car in the Maruti Suzuki stable to cross the million units mark. Previously, the Maruti 800 and the Omni had exceeded the million units mark. Besides its success in India, over 152,000 Altos made at Maruti Suzuki were delivered internationally, enjoying good outcomes in Algeria and Chile.

Maruti Exports Limited is the subsidiary of Maruti Udyog Limited with its major focus on exports and it does not operate in the domestic Indian market. The first commercial consignment of 480 cars were sent to Hungary. By sending a consignment of 571 cars to the same country, Maruti crossed the benchmark of 3,000,000 cars. Since its inception export was one of the aspects the government has been keen to encourage. Every political party expected Maruti to earn foreign exchange. Angola, Benin, Djibouti, Ethiopia, Europe, Kenya, Morocco, Sri Lanka, Uganda, Chile, Guatemala, Costa Rica and El Salvador are some of the markets served by Maruti Exports.

Other subsidiary companies of the Suzuki Motor Corporation, Japan in India are:

- SUZUKI POWERTRAIN INDIA LIMITED: Manufacturers engines for cars
- SUZUKI MOTORCYCLE INDIA PRIVATE LIMITED: Manufactures two wheelers under brand name 'Suzuki'. Its two wheeler models launched in India are 'GS 150R, Intruder, Hayabusa 1300 cc, 125 cc Access, 125 cc Motorcycle Zeus.

American Suzuki Motor Corp. history

American Suzuki headquarters is located in Brea, California. Through an agreement with General Motors, Suzuki began selling a version of their Suzuki Cultus in the United States as the Chevrolet Sprint in 1985. This model was initially sold as a 3-door hatchback and would be Chevrolet's smallest model.

2004 Suzuki XL-7

The Samurai was also introduced in 1985 for the 1986 model year and was the first car introduced to the United States by the newly created American Suzuki Corp. No other Japanese company sold more cars in the United States in its first year than Suzuki. The Samurai was available as a convertible or hardtop and the company slogan was *Never a Dull Moment*. The Samurai was successful until Consumer Reports alleged the Samurai of being susceptible to roll over in a 1988 test. This led to a much publicized 1996 lawsuit, not settled until 2004.

In 1989, American Suzuki introduced the Swift which was the 2nd generation Suzuki Cultus. The Swift was available as a GTi and GLX hatchback with a 4-door sedan following in 1990. A new small SUV called the Sidekick was also introduced in 1989. 1991 saw the introduction of the 4-door Suzuki Sidekick, the first 4-door mini-SUV in North America. The Swift and Sidekick were cousins to GM's Geo Metro and Geo Tracker and were mostly produced in Ingersoll, Ontario, Canada by Suzuki and GM's joint venture, CAMI. The Swift GT/GTi and 4-door models were imported from Japan. Negative evaluations from Consumer Reports of the Suzuki Samurai led to some temporary setbacks at American Suzuki as annual sales in the following years dropped to below 20,000 units.

In 1995, American Suzuki introduced the Esteem and redesigned the Swift. The Swift GT was dropped and this version Swift was specific only to North America where it was built at CAMI. These models were the first Suzuki vehicles to be marketed in North America with dual front airbags. A station wagon version of the Esteem was introduced in 1996. Worldwide Suzuki production reached more than 975,000 cars this year.

Also in 1996, American Suzuki released the 2-door SUV X-90 and a revised Sidekick Sport model with dual airbags, a 120 hp (89 kW) 1.8 liter engine, 16 inch wheels and two-tone paint. The Sidekick was replaced by the Vitara and the Grand Vitara for 1999. The Grand Vitara would be Suzuki's first model with a V6-cylinder engine and available 4-wheel ABS brakes.

The Grand Vitara XL-7 was introduced in 2001 as a stretched version of the Grand Vitara. The Grand Vitara XL-7 had a larger 2.7 liter V6-cylinder engine and 3-row seating. This would be Suzuki's largest vehicle to date and the first compact SUV to offer 3-row seating.

The Swift was dropped from the model lineup in 2001 and the Esteem was replaced in 2002 by the new Aerio, which was offered as a 4-door sedan and 5-door crossover with 4-wheel-drive as an option.

In 2004, General Motors and Suzuki jointly purchased the bankrupt Daewoo Motors renaming the venture GMDAT. American Suzuki rebadged the compact Daewoo Nubira/Daewoo Lacetti as the Forenza and the mid-size Daewoo Magnus as the Verona. The Forenza gained station wagon and hatchback body style in 2005, with the hatchback sold under the Reno name.

2006 was the first year American Suzuki sold more than 100,000 vehicles in the United States. Suzuki redesigned the Grand Vitara in 2006 as well as introduced the all-new Suzuki SX4 and Suzuki XL7 in 2007. The Suzuki SX4 is produced as a joint venture with Fiat and the XL7 (notice the shortening of the name from Grand Vitara XL-7) was produced as a joint venture with GM at CAMI Automotive Inc. in Ingersoll. Suzuki put XL7 production on indefinite hiatus in mid-2009 due to low demand and subsequently sold off its share of CAMI back to GM later that year.

Despite a difficult domestic US automarket, Suzuki has been keeping pace with its 2007 sales numbers including recording their best May ever in May 2008.

Pakistani Suzuki Motor Company Limited

Following the terms of the Joint Venture Agreement between Suzuki Motor Corporation of Japan (SMC) and Pakistan Automobile Corporation (PACO), Pak Suzuki Motor Company Limited (PSMCL) was incorporated as a public limited company in August 1983.

The new company assumed the assets, including production facilities ,of Awami Autos Limited. PSMCL started commercial operations in January 1984 with the primary objective of passenger cars, pick ups, vans and 4x4 vehicles.

The groundbreaking ceremony of the company's green field automobile plant at Bin Qasim was performed by the then prime Minister of Pakistan in early 1989.

On completion of first phase of this plant in early 1990, in-house assembly Suzuki engines started. The new plant was completed in 1992, and Suzuki production was transferred to new plant — and three-box 1300 cc Margalla car was also added to its range of production.

In September 1992 the company was privatized and placed directly under the Japanese Management. At the time of privatization SMC increased its equity from 25% to 40% Subsequently, SMC progressively increased its equity to 73.09% by December 31, 2001.

The Bin Qasim Plant further expanded its production capacity to 50,000 vehicles per year in July 1994 and 300,000 vehicles had been manufactured at this plant by December 2003.

Today Paksuzuki has one of the most modern automobile manufacturing plants in South Asia and currently exports its cars to countries like Bangladesh, Ghana, Nigeria & Maldives.

Suzuki Canada Inc. history

- 1973 – June 1, Suzuki Canada Ltd. was incorporated with offices at Downsview, Ontario. Product lines included motorcycles, parts and accessories to Suzuki dealers throughout Canada.
- 1974 – Vancouver branch office and warehouse inaugurated to service dealers in western Canada.
- 1980 – Autumn - Suzuki Canada began its automotive sales with the marketing and sales of four-wheel-LJ80 in eastern Canada. November 1, the name of company changed from Suzuki Canada Ltd. to Suzuki Canada Inc.
- 1982 – Introduction of a line of Suzuki all-terrain vehicles (ATVs) in Canada.
- 1983 – Introduction of a line of Suzuki outboard motors in western Canada. February 1, 1983 - Western Branch moved to enlarged facilities in Richmond, British Columbia.
- 1984 – Began the sales of 'Suzuki Forsa' (Suzuki Cultus) automobile.
- 1986 – A $600 million Suzuki-GM joint venture CAMI Automotive Inc. announced for the manufacturing of vehicles. Production was set to begin in 1989 at Ingersoll, Ontario.
- 1987 – January 25 - Suzuki Canada Inc. moved to a new 110000 sq ft (10000 m^2). head office and warehouse facility at Richmond Hill, Ontario.
- 1988 – Autumn - Suzuki began selling the CAMI-built 2-door Suzuki Sidekick.
- 2009 – Autumn - Suzuki sold its participation in CAMI to GM

OEM deals

Since 1985, Suzuki has shared or produced automobiles for other manufacturers around the world.

General Motors

Chevrolet Sprint - United States/Canada (Suzuki Cultus)

Pontiac Firefly - Canada (Suzuki Cultus)

Geo Metro - United States (Suzuki Cultus)

Holden Barina - Australia & New Zealand (Suzuki Cultus)

Chevrolet Swift - South America (Suzuki Cultus)

Chevrolet Cruze - Japan (Suzuki Ignis)

Holden Cruze - Australia (Suzuki Ignis)

Chevrolet MW - Japan (Suzuki Wagon R)

Bedford Rascal - Europe (Suzuki Carry)

Bedford Rascal - United Kingdom (Suzuki Carry)

Holden Scurry - Australia (Suzuki Carry)

Chevrolet Supercarry - South America (Suzuki Carry)

Geo Tracker - United States (Sidekick/Vitara)

Chevrolet Tracker - United States/Canada (Sidekick/Vitara)

GMC Tracker - Canada (Sidekick/Vitara)

Asüna Sunrunner - Canada (Sidekick/Vitara)

Pontiac Sunrunner - Canada (Sidekick/Vitara)

Chevrolet Vitara - South America (Sidekick/Vitara)

Chevrolet Grand Nomad - South America (Suzuki XL7)

Holden Drover - Australia & New Zealand (Suzuki Sierra/Jimny)

Opel Agila - Europe (Suzuki Wagon R and Suzuki Splash)

Chevrolet MW - Japan (Suzuki Wagon R)

Vauxhall Agila - United Kingdom (Suzuki Wagon R and Suzuki Splash)

Subaru

Subaru Justy - Europe (Suzuki Swift)

Mazda

Mazda Proceed Levante - Japan (Suzuki Vitara)

Mazda Carol - Japan (Suzuki Alto)

Autozam AZ-1 - Japan (Suzuki Cara)

Autozam Scrum - Japan (Suzuki Every)

Autozam AZ-Wagon - Japan (Suzuki MR Wagon)

Mazda AZ-Offroad - Japan (Suzuki Jimny)

Mazda Spiano - Japan (Suzuki Lapin)

Mazda Laputa - Japan (Suzuki Kei)

Nissan

Nissan Moco - Japan (Suzuki MR Wagon)

Nissan Pino - Japan (Suzuki Alto)

Nissan Roox - Japan (Suzuki Palette)

Maruti Suzuki

Maruti 800 - India (Suzuki Alto)

Maruti Omni - India (Suzuki Carry)

Maruti Gypsy - India (Suzuki Jimny)

Maruti 1000 - India (Suzuki Cultus)

Maruti Zen - India (Suzuki Alto)

- All Maruti models since the Zen are referred to as Maruti Suzuki.

Volkswagen

Volkswagen Rocktan (Suzuki SX4) - currently in development.

Automobiles

- Suzuki models
  - Aerio/Liana
  - Alto
  - Alto Lapin
  - APV
  - Cappuccino
  - Carry
  - Cervo
  - Suzuki Cultus (aka Suzuki Forsa, Suzuki Swift, Geo Metro, Pontiac Firefly, et al.)
  - Escudo
  - Suzuki Equator
  - Esteem/Cultus Crescent
  - Fronte
  - Grand Vitara
  - Ignis
  - Jimny
  - Kei
  - Kizashi
  - LJ-Series
  - Mehran
  - MightyBoy
  - MR Wagon
  - Palette
  - Sidekick
  - Splash
  - SX4
  - SX4 Crossover
  - SX4 Sport
  - Suzuki Twin
  - Wagon R
  - X-90
  - XL7
- Daewoo based North American models

    - Swift+
    - Forenza/Reno
    - Verona
- Chevrolet based South American models
    - Fun

Motorcycles

Suzuki started manufacturing motorcycles in 1952, the first models being motorized bicycles. During the 1950s, 1960s and the better part of the 1970s, the company manufactured motorcycles with two-stroke engines only, the biggest two-stroke model being the water-cooled triple-cylinder GT750.

Suzuki's flagship motorcycle, the GSX1300R Hayabusa.

A large factor in Suzuki's success in two-stroke competition was the East German Grand Prix racer Ernst Degner, who defected to the West in 1961, bringing with him expertise in two-stroke engines from the East German manufacturer MZ. Suzuki hired Degner, and he won the 50 cc class F.I.M. road racing World Championship for them in the 1962 season. Suzuki became the first Japanese manufacturer to win a motocross world championship when Joel Robert won the 1970 250 cc title. In the 1970s, Suzuki established themselves in the motorcycle racing world with Barry Sheene and Roger De Coster winning world championships in the premier 500 cc division in road racing and motocross respectively. Suzuki continues to compete in MotoGP and last won the title in the 2000 season. Since 2006, the team is sponsored by Rizla and is known as Rizla Suzuki MotoGP team.

It was not until 1976 that Suzuki introduced its first motorcycle with a four-stroke engine, the GS400 and GS750.

In 1994, Suzuki partnered with Nanjing Jincheng Machinery to create a Chinese motorcycle manufacturer and exporter called Jincheng Suzuki.

Models

Main article: List of Suzuki motorcycles

Notable Suzuki motorcycles include some of the following:

- Hayabusa (GSX-1300R) – a sport motorcycle capable of 190 mph (310 km/h) in 1999, and limited to 186 mph (299 km/h) since 2000.
- GSX-R1000 – the largest model of the GSX-R series, first launched in 2000.
- GSX-R750 – the grandfather of the GSX-R1000, this designation is more than 25 years old and this model is being updated/redesigned entirely every two to four years.
- GSX-R600 – a smaller version of the GSX-R750. Comparable to Honda's CBR600RR, and Kawasaki's ZX-6.
- GSX-650F – introduced in 2008, this new sport touring model fills the void of the retired Katana, competing with the Yamaha FZ6/Fazer and the Kawasaki ZZR600. The 2009 model has ABS as a standard feature.
- SV650 – introduced in 1999 as a budget entry in the emerging naked bike market and, as of 2008, offered both naked and fully faired. Since 2009 it is also offered in the Gladius variant.
- Burgman – series of urban scooters with engine capacities from 125 cc up to 638 cc produced in Japan, Italy and Spain.
- RGV250 – the road-racing replica of Kevin Schwantz's RGV500 GP race bike

All-terrain vehicles (ATVs)

- Suzuki Eiger 400
- Suzuki LT 230
- Suzuki LT-R450 (race ready)
- Suzuki LT250R

Event sponsorship

Suzuki is a major sponsor of luge, biathlon, and cross country skiing sporting events.

See also

- List of Suzuki engines
- Suzuki World Rally Team
- Suzuki T Series
- Suzuki T20
- Suzuki GT Series

External links

- Suzuki Global website [3]
- Suzuki autos [4] at the Open Directory Project
- Suzuki motorcycles [5] at the Open Directory Project

pnb:سوزوکی

Yamaha Motor Company

Type	Public
Founded	July 1, 1955
Headquarters	Iwata, Shizuoka, Japan
Area served	Global
Products	Automobiles, ATVs, Motorbikes, Vehicle Engines, Personal water craft
Revenue	12 billion US$ (2005)
Operating income	900 million US$ (2005)
Net income	550 million US$ (2005)
Employees	39,300 (2005)
Website	Yamaha Motor Global [1]

Yamaha Motor Company Limited (ヤマハ発動機株式会社 *Yamaha Hatsudōki Kabushiki-gaisha*) (TYO: 7272 [2]), is a Japanese motorized vehicle-producing company. Yahama Motor is part of the Yamaha Corporation and its headquarter is located in Iwata, Shizuoka. Along with expanding Yamaha Corporation into the world's biggest piano maker, then Yamaha CEO Genichi Kawakami took Yamaha into the field of motorized vehicles on July 1, 1955. The company's intensive research into metal alloys for use in acoustic pianos had given Yamaha wide knowledge of the making of lightweight, yet sturdy and reliable metal constructions. This knowledge was easily applied to the making of metal frames and motor parts for motorcycles. It produces motorcycles, all-terrain vehicles, boats, snowmobiles, outboard motors, and personal watercraft.

The Yamaha corporate logo is composed of three tuning forks placed on top of each other in a triangular pattern.

In 2000, Toyota and Yamaha Corporation made a capital alliance in which Toyota paid Yamaha Corporation 10.5 billion yen for a 5 per cent share in Yamaha Motor Company while Yamaha and Yamaha Motor each bought 500,000 shares of Toyota stock in return.

Racing heritage

See also: Yamaha Motor Racing

Yamaha has a long racing heritage where it has had its machines and team win many different competitions in many different areas, particularly in motorcycle racing. Yamaha has had great success with riders such as Bob Hannah, Heikki Mikkola, Kenny Roberts, Eddie Lawson, Wayne Rainey, Jeremy McGrath, Stefan Merriman, Chad Reed, Valentino Rossi, Ben Spies, and currently James Stewart. They won the supercross championship two years in a row (2008 and 2009) with the YZ 450F(One with Chad Reed, and the other with James Stewart). Yamaha has won a total of 36 World Championships, including 3 in MotoGP and 9 in the preceding 500cc 2-stroke class, and 1 in World Superbike.

Yamaha created the innovations which lead to the modern motocross bike, as they were the first to build a production monoshock motocross bike (1975 for 250 and 400, 1976 for 125) and one of the first to have a water-cooled motocross production bike (1977 in works bikes, 1981 in off-the-shelf bikes).

Since 1962, Yamaha produced production road racing grand prix motorcycles that any licensed road racer could purchase. In 1970, non-factory "privateer" teams dominated the 250cc World Championship with Great Britain's Rodney Gould winning the title on a Yamaha TD2.

Yamaha also sponsors several professional ATV riders in several areas of racing, such as cross country racing and motocross. Yamaha has had good success in cross country with their YFZ450, being ridden by Bill Ballance, winning 9 straight titles since 2000. Yamaha's other major rider, Traci Cecco, has ridden the YFZ450 to 7 titles, with the first in 2000. In ATV motocross, Yamaha has had success with Dustin Nelson and Pat Brown, both who race the YFZ450. Pat Brown's best season was a 3rd place title in 2007, while Nelson has had two 1st place titles in the Yamaha/ITP Quadcross, one in 2006 and the other in 2008.

The company also produced Formula One engines from 1989 to 1997, initially for the Zakspeed team and later for Tyrrell. These never won a race, but drivers including Damon Hill, Ukyo Katayama, Mark Blundell and Andrea de Cesaris scored some acceptable results with them.

Motorcycle models

Main article: List of Yamaha motorcycles

Yamaha has made an extensive number of two- and four-stroke scooters, on-road and off-road motorcycles. The Yamaha XS 650, introduced in 1970, was an early success. The Yamaha RX-S 100 introduced in the RX models but with an energy induction in 1980s. In 2009, Yamaha introduced the first production in-line four cylinder with a cross-plane crankshaft orientation, technology derived from their MotoGP racebike.

Also in 2009, Yamaha released their new model of sportbike based from the previous R6 motor. This new model is known as the FZ6R. The FZ6R with 600cc and a newly designed fuel-injected 4-cylinder engine is at the top of Yamaha's innovation. Both the '09 and now '10 models, have features to attract first-time riders with digital display and lower seats for more comfort, and even new body work with designs to attract women riders. [3]

Scooters

See also List of scooters

- Yamaha PAS (Nickel metal hydride battery)
- PAS Lithium (Lithium ion battery)
- PAS Business (Ni-Cd battery)
- Yamaha YQ50 Aerox R
- Yamaha Boxer
- Yamaha Champ
- Yamaha Champ CX
- Yamaha Jog
- Yamaha Jog R
- Yamaha Jog Aprio
- Yamaha ZX Super Jog
- Yamaha Neo's
- Yamaha BW'S/Yamaha Zuma
- Yamaha Morphous
- Yamaha XF50X (C3/Vox/Giggle)
- Yamaha FS1 (Yamaha FS1E)
- Yamaha Lagenda
- Yamaha QT50
- Yamaha X-City 250 cc
- Yamaha T-Max 500 cc

Personal water craft

- Yamaha WaveRunner

All-terrain vehicles

- BW80 / 200 / 350
- YFZ450
- Raptor 80 / 250 / 350 / 660 / 700R
- Blaster 200
- Yamaha Timberwolf 250

- Banshee 350
- Warrior 350
- Bruin 350
- Kodiak 400 / 450
- Grizzly 80 / 125 / 350 / 400 / 450 / 550 / 600 / 660 / 700
- Big Bear 350 / 400
- Wolverine 350 / 450
- Tri-Z 250

Snowmobiles

Yamaha has recently claimed[*citation needed*] a 100% four-stroke snowmobile line-up, making them the only snowmobile manufacturer to do so. In Canada though, there are still three models that Yamaha manufactures that are still two-stroke. They are the Bravo, VK 540 and the Venture XL. Yamaha had introduced four-strokes to their line-up in 2003 and the line-up became four-stroke based for model year 2005. Many sayWikipedia:Avoid weasel words that Yamaha has proven snowmobiles can be clean, efficient, and reliable all while maintaining strong performance. The RX-1 released in 2003 was the first performance-oriented four-stroke snowmobile to ever hit the market. It was not, however, the first modern four-stroke snowmobile produced. That honor belongs to Arctic Cat for their Yellowstone Special, released in 2000, which was designed as a rental sled that could meet Yellowstone National Park's stringent emission requirement. However, the Yamaha received much criticism for its weight disadvantage when compared to similar two-strokes, despite its excellent fuel economy and low-range torque. Yamaha is now on the cutting edge of four-stroke technology with the introducing of their 80FI engine which is equipped on the Phazer and Venture Lite models. This engine has one of the highest specific output of any four-stroke in production, with 160 HP/L, Yamaha achieves this even without the use of a forced induction system. Yamaha is also a key player in the "four-stroke wars", which are a series of advertisements from opponent Ski-Doo who claim their E-tec and power-tec equipped two-strokes are still cleaner and more efficient than four-strokes, while Yamaha still claims the four-strokes are cleaner. Yamaha also broke a multi-year absence from sno-cross in the winter of 2006/2007 with their introduction of a factory race team headed by former Arctic Cat racer Robbie Malinoski.

Yamaha was the first brand to win with a 4-stroke in a professional snowcross race. This happened in 2006 at the WPSA snow cross Championship

Current line-up

- Apex
- Nytro
- FX Nytro
- Phazer (4th Generation)
- RS Vector
- RS Venture
- VK Professional
- YFZ R 450

Significant previously produced models

- Bravo
- V-Max
- SRX
- GPX 433-338
- GP
- SL
- EXCITER

Automobiles

Yamaha has also built engines for other manufacturers' vehicles, most notably the V-6 and V-8 engine for the Ford Taurus SHO. The Volvo XC90 uses a larger version of the same Yamaha V-8 engine. They also built Formula One racing engines from the late 1980s to the mid 1990s, with little on-track success. In 1991, Yamaha developed its F1 engined supercar called the OX99-11 where two drivers sit in tandem in front of the engine, but the project was cancelled due to the world recession and lack of interest.

Yamaha also tunes engines for other manufacturers, Toyota being one of them. Yamaha logos are, for instance, found on the Toyota S engines. as well as the 2ZZ-GE utilized by Toyota, Pontiac, and Lotus.

Yamaha developed a prototype for a two-seater sports car with help of Albrecht Goertz. While the Yamaha/Nissan partnership never progressed beyond the prototype stage, Toyota took up the design and released the Toyota 2000GT.

Other products

Main article: List of Yamaha products

- Wheelchairs
- Snowblowers
- Remote-controlled helicopters
- Outboard motors
- KT series 2 stroke karts
- Water purifiers
- Industrial equipment

External links

- Yamaha Motor Co. [1] global site
- Yamaha Motorcycles [4] at the Open Directory Project

Harley-Davidson

Type	Public (NYSE: HOG [1])
Founded	1903
Founder(s)	William S. Harley Arthur Davidson Walter Davidson William A. Davidson
Headquarters	Milwaukee, Wisconsin, United States
Key people	Keith E. Wandell, CEO
Products	Motorcycles
Revenue	▼ US$4.29 Billion (*FY 2009*)
Operating income	▼ US$70.6 million (*FY 2009*)
Employees	9,700 (2006)
Subsidiaries	MV Agusta
Website	www.harley-davidson.com [2]

Harley-Davidson (NYSE: HOG [1], formerly HDI), often abbreviated **H-D** or **Harley**, is an American motorcycle manufacturer. Founded in Milwaukee, Wisconsin, during the first decade of the 20th century, it was one of two major American motorcycle manufacturers to survive the Great Depression. Harley-Davidson also survived a period of poor quality control and competition from Japanese manufacturers.

The company sells heavyweight (over 750 cc) motorcycles designed for cruising on the highway. Harley-Davidson motorcycles (popularly known as "Harleys") have a distinctive design and exhaust note. They are especially noted for the tradition of heavy customization that gave rise to the chopper style of motorcycle. Except for the modern VRSC model family, current Harley-Davidson motorcycles reflect the styles of classic Harley designs. Harley-Davidson's attempts to establish itself in the light motorcycle market have met with limited success and have largely been abandoned since the 1978 sale of its Italian Aermacchi subsidiary.

Harley-Davidson sustains a loyal brand community which keeps active through clubs, events, and a museum. Licensing of the Harley-Davidson logo accounts for almost 5% of the company's net revenue.

History

Beginning

Clockwise from top left: William S. Harley, William A. Davidson, Walter Davidson, Sr., Arthur Davidson

In 1901, William S. Harley, age 21, drew up plans for a small engine with a displacement of 7.07 cubic inches (116 cc) and four-inch (102 mm) flywheels. The engine was designed for use in a regular pedal-bicycle frame. Over the next two years Harley and his childhood friend Arthur Davidson labored on their motor-bicycle using the northside Milwaukee machine shop at the home of their friend, Henry Melk. It was finished in 1903 with the help of Arthur's brother, Walter Davidson. Upon completion the boys found their power-cycle unable to conquer Milwaukee's modest hills without pedal assistance. Will Harley and the Davidsons quickly wrote off their first motor-bicycle as a valuable learning experiment.

Work immediately began on a new and improved second-generation machine. This first "real" Harley-Davidson motorcycle had a bigger engine of 24.74 cubic inches (405 cc) with 9.75 inches (25 cm) flywheels weighing 28 lb (13 kg). The machine's advanced loop-frame pattern was similar to the 1903 Milwaukee Merkel motorcycle (designed by Joseph Merkel, later of Flying Merkel fame). The bigger engine and loop-frame design took it out of the motorized-bicycle category and would help define what a modern motorcycle should contain in the years to come. The boys also received help with their bigger engine from outboard motor pioneer Ole Evinrude, who was then building gas engines of his own design for automotive use on Milwaukee's Lake Street.

The prototype of the new loop-frame Harley-Davidson was assembled in a 10 × 15 ft (3.0 × 4.6 m) shed in the Davidson family backyard. Most of the major parts, however, were made elsewhere, including some probably fabricated at the West Milwaukee railshops where oldest brother William A. Davidson was then toolroom foreman. This prototype machine was functional by September 8, 1904, when it competed in a Milwaukee motorcycle race held at State Fair Park. It was ridden by Edward Hildebrand and placed fourth. This is the first documented appearance of a Harley-Davidson motorcycle in the historical record.

In January 1905, small advertisements were placed in the "Automobile and Cycle Trade Journal" that offered bare Harley-Davidson engines to the do-it-yourself trade. By April, complete motorcycles were in production on a very limited basis. That year the first Harley-Davidson dealer, Carl H. Lang of Chicago, sold three bikes from the dozen or so built in the Davidson backyard shed. (Some years later the original shed was taken to the Juneau Avenue factory where it would stand for many decades as a tribute to the Motor Company's humble origins. Unfortunately, the first shed was accidentally destroyed by contractors in the early 1970s during a clean-up of the factory yard.)

In 1906, Harley and the Davidson brothers built their first factory on Chestnut Street (later Juneau Avenue). This location remains Harley-Davidson's corporate headquarters today. The first Juneau Avenue plant was a 40 × 60 ft (12 × 18 m) single-story wooden structure. The company produced about 50 motorcycles that year.

1907 model.

In 1907, William S. Harley graduated from the University of Wisconsin–Madison with a degree in mechanical engineering. That year additional factory expansion came with a second floor and later with facings and additions of Milwaukee pale yellow ("cream") brick. With the new facilities production increased to 150 motorcycles in 1907. The company was officially incorporated that September. They also began selling their motorcycles to police departments around this time, a market that has been important to them ever since.

Harley-Davidson 1000 cc HT 1916

Production in 1905 and 1906 were all single-cylinder models with 26.84 cubic inches (440 cc) engines. In February 1907 a prototype model with a 45-degree V-Twin engine was displayed at the Chicago Automobile Show. Although shown and advertised, very few V-Twin models were built between 1907 and 1910. These first V-Twins displaced 53.68 cubic inches (880 cc) and produced about 7 horsepower (5.2 kW). This gave about double the power of the first singles. Top speed was about 60 mph (100 km/h). Production jumped from 450 motorcycles in 1908 to 1,149 machines in 1909.

By 1911, some 150 makes of motorcycles had already been built in the United States – although just a handful would survive the 1910s.

In 1911, an improved V-Twin model was introduced. The new engine had mechanically operated intake valves, as opposed to the "automatic" intake valves used on earlier V-Twins that opened by engine vacuum. With a displacement of 49.48 cubic inches (811 cc), the 1911 V-Twin was smaller than earlier twins, but gave better performance. After 1913 the majority of bikes produced by Harley-Davidson would be V-Twin models.

By 1913, the yellow brick factory had been demolished and on the site a new 5-story structure of reinforced concrete and red brick had been built. Begun in 1910, the red brick factory with its many additions would take up two blocks along Juneau Avenue and around the corner on 38th Street. Despite the competition, Harley-Davidson was already pulling ahead of Indian and would dominate motorcycle racing after 1914. Production that year swelled to 16,284 machines.

World War I

In 1917, the United States entered World War I and the military demanded motorcycles for the war effort. Harleys had already been used by the military in the Pancho Villa Expedition but World War I was the first time the motorcycle had been adopted for combat service.[citation needed] Harley-Davidson provided about 15,000 machines to the military forces during World War I.

Ralph Hepburn on his Harley racing bike in this 1919 photo.

1920s

Harley-Davidson 1000 cc HT 1923

By 1920, Harley-Davidson was the largest motorcycle manufacturer in the world. Their motorcycles were sold by dealers in 67 countries. Production was 28,189 machines.

In 1921, a Harley-Davidson, ridden by Otto Walker, was the first motorcycle ever to win a race at an average speed of over 100 mph (160 km/h).

During the 1920s, several improvements were put in place, such as a new 74 cubic inch (1200 cc) V-Twin, introduced in 1922, and the "Teardrop" gas tank in 1925. A front brake was added in 1928.[citation needed]

In the late summer of 1929, Harley-Davidson introduced its 45 cubic inches (737 cc) flathead V-Twin to compete with the Indian 101 Scout and the Excelsior Super X. This was the "D" model, produced from 1929 to 1931. Riders of Indian motorcycles derisively referred to this model as the "three cylinder Harley" because the generator was upright and parallel to the front cylinder. The 2.745 in (69.7 mm) bore and 3.8125 in (96.8 mm) stroke would continue in most versions of the 750 engine; exceptions include the XA and the XR750.[citation needed]

The Great Depression

The Great Depression began a few months after the introduction of their 45 cubic inch model. Harley-Davidson's sales plummeted from 21,000 in 1929 to 3,703 in 1933. Despite those dismal numbers, Harley-Davidson proudly unveiled its lineup for 1934, which included a Flathead with Art Deco styling.

Harley-Davidson 1200 cc SV 1931

In order to survive the remainder of the Depression, the company manufactured industrial powerplants based on their motorcycle engines. They also designed and built a three-wheeled delivery vehicle called the Servi-Car, which remained in production until 1973.

Harley-Davidson WL

In the mid 1930s, Alfred Rich Child opened a production line in Japan with the 74 cubic inches (1210 cc) VL. The Japanese license-holder severed its business relations with Harley-Davidson in 1936 and continued manufacturing the VL under the Rikuo name.

An 80 cubic inches (1300 cc) flathead engine was added to the line in 1935, by which time the single-cylinder motorcycles had been discontinued.

In 1936, the 61E and 61EL models with the "Knucklehead" OHV engines was introduced. Valvetrain problems in early Knucklehead engines required a redesign halfway through its first year of production and retrofitting of the new valvetrain on earlier engines.

By 1937, all Harley-Davidson's flathead engines were equipped with dry-sump oil recirculation systems similar to the one introduced in the "Knucklehead" OHV engine. The revised 74 cubic inches (1210 cc) V and VL models were renamed U and UL, the 80 cubic inches (1300 cc) VH and VLH to be renamed UH and ULH, and the 45 cubic inches (740 cc) R to be renamed W.

In 1941, the 74 cubic inches (1210 cc) "Knucklehead" was introduced as the F and the FL. The 80 cubic inches (1300 cc) flathead UH and ULH models were discontinued after 1941, while the 74" U & UL flathead models were produced up to 1948.

World War II

Harley copied the BMW R71 to produce its XA model.

One of only two American cycle manufacturers to survive the Great Depression, Harley-Davidson again produced large numbers of motorcycles for the US Army in World War II and resumed civilian production afterwards, producing a range of large V-twin motorcycles that were successful both on racetracks and for private buyers.

Harley-Davidson, on the eve of World War II, was already supplying the Army with a military-specific version of its 45 cubic inches (740 cc) WL line, called the WLA. (The A in this case stood for "Army".) Upon the outbreak of war, the company, along with most other manufacturing enterprises, shifted to war work. Over 90,000 military motorcycles, mostly WLAs and WLCs (the Canadian version) would be produced, many to be provided to allies. Harley-Davidson received two Army-Navy 'E' Awards, one in 1943 and the other in 1945, which were awarded for Excellence in Production.

Harley produced the WLC for the Canadian military.

Shipments to the Soviet Union under the Lend-Lease program numbered at least 30,000.[citation needed] The WLAs produced during all four years of war production generally have 1942 serial numbers. Production of the WLA stopped at the end of World War II, but was resumed from 1950 to 1952 for use in the Korean War.

The U.S. Army also asked Harley-Davidson to produce a new motorcycle with many of the features of BMW's side-valve and shaft-driven R71. Harley largely copied the BMW engine and drive train and produced the shaft-driven 750 cc 1942 Harley-Davidson XA. This shared no dimensions, no parts and no design concepts (except side valves) with any prior Harley-Davidson engine. Due to the superior cooling of the flat-twin engine with the cylinders across the frame, Harley's XA cylinder heads ran 100 °F (56 °C) cooler than its V-twins. The XA never entered full production: the motorcycle by that time had been eclipsed by the Jeep as the Army's general purpose vehicle, and the WLA—already in production—was sufficient for its limited police, escort, and courier roles. Only 1,000 were made and the XA never went into full production. It remains the only shaft-driven Harley-Davidson ever made.

Small Harleys - Hummers and Aermacchis

See also: Harley-Davidson Hummer

See also: Harley-Davidson Topper

Harley-Davidson Hummer

As part of war reparations, Harley-Davidson acquired the design of a small German motorcycle, the DKW RT125 which they adapted, manufactured, and sold from 1947 to 1966. Various models were made, including the Hummer from 1955 to 1959, but they are all colloquially referred to as "Hummers" at present. BSA in the United Kingdom took the same design as the foundation of their BSA Bantam.

1971 Aermacchi Harley-Davidson Turismo Veloce

In 1960, Harley-Davidson consolidated the Model 165 and Hummer lines into the Super-10, introduced the Topper scooter, and bought fifty percent of Aeronautica Macchi's motorcycle division. Importation of Aermacchi's 250 cc horizontal single began the following year. The bike bore Harley-Davidson badges and was marketed as the Harley-Davidson Sprint. The engine of the Sprint was increased to 350 cc in 1969 and would remain that size until 1974, when the four-stroke Sprint was discontinued.

After the Pacer and Scat models were discontinued at the end of 1965, the Bobcat became the last of Harley-Davidson's American-made two-stroke motorcycles. The Bobcat was manufactured only in the 1966 model year.

Harley-Davidson replaced their American-made lightweight two-stroke motorcycles with the Aermacchi-built two-stroke powered M-65, M-65S, and Rapido. The M-65 had a semi-step-through frame and tank. The M-65S was a M-65 with a larger tank that eliminated the step-through feature. The Rapido was a larger bike with a 125 cc engine. The Aermacchi-built Harley-Davidsons became entirely two-stroke powered when the 250 cc two-stroke SS-250 replaced the four-stroke 350 cc Sprint in 1974.

Harley-Davidson purchased full control of Aermacchi's motorcycle production in 1974 and continued making two-stroke motorcycles there until 1978, when they sold the facility to Cagiva.

Tarnished reputation

In 1952, following their application to the US Tariff Commission for a 40% tax on imported motorcycles, Harley-Davidson was charged with restrictive practices. Hollywood also damaged Harley's image with many outlaw biker gang films produced from the 1950s through the 1970s, following the Hollister riot on July 4, 1947. "Harley-Davidson" for a long time was synonymous with the Hells Angels and other outlaw motorcyclists.[*citation needed*]

Replica of the "Captain America" bike from the film *Easy Rider*

AMF H-D Electra Glide

In 1969, American Machinery and Foundry (AMF) bought the company, streamlined production, and slashed the workforce. This tactic resulted in a labor strike and a lower quality of bikes. The bikes were expensive and inferior in performance, handling, and quality to Japanese motorcycles. Sales declined, quality plummeted, and the company almost went bankrupt. The "Harley-Davidson" name was mocked as "Hardly Ableson", "Hardly Driveable," and "Hogly Ferguson", and the nickname "Hog" became pejorative.[*citation needed*]

In 1977, Harley-Davidson produced what has become one of its most controversial models, the Confederate Edition. The bike was essentially a stock Harley with Confederate-specific paint and details.

Restructuring and revival

In 1981, AMF sold the company to a group of thirteen investors led by Vaughn Beals and Willie G. Davidson for $80 million. Inventory was strictly controlled using the just-in-time system.

In the early eighties, Harley-Davidson claimed that Japanese manufacturers were importing motorcycles into the US in such volume as to harm or threaten to harm domestic producers. After an investigation by the US International Trade Commission, President Reagan imposed in 1983 a 45% tariff on imported bikes and bikes over 700 cc engine capacity. Harley Davidson subsequently rejected offers of assistance from Japanese motorcycle makers.

Rather than trying to match the Japanese, the new management deliberately exploited the "retro" appeal of the machines, building motorcycles that deliberately adopted the look and feel of their earlier machines and the subsequent customizations of owners of that era. Many components such as brakes, forks, shocks, carburetors, electrics and wheels were outsourced from foreign manufacturers and quality increased, technical improvements were made, and buyers slowly returned.

Ford F-150 Super Crew
Harley-Davidson edition

The "Sturgis" model, boasting a dual belt-drive, was introduced. By 1990, with the introduction of the "Fat Boy", Harley once again became the sales leader in the heavyweight (over 750 cc) market. At the time of the Fat Boy model introduction a story rapidly spread that its silver paint job and other features were inspired by the World War II American B-29 bomber; and that the Fat Boy name was a combination of the names of the atomic bombs (Fat Man and Little Boy) that were dropped on Nagasaki and Hiroshima respectively. However, the Urban Legend Reference Pages lists this story as an urban legend.

1993 saw the replacement of the FXR frame with the Dyna, though it was revived briefly from 1999 to 2000 for special limited editions (FXR2,FXR3 & FXR4).

In 2000, Ford Motor Company added a Harley-Davidson edition to the Ford F-Series F-150 line, complete with the Harley-Davidson logo. This truck was a Super Cab for model year 2000. In 2001, Ford changed the truck to a Super Crew and in 2002 added a super-charged engine (5.4 L) which continued until 2003. The 2003 model bore badges celebrating the 100th anniversaries of both companies. In 2004, the Ford/Harley was changed to a Super-Duty, which continues through 2009. Ford again produced a Harley-Davidson Edition F-150 for their 2006 model-year, as well.

Building started on $75 million 130,000 square-foot (12,000 m^2) Harley-Davidson Museum in the Menomonee River Valley on June 1, 2006. It opened in 2008 and houses the company's vast collection of historic motorcycles and corporate archives, along with a restaurant, café and meeting space.

Buell Motorcycle Company

Main article: Buell Motorcycle Company

Harley-Davidson's association with sportbike manufacturer Buell Motorcycle Company began in 1987 when they supplied Buell with fifty surplus XR1000 engines. Buell continued to buy engines from Harley-Davidson until 1993, when Harley-Davidson bought forty-nine percent of the Buell Motorcycle Company. Harley-Davidson increased its share in Buell to ninety-eight percent in 1998, and to complete ownership in 2003.

In an attempt to attract newcomers to motorcycling in general and to Harley-Davidson in particular, Buell developed a low-cost, low-maintenance motorcycle. The resulting single-cylinder Buell Blast was introduced in 2000, and was made through 2009, which, according to Buell, is to be the final year of production. On October 15, 2009, the company issued an official statement that it would be discontinuing the Buell line and ceasing production immediately.

Claims of stock price manipulation

During its period of peak demand, during the late 1990s and early 2000s, Harley-Davidson embarked on a program of expanding the number of dealerships throughout the country. At the same time, its current dealers typically had waiting lists that extended up to a year for some of the most popular models. Harley-Davidson, like the auto manufacturers, records a sale not when a consumer buys their product, but rather when it is delivered to a dealer. Therefore, it is possible for the manufacturer to inflate sales numbers by requiring dealers to accept more inventory than desired in a practice called channel stuffing. When demand softened following the unique 2003 model year, this news led to a dramatic decline in the stock price. In April 2004 alone, the price of HOG shares dropped from over $60 to under $40. Immediately prior to this decline, retiring CEO Jeffrey Bleustein profited $42 million on the exercise of employee stock options. Harley-Davidson was named as a defendant in numerous class action suits filed by investors who claimed they were intentionally defrauded by Harley-Davidson's management and directors. By January 2007, the price of Harley-Davidson shares reached $70.

2007 workers' strike

On February 2, 2007, upon the expiration of their union contract, about 2,700 employees at Harley-Davidson Inc.'s largest manufacturing plant in York, PA went on strike after failing to agree on wages and health benefits. During the pendency of the strike, the company refused to pay for any portion of the striking employees' health care.

The day before the strike, after the union voted against the proposed contract and to authorize the strike, the company shut down all production at the plant. The York facility employs more than 3,200 workers, both union and non-union.

Harley-Davidson announced on February 16, 2007, that it had reached a labor agreement with union workers at its largest manufacturing plant, a breakthrough in the two-week-old strike. The strike disrupted Harley-Davidson's national production and had ripple effects as far away as Wisconsin, where 440 employees were laid off, and many Harley suppliers also laid off workers because of the strike.

MV Agusta Group acquisition

On July 11, 2008 Harley-Davidson announced they had signed a definitive agreement to acquire the MV Agusta Group for $109M USD (€70M). MV Agusta Group contains two lines of motorcycles: the high-performance MV Agusta brand and the lightweight Cagiva brand. The acquisition was completed on August 8.

On October 15, 2009, Harley-Davidson announced that it would divest its interest in MV Agusta. Harley-Davidson Inc. finished its sale of Italian motorcycle maker MV Agusta to Claudio Castiglioni. Castiglioni is the company's former owner and had served as MV Agusta's chairman since Harley-Davidson purchased it in 2008.[*citation needed*]

Steps towards export to India

In August 2009, Harley-Davidson announced plans to enter the market in India, where, according to press releases, it expects to start selling its motorcycles in 2010. The company has established a subsidiary to be located in Gurgaon, near Delhi, and has begun the process of seeking dealers. Plans to enter the Indian market have been delayed for several years, due to high tariffs and emissions regulations. The pollution regulations have recently changed, but the tariff problem is yet unresolved.

In 2007, U.S. Trade Representative Susan Schwab and the Minister for Commerce and Industry of India, Kamal Nath, had agreed that Harley-Davidson motorcycles will be allowed access to the Indian market in exchange for the export of Indian mangoes. However, India had not specified emission standards for motorcycles over 500 cc displacement, effectively prohibiting the import of Harley-Davidsons, along with most models of other manufacturers. Plans to export to India were also held up by import duties of 60% and taxes of 30%, which effectively doubled the sale price. A Harley-Davidson spokesman said the company thinks demand is high enough to overcome the tariffs, and chief operating officer Matt Levatich said they would continue to push for lower tariffs.

Harley Davidson is introducing 12 models in India from the range of five motorcycle families, namely Sportster, Dyna, VRSC, Softail and CVO. The motorcycles are completely built units and will be imported to India, thus attracting a tax over 100% in the price range of 695,000 rupees and 3,495,000 rupees ex-showroom. The bookings might start from April 2010 and the motorcycle delivery will commence from June 2010. To begin with, Harley Davidson would have five dealerships (Delhi, Mumbai, Bangalore, Hyderabad and Chandigarh) with the aim of increasing the dealerships to more than 20 in the next five years.

Financial crisis

According to Interbrand, the value of the Harley-Davidson brand fell by 43% to $4.34 billion in 2009. The fall in value is believed to be connected to the 66% drop in the company profits in two quarters of the previous year. On April 29, 2010, Harley-Davidson stated that they must cut $54 million in manufacturing costs from its production facilities in Wisconsin, and that they would explore alternate U.S. sites to accomplish this. The announcement came in the wake of a massive company-wide restructuring, which began in early 2009 and involved the closing of two factories, one distribution center, and the planned elimination of nearly 25% of its total workforce (around 3,500 employees). The company announced on September 14, 2010 that it would remain in Wisconsin.

Harley-Davidson engines

Main article: Harley-Davidson engine timeline

V-twin in a HD Road King

The classic Harley-Davidson engines are two-cylinder, V-twin engines with the pistons mounted in a 45° "V". The crankshaft has a single pin, and both pistons are connected to this pin through their connecting rods.

This design causes the pistons to fire at uneven intervals. This is due to an engineering tradeoff to create a large, high-torque engine in a small space. This design choice is entirely vestigial from an engineering standpoint, but has been sustained because of the strong connection between the distinctive sound and the Harley-Davidson brand. This design, which is covered under several United States patents, gives the Harley-Davidson V-twin its unique choppy "potato-potato" sound. To simplify the engine and reduce costs, the V-twin ignition was designed to operate with a single set of points and no distributor. This is known as a dual fire ignition system, causing both spark plugs to fire regardless of which cylinder was on its compression stroke, with the other spark plug firing on its cylinder's exhaust stroke, effectively "wasting a spark". The exhaust note is basically a throaty growling sound with some popping. The 45° design of the engine thus creates a plug firing sequencing as such: The first cylinder fires, the second (rear) cylinder fires 315° later, then there is a 405° gap until the first cylinder fires again, giving the engine its unique sound.

Harley-Davidson has used various ignition systems throughout its history - be it the early points/condenser system, (Big Twin up to 1978 and Sportsters 1970 to 1978), magneto ignition system used on 1958 to 1969 Sportsters, early electronic with centrifugal mechanical advance weights, (all models 1978 and a half to 1979), or the late electronic with transistorized ignition control module, more familiarly known as the black box or the brain, (all models 1980 to present).

Starting in 1995, the company introduced Electronic Fuel Injection (EFI) as an option for the 30th anniversary edition Electra Glide. With the introduction of the 2007 product line, EFI is now standard on all models, including Sportsters.

In 1991, Harley-Davidson began to participate in the Sound Quality Working Group, founded by Orfield Labs, Bruel and Kjaer, TEAC, Yamaha, Sennheiser, SMS and Cortex. This was the nation's first group to share research on psychological acoustics. Later that year, Harley-Davidson participated in a series of sound quality studies at Orfield Labs, based on recordings taken at the Talladega Superspeedway, with the objective to lower the sound level for EU standards while analytically capturing the "Harley Sound."[citation needed] This research resulted in the bikes that were introduced in compliance with EU standards for 1998.

On February 1, 1994, the company filed a sound trademark application for the distinctive sound of the Harley-Davidson motorcycle engine: "The mark consists of the exhaust sound of applicant's motorcycles, produced by V-twin, common crankpin motorcycle engines when the goods are in use". Nine of Harley-Davidson's competitors filed comments opposing the application, arguing that cruiser-style motorcycles of various brands use a single-crankpin V-twin engine which produce a similar sound. These objections were followed by litigation. In June 2000, the company dropped efforts to federally register its trademark.

Big V-twins

Electra Glide "Ultra Classic" in Bristol

- F-head, also known as JD, pocket valve and IOE (intake over exhaust), 1914–1929 (1000 cc), and 1922–1929 (1200 cc)
- Flathead, 1930–1948 (1200 cc) and 1935–1941 (1300 cc).
- Knucklehead, 1936–1947 61 cubic inch (1000 cc), and 1941–1947 74 cubic inch (1200 cc)
- Panhead, 1948–1965 61 cubic inch (1000 cc), and 1948–1965, 74 cubic inch (1200 cc)
- Shovelhead, 1966–1984, 74 cubic inch (1200 cc) and 80 cubic inch (1345 cc) since late 1978
- Evolution (a.k.a. "Evo" and "Blockhead"), 1984–2000, 80 cubic inch (1340 cc)
- Twin Cam 88 (a.k.a. "Fathead") 1999–2006, 88 cubic inch (1450 cc)
- Twin Cam 88B (counter balanced version of the Twin Cam 88) 2000–2006, 88 cubic inch (1450 cc)
- Twin Cam 95, since 2000, 95 cubic inch (1550 cc) (engines for early C.V.O. models)
- Twin Cam 96, since 2007, 96 cubic inch (1584 cc)
- Twin Cam 103, 2003–2006, 2009, 103 cubic inch (1690 cc) (engines for C.V.O. models)
- Twin Cam 110, since 2007, 110 cubic inch (1802 cc) (engines for C.V.O. models)

Small V-twins

Evolution Sportster cruising around downtown Buenos Aires

- D Model, 1929–1931, 750 cc
- R Model, 1932–1936, 750 cc
- W Model, 1937–1952, 750 cc, solo (2 wheel, frame only)
- G (Servi-Car) Model, 1932–1973, 750 cc
- K Model, 1952–1953, 750 cc
- KH Model, 1954–1956, 900 cc
- Ironhead, 1957–1971, 900 cc; 1971–1985, 1000 cc
- Evolution, since 1986, 883 cc, 1100 cc and 1200 cc

Revolution engine

V-Rod on the show room floor

The Revolution engine is based on the VR-1000 Superbike race program, developed by Harley-Davidson's Powertrain Engineering team and Porsche Engineering in Stuttgart, Germany. It is a liquid cooled, dual overhead cam, internally counterbalanced 60 degree V-twin engine with a displacement of 69 cubic inch (1130 cc), producing 115 hp (86 kW) at 8250 rpm at the crank, with a redline of 9000 rpm. It was introduced for the new V-Rod line in 2001 for the 2002 model year, starting with the single VRSCA (V-Twin Racing Street Custom) model.

A 1250 cc Screamin' Eagle version of the Revolution engine was made available for 2005 & 2006, and was present thereafter in a single production model from 2005 to 2007. In 2008, the 1250 cc Revolution Engine became standard for the entire VRSC line. Harley-Davidson claims 123 hp (92 kW) at the crank for the 2008 VRSCAW model. The VRXSE *Destroyer* is equipped with a stroker (75 mm crank) Screamin' Eagle 79 cubic inch (1300 cc) Revolution Engine, producing over 165 hp (123 kW).

Model designations

Harley model designations are a sequence of letters and numbers, combined in limited ways. The sequences can be long, as in the 2006 model designation FLHTCUSE.

The first letter may be one of the following:

K ('50s flathead small twin), E, F (1936-* single cam OHV big twin), U, V (1930-48 four cam flathead big twin), D, G, R, W (flathead small twin), X (Sportster OHV), or V (VRSC)

since 1984 only F (Big Twin), X (Sportster) and V (V_ROD) have been used regularly.

Letters are appended singly or in pairs, as follows:

B (BLACKED OUT ie Street Bob, Night Train, and Cross Bones models), C (Classic or Custom), CW (Custom Wide (2008 Softail Rocker)) D (Dyna chasis or Softail Deuce), E (Electric start), F (Fat Boy (1990–present); Fat Bob (2008–present) or Foot-shift (1972 and prior)), H (HANDLE BAR/ FRONT END MOUNTED FAIRING. ie bat wing fairing/quick release windshield.), I (Fuel injection), L (Low Rider)), N {(Nostalgia as in Softail Deluxe/Nostalgia/Special) and Nightster in Sportster family} P (Police), R (Race, Road King, or Rubber-mount), S (Sport, Springer), ST (Softail), T (FRAME MOUNTED FAIRING), WG (Wide Glide), SE (Screamin' Eagle), U (Ultra) X (FLHX Street Glide), sport in Dyna models, and Street Glide in Touring models.) XT (T-Sport Dyna Model).

Custom Vehicle Operations models can also have a number (2,3,4) added.

Note that these conventions for model designations are broken regularly by the company.

Current model designations

2001 883 Sportster Hugger

- **Sportster** With the exception of the street-going XR1000 of the 1980s and the XR1200 most Sportsters made for street use have the prefix XL in their model designation. For the Sportster Evolution engines used since the mid 1980s, there have been two engine sizes. Motorcycles with the smaller engine are designated XL883, while those with the larger engine were initially designated XL1100. When the size of the larger engine was increased from 1,100 cc to 1,200 cc, the designation was changed accordingly from XL1100 to XL1200. Subsequent letters in the designation refer to model variations within the Sportster range, e.g. the XL883C refers to an 883 cc Sportster Custom, while the XL1200S designates the now-discontinued 1200 Sportster Sport.
- **Dyna** models utilize the big-twin engine (F), small-diameter telescopic forks similar to those used on the Sportster (X), and the Dyna chassis (D). Therefore, all Dyna models have designations that

begin with FXD, *e.g.*, FXDWG (Dyna Wide Glide) and FXDL (Dyna Low Rider).

- **Softail** models utilize the big-twin engine (F) and the Softail chassis (ST).
  - Softail models that use small-diameter telescopic forks similar to those used on the Sportster (X) have designations that begin with FXST, *e.g.*, FXSTB (Night Train), FXSTD (Deuce), and FXSTS (Springer).
  - Softail models that use large-diameter telescopic forks similar to those used on the touring bikes (L) have designations beginning with FLST, *e.g.*, FLSTF (Fat Boy), FLSTC (Heritage Softail Classic), and FLSTN (Softail Deluxe).
  - Softail models that use Springer forks with a 21-inch (530 mm) wheel have designations that begin with FXSTS, *e.g.*, FXSTS (Springer Softail) and FXSTSB (Bad Boy).
  - Softail models that use Springer forks with a 16-inch (410 mm) wheel have designations that begin with FLSTS, *e.g.*, FLSTSC (Springer Classic) and FLSTSB (Cross Bones).
- **Touring** models use Big-Twin engines and large-diameter telescopic forks. All Touring designations begin with the letters FL, *e.g.*, FLHR (Road King) and FLTR (Road Glide).
- **Revolution** models utilize the Revolution engine (VR), and the street versions are designated Street Custom (SC). After the VRSC prefix common to all street Revolution bikes, the next letter denotes the model, either A (base V-Rod: discontinued), AW (base V-Rod + W for Wide with a 240mm rear tire), B (discontinued), D (Night Rod: discontinued), R (Street Rod: discontinued), SE and SEII(CVO Special Edition), or X (Special edition). Further differentiation within models are made with an additional letter, *e.g.*, VRSCDX denotes the Night Rod Special.
  - The factory drag bike, the VRXSE Destroyer, uses X instead of SC to denote a non-street bike and SE to denote a CVO Special Edition

Model families

Modern Harley-branded motorcycles fall into one of five model families: Touring, Softail, Dyna, Sportster and VRSC. Model families are distinguished by the frame, engine, suspension, and other characteristics.

Touring

See also: Harley-Davidson FL

Hamburg Police Electra Glide.

The touring family, also known as "dressers", includes three Road King models and Electra Glide models offered in various trim. The Road Kings have a "retro cruiser" appearance and are equipped with a large clear windshield. Road Kings are reminiscent of big-twin models from the 1940s and '50s. Electra Glides can be identified by their full front fairings. Most Electra Glides sport a fork-mounted fairing referred to as the "Batwing" due to its unmistakable shape. The Road Glide has a frame-mounted fairing, referred to as the "Sharknose". The Sharknose includes a unique, dual front headlight.

Touring models are distinguishable by their large saddlebags, rear coil-over air suspension and are the only models to offer full fairings with Radios/CBs. All touring models use the same frame, first introduced with a Shovelhead motor in 1980, and carried forward with only modest upgrades until 2009, when it was extensively redesigned. The frame is distinguished by the location of the steering head in front of the forks and was the first H-D frame to rubber mount the drivetrain to isolate the rider from the vibration of the big V-twin.

The frame was modified for the 1994 model year when the oil tank went under the transmission and the battery was moved inboard from under the right saddlebag to under the seat. In 1997, the frame was again modified to allow for a larger battery under the seat and to lower seat height. In 2007, Harley introduced the 96 cubic inch motor, as well the 6 speed transmission to give the rider better speeds on the highway.

In years past, these touring models have become favorites with several local and state police agencies, such as the Chicago Police Department, the Los Angeles Police Department, the Iowa State Patrol, and several others.

In 2006, Harley introduced the FLHX, a bike designed by Willie G. Davidson to be his personal ride, to its touring line.

In 2008, Harley added anti-lock braking systems and cruise control as a factory installed option on all touring models. Also new for 2008 is the 6-gallon fuel tank for all touring models.

For the 2009 model year, Harley-Davidson has redesigned the entire touring range with several changes, including a new frame, new swingarm, a completely revised engine-mounting system, 17-inch (430 mm) front wheels for all but the FLHRC, and a 2-1-2 exhaust. The changes result in greater load carrying capacity, better handling, a smoother engine, longer range and less exhaust heat transmitted to the rider and passenger. Also released for the 2009 model year is the FLHTCUTG Tri-Glide Ultra Classic, the first three-wheeled Harley since the Servi-Car was discontinued in 1973. The model features a unique frame and a 103 ci engine exclusive to the trike.

Softail

Main article: Softail

These big-twin motorcycles capitalize on Harley's strong value on tradition. With the rear-wheel suspension hidden under the transmission, they are visually similar to the "hardtail" choppers popular in the 1960s and 1970s, as well as from their own earlier history. In keeping with that tradition, Harley offers Softail models with "Springer" front ends and "Heritage" styling that incorporate design cues from throughout their history.

Dyna

Main article: Harley-Davidson Super Glide

Dyna motorcycles feature big-twin engines and traditional styling. They can be distinguished from the Softail by the traditional coil-over suspension that connects the swingarm to the frame, and from the Sportster by their larger engines. On these models, the transmission also houses the engine's oil reservoir.

In 2006, Harley-Davidson released a line-up of five Dyna models: Super Glide, Super Glide Custom, Street Bob, Low Rider, and Wide Glide.

In 2008, the Dyna Fat Bob was introduced to the Dyna line-up featuring aggressive styling, including a new 2-1-2 exhaust, twin headlamps, a 180 mm rear tire and a 130 mm front tire.

The Dyna family uses the 88 cubic inch twin cam from 99-06. From 2007-and on the displacement was increased to 96 cubic inches. This was the result of the factory increasing the stroke to 4 3/8" inches.

Sportster

Main article: Harley-Davidson Sportster

Introduced in 1957, the Sportster is the longest-running model family in the Harley-Davidson lineup.[citation needed] They were conceived as racing motorcycles, and were popular on dirt and flat-track race courses through the 1960s and 1970s. Smaller and lighter than the other Harley models, contemporary Sportsters make use of 883 cc or 1,200 cc Evolution engines and, though often modified, remain similar in appearance to their racing ancestors.

Up until the 2003 model year, the engine on the Sportster was rigidly mounted to the frame. The 2004 Sportster received a new frame accommodating a rubber-mounted engine. Although this made the bike heavier and reduced the available lean angle, it reduced the amount of vibration transmitted to the frame and the rider. The rubber mounted engine provides a significantly smoother ride for rider and passenger, allowing longer trips.

In the 2007 model year, Harley-Davidson celebrated the 50th anniversary of the Sportster and produced a limited edition called the XL50, of which only 2000 were made for sale worldwide. Each motorcycle was individually numbered and came in one of two colors, Mirage Pearl Orange or Vivid Black. Also in 2007, electronic fuel injection was introduced to the Sportster family, and the Nightster model was introduced in mid-year. In 2009, Harley-Davidson added the Iron 883 to the Sportster line, the newest in the Dark Custom series.

In the 2008 model year, Harley-Davidson released the XR1200 Sportster in Europe, Africa, and the Middle East. The XR1200 had an Evolution engine tuned to produce 91 bhp (68 kW), four-piston dual front disc brakes, and an aluminum swing arm. *Motorcyclist* featured the XR1200 on the cover of its July 2008 issue and was generally positive about it in their "First Ride" story, in which Harley-Davidson was repeatedly asked to sell it in the United States. One possible reason for the delayed availability in the United States was the fact that Harley-Davidson had to obtain the "XR1200" naming rights from Storz Performance, a Harley customizing shop in Ventura, Calif. The XR1200 was released in the United States in 2009 in a special color scheme including Mirage Orange highlighting its dirt-tracker heritage. The first 750 XR1200 models in 2009 were pre-ordered and came with a number 1 tag for the front of the bike, autographed by Kenny Coolbeth and Scott Parker and a thank you/welcome letter from the company, signed by Bill Davidson.[*citation needed*]

VRSC

Main article: Harley-Davidson VRSC

Introduced in 2001, the VRSC family bears little resemblance to Harley's more traditional lineup. Competing against Japanese and American muscle bikes and seeking to expand its market appeal, the "V-Rod" makes use of an engine developed jointly with Porsche that, for the first time in Harley history, incorporates overhead cams, and liquid cooling. The V-Rod is visually distinctive, easily identified by the 60-degree V-Twin engine, the radiator and the hydroformed frame members that support the round-topped air cleaner cover. Based on the VR-1000 racing motorcycle, it continues to be a platform around which Harley-Davidson builds drag-racing competition machines. The V-Rod has gathered an enthusiastic following in the U.S., Europe and Australia, and an annual Rally at the Kansas City production facility has been organized by Max Millender and the members of a 21,000+ member strong internet discussion forum www.1130cc.com [3]. Bill Davidson has presented Mr Millender with a signed airbox cover to recognize the contribution the forum has made to the VRSC platform which continues to evolve with models like the Night Rod Special (VRSCDX).

In 2008, Harley added anti-lock braking systems as a factory installed option on all VRSC models. Harley also increased the displacement of the stock engine from 1130 to 1250 cc (69 to 76 cu in), which had only been previously available from Screamin' Eagle, and added a slipper clutch as standard equipment.

VRSC Models Include:

VRSCA: V-Rod (2002–2006), VRSCAW: V-Rod (2007–2010), VRSCB: V-Rod (2004–2005), VRSCD: Night Rod (2006–2008), VRSCDX: Night Rod Special (2007–2010), VRSCSE: Screamin' Eagle CVO V-Rod (2005), VRSCSE2: Screamin' Eagle CVO V-Rod (2006), VRSCR: Street Rod (2006–2007), VRSCX: Screamin' Eagle Tribute V-Rod (2007), VRSCF: V-Rod Muscle (2009–2010).

VRXSE

The VRXSE V-Rod Destroyer is Harley-Davidson's production drag racing motorcycle, constructed to run the quarter mile in under ten seconds. It is based on the same revolution engine that powers the VRSC line, but the VRXSE uses the Sceamin' Eagle 1,300 cc "stroked" incarnation, featuring a 75 mm crankshaft, 105 mm Pistons, and 58 mm throttle bodies.

The V-Rod Destroyer is not a street legal motorcycle.

Environmental record

The Environmental Protection Agency conducted emissions-certification and representative emissions test in Ann Arbor, Michigan, in 2005. Subsequently, Harley-Davidson produced an "environmental warranty." The warranty ensures each owner that the vehicle is designed and built free of any defects in materials and workmanship that would cause the vehicle to not meet EPA standards. In 2005, the EPA and the Pennsylvania Department of Environmental Protection (PADEP) confirmed Harley-Davidson to be the first corporation to voluntarily enroll in the One Clean-Up Program [4]. This program is designed for the clean-up of the affected soil and groundwater at the former York Naval Ordnance Plant. The program is backed by the state and local government along with participating organizations and corporations.

Paul Gotthold, Director of Operations for the EPA, congratulated the motor company:

> "Harley-Davidson has taken their environmental responsibilities very seriously and has already made substantial progress in the investigation and cleanup of past contamination. Proof of Harley's efforts can be found in the recent EPA determination that designates the Harley property as 'under control' for cleanup purposes. This determination means that there are no serious contamination problems at the facility. Under the new One Cleanup Program, Harley, EPA, and PADEP will expedite the completion of the property investigation and reach a final solution that will permanently protect human health and the environment."

Harley-Davidson has also purchased most of Castalloy, which is a South Australian producer of cast motorcycle wheels and hubs. The South Australian government has set forth "protection to the purchaser (Harley-Davidson) against environmental risks."

Factory tours & museum

Harley-Davidson Museum in Milwaukee

Harley-Davidson offers factory tours at four of its manufacturing sites, and the Harley-Davidson Museum, which opened in 2008, exhibits Harley-Davidson's history, culture, and vehicles, including the motor company's corporate archives.

- York, Pennsylvania - Vehicle Operations: Manufacturing site for Touring class, Softail, and custom vehicles.
- Tomahawk, Wisconsin - Tomahawk Operations: Facility that makes sidecars, saddlebags, windshields, and more.
- Kansas City, Missouri - Vehicle and Powertrain Operations: Manufacturing site of Sportster, VRSC, and other vehicles.
- Menomonee Falls, Wisconsin - Pilgrim Road Powertrain Operations plant, two types of tours.
- Milwaukee, Wisconsin - Harley-Davidson Museum: Archive; exhibits of people, products, culture and history; restaurant & café; and museum store.

Due to the consolidation of operations, the Capitol Drive Tour Center in Wauwatosa, Wisconsin was closed in 2009.

Harley-Davidson culture

According to a recent Harley-Davidson study, in 1987 half of all Harley riders were under age 35. Now, only 15% of Harley buyers are under 35, and as of 2005, the median age had risen to 46.7.

The income of the average Harley-Davidson rider has risen, as well. In 1987, the median household income of a Harley-Davidson rider was $38,000. By 1997, the median household income for those riders had more than doubled, to $83,000.Wikipedia:Please clarify

Harley-Davidson attracts a loyal brand community, with licensing of the Harley-Davidson logo accounting for almost 5% of the company's net revenue ($41 million in 2004). Harley-Davidson supplies many American police forces with their motorcycle fleets.

Harley-Davidson motorcycles has long been associated with the sub-cultures of the:

- Biker
- Motorcycle club
- Outlaw motorcycle clubs, bikers, one percenters

Origin of "Hog" nickname

Beginning in 1920, a team of farm boys, including Ray Weishaar, who became known as the "hog boys," consistently won races. The group had a live hog as their mascot. Following a win, they would put the hog on their Harley and take a victory lap. In 1983, the Motor Company formed a club for owners of its product taking advantage of the long-standing nickname by turning "hog" into the acronym HOG., for Harley Owners Group. Harley-Davidson attempted to trademark "hog", but lost a case against an independent Harley-Davidson specialist, The Hog Farm of West Seneca, NY, in 1999 when the appellate panel ruled that "hog" had become a generic term for large motorcycles and was therefore unprotectable as a trademark.

On August 15, 2006, Harley-Davidson Inc. had its NYSE ticker symbol changed from HDI to HOG.

WHQG, a mainstream rock radio station which serves the Milwaukee metropolitan area, uses the moniker in their official callsign (102.9 The Hog) as a tribute to their home town motorcycle manufacturer, as well as its fans and riders.

Harley-Davidson Riders Club of Great Britain

The Harley-Davidson Riders Club of Great Britain [5] (est 1949) was the first British riders club (as opposed to motorcycle club) and organized national rallies and ride-outs from the outset. The 1982 rally began a popular run of events, probably due to the good fortune of having William G. Davidson attending his first rally outside the U.S., in Great Britain. He is thought to have been more than curious to discover how the secret "Evolution Motor" had found its world exclusive on the cover of the spring edition of the HDRCGB magazine, the "Harleyquin", but having a forgiving nature, Willie G. returned in 1984, along with Vaughn Beals and Len Thomson to officially show off the Evolution engine by bringing a test ride fleet to the second Brighton International Super Rally run by H.D.R.C.G.B. [6]. The demonstration rides were the first at any European Rally. The club now has circa 1800 members throughout the U. K., U.S.A. and Europe not forgetting their founder member in Australia. The club is split into regions and most hold rallies during the summer culminating in the clubs International Rally. [7]

Harley Owners Group

Harley-Davidson 2004 Heritage

Harley-Davidson established the Harley Owners Group (HOG) in 1983 to build on the strong loyalty and fraternity of Harley-Davidson enthusiasts as a means to promote not just a consumer product, but a lifestyle. The HOG has also served to open new revenue streams for the company, with the production of tie-in merchandise offered to club members, numbering over one million strong. Other motorcycle brands, and other and consumer brands outside motorcycling, have tried to imitate the Harley-Davidson's success in this endeavor by creating factory-sponsored community marketing clubs of their own. HOG members typically spend 30% more than other Harley owners, on such items as clothing and Harley-Davidson-sponsored events.

In 1991, HOG went international, with the first official European HOG Rally in Cheltenham, England. Today, more than one million members and more than 1400 chapters worldwide make HOG the largest factory-sponsored motorcycle organization in the world.

HOG benefits include organized group rides, exclusive products and product discounts, insurance premium discounts, and the Hog Tales newsletter. A one year full membership is included with the purchase of a new, unregistered Harley-Davidson.

In 2008, HOG celebrated its 25 anniversary in conjunction with the Harley 105th in Milwaukee Wisconsin.

Anniversary Celebrations

Beginning with Harley-Davidson's 90th anniversary in 1993, Harley-Davidson has had celebratory rides to Milwaukee called the "Ride Home". This new tradition has continued every 5 years, and is referred to unofficially as "Harleyfest," in line with Milwaukee's other festivals (Summerfest, German fest, Festa Italiana, etc.). This event brings Harley riders from all around the world. The 105th anniversary celebration was held on August 28–31, 2008, and included events in Milwaukee, Waukesha, Racine, and Kenosha counties, in Southeast Wisconsin.

Video games

There were several games inspiring *Harley-Davidson* motorcycles. The first one being *Harley-Davidson: The Road to Sturgis*, released for the Amiga in 1989. Several other *Harley-Davidson* games were released for the PC, PlayStation 2, and the Wii.

A couple of arcade games that inspired *Harley-Davidson* motorcycles were released by Sega. One being *Harley-Davidson & L.A. Riders*, and the other being *Harley-Davidson: King of the Road.*

Labor Hall of Fame

Because William S. Harley, Arthur Davidson, William A. Davidson and Walter Davidson, Sr. used and believed in H-D products and relied on the dedication of its employees to produce quality motorcycles, the four men were inducted into the Labor Hall of Fame.

See also

- List of Harley-Davidson motorcycles
- Category:Harley-Davidson engines

References

- Bach, Sharon, & Ostermann, Ken, eds. 1993. *The Legend Begins: Harley-Davidson Motorcycles, 1903–1969* (Harley-Davidson, Inc.)
- Mitchel, D. (1997). *Harley-Davidson Chronicle - An American Original.* Publications International Limited. ISBN 0-7853-2514-X.
- Wagner, Herbert, 2003. *At the Creation: Myth, Reality, and the Origin of the Harley-Davidson Motorcycle, 1901–1909* (Wisconsin Historical Society Press)
- Wilson, H. "The Encyclopedia of the Motorcycle" Dorling-Kindersley Limited, 1995 ISBN 0 7513 0206 6

External links

- Official Harley-Davidson Inc. Corporate website [2]
- Harley-Davidson [8] at the Open Directory Project

BMW Motorrad

Type	Motorcycle brand
Owner	BMW AG
Markets	Global
Website	bmw-motorrad.com [1]

BMW Motorrad is the motorcycle business unit of the German company BMW, part of its Corporate and Brand Development division. The current General Director of the unit is Hendrik von Kuenheim. BMW Motorrad has produced motorcycles since 1923, and revenues for 2009 were €1,069 million from the sale of 87,306 motorcycles, a drop on the 2008 figure of €1,230 million from the sales of 101,685 motorcycles.

History

Main article: History of BMW motorcycles

BMW's first motorcycle, the R32

The company began as an aircraft engine manufacturer in the early 20th century and through World War I. BMW manufactured its first motorcycle in 1923, the R32, which featured flat-twin boxer engine. BMW Motorrad still uses the flat-twin boxer configuration, but now manufactures motorcycles with a variety of engine configurations.

Current production

All BMW Motorrad's motorcycle production takes place at its plant in Berlin, Germany, although some engines are manufactured in Austria, China, and Taiwan.

BMW's best selling motorcycle, the R1200GS

BMW Motorrad produced 82,631 motorcycles in 2009, compared with 104,220 in 2008, a fall of 20.7% The most popular model is the R1200GS and its sibling R1200GS Adventure, which sold 24,467 units – accounting for 28% of BMW's annual production. Current production includes a variety of shaft, chain, and belt driven models, with engines from 450 cc to 1,300 cc; and models designed for off-road, dual-purpose, sport, and touring activities.

In 2008, BMW introduced the DOHC Boxer HP2 Sport, and entered the serious off-road competition motorcycle market with the release of the BMW G450X motorcycle.

BMW Motorrad motorcycles are categorized into product families, and each family is assigned a different letter prefix. The current families are:

- F series – parallel-twin engines of 800 cc capacity, featuring either chain or belt drive. Models are F650GS, F800GS, F800R, F800S and F800ST.
- G series – single-cylinder engines of 450–650 cc capacity featuring chain drive. Models are G450X, G650GS (available in some markets), G650 Xmoto, G650 Xchallenge and G650 Xcountry. The 450 cc engines are manufactured by Kymco in Taiwan. The 650 cc engines are manufactured by Loncin Holdings, Ltd in China.
- R series – twin-cylinder boxer engines of 1,200 cc capacity featuring shaft drive. Models are R1200GS, R1200R, R1200RT and R1200S.
- K series – four-cylinder engines of 1,200–1,300 cc capacity featuring shaft drive. Models are K1200LT, K1300GT, K1300R and K1300S. In 2010, BMW Motorrad announced the six-cylinder 1,649 cc K1600GT and K1600GTL, which will enter production in 2011.
- S1000RR – sport bike with transverse-mounted, 999 cc inline-four engine.

Racing

Team BMW Motorrad Motorsport

2010 name	Team Alpha BMW
Base	Rosenheim, Germany
Team principal/s	Berti Hauser
Race riders	111 Rubén Xaus 11 Troy Corser
Motorcycle	BMW S1000RR
Tyres	Pirelli
Riders' Championships	0

BMW Motorrad regularly enters its motorcycles in the Dakar Rally, an annual car, truck, and motorcycle race that runs from Europe to Africa and has featured riders such as Simon Pavey and motorcycling celebrity Charley Boorman. BMW Motorrad motorcycles have won the Dakar Rally six times.

In 2007, BMW Motorrad announced its entry to the 2009 Superbike World Championship season, where it is racing the BMW S1000RR. The 2009 season factory team is known as Team Alpha BMW and includes Spanish rider Ruben Xaus and Australian rider Troy Corser. In 2010, Xaus and Corser were joined on the track by Team Reitwagen BMW riders Andrew Pitt and Roland Resch, also riding the S1000RR.

External links

- BMW Motorrad International [1]
- BMW motorcycles [2] at the Open Directory Project

Article Sources and Contributors

Motorcycle *Source*: http://en.wikipedia.org/?oldid=390240121 *Contributors*: Bongwarrior

Motorcycling *Source*: http://en.wikipedia.org/?oldid=388627454 *Contributors*: 1 anonymous edits

Motorcycle history *Source*: http://en.wikipedia.org/?oldid=389558271 *Contributors*:

Gottlieb Daimler *Source*: http://en.wikipedia.org/?oldid=390383378 *Contributors*:

Wilhelm Maybach *Source*: http://en.wikipedia.org/?oldid=383565731 *Contributors*: 1 anonymous edits

Hildebrand & Wolfmüller *Source*: http://en.wikipedia.org/?oldid=371257116 *Contributors*: John of Reading

Motorcycle construction *Source*: http://en.wikipedia.org/?oldid=389739500 *Contributors*:

Motorcycle design *Source*: http://en.wikipedia.org/?oldid=387596947 *Contributors*: 1 anonymous edits

Types of motorcycles *Source*: http://en.wikipedia.org/?oldid=387857353 *Contributors*: Dbratland

Electric motorcycles and scooters *Source*: http://en.wikipedia.org/?oldid=389519314 *Contributors*:

Legal definition of motorcycle *Source*: http://en.wikipedia.org/?oldid=390066627 *Contributors*: Fetchcomms

Motorcycle safety *Source*: http://en.wikipedia.org/?oldid=387280455 *Contributors*: Rjwilmsi

Single-track vehicle *Source*: http://en.wikipedia.org/?oldid=338537532 *Contributors*: Malcolma

Bicycle and motorcycle dynamics *Source*: http://en.wikipedia.org/?oldid=389118461 *Contributors*:

Touring motorcycle *Source*: http://en.wikipedia.org/?oldid=389345988 *Contributors*: Dbratland

Cruiser (motorcycle) *Source*: http://en.wikipedia.org/?oldid=380513199 *Contributors*:

Motorcycle sport *Source*: http://en.wikipedia.org/?oldid=384095007 *Contributors*:

Honda *Source*: http://en.wikipedia.org/?oldid=389759793 *Contributors*: CliffC

Kawasaki Heavy Industries *Source*: http://en.wikipedia.org/?oldid=388848951 *Contributors*: Ron versatile

Suzuki *Source*: http://en.wikipedia.org/?oldid=390318652 *Contributors*:

Yamaha Motor Company *Source*: http://en.wikipedia.org/?oldid=388756918 *Contributors*: The Thing That Should Not Be

Harley-Davidson *Source*: http://en.wikipedia.org/?oldid=389673622 *Contributors*:

BMW Motorrad *Source*: http://en.wikipedia.org/?oldid=389115993 *Contributors*:

Image Sources, Licenses and Contributors

Image:Triumph T 110 650 cc 1954.jpg *Source*: http://bibliocm.bibliolabs.com/mwAnon/index.php?title=File:Triumph_T_110_650_cc_1954.jpg *License*: Creative Commons Attribution-Sharealike 3.0 *Contributors*: Yesterdays Antique Motorcycles

Image:URAL650-SPORTSMAN.jpg *Source*: http://bibliocm.bibliolabs.com/mwAnon/index.php?title=File:URAL650-SPORTSMAN.jpg *License*: Public Domain *Contributors*: Junji Matsumoto"COLONEL-J" From Japan

Image:Daimler-1-motorcycle-1.jpg *Source*: http://bibliocm.bibliolabs.com/mwAnon/index.php?title=File:Daimler-1-motorcycle-1.jpg *License*: GNU Free Documentation License *Contributors*: User:Softeis

Image:ZweiRadMuseumNSU NSU-SportMax 1955.JPG *Source*: http://bibliocm.bibliolabs.com/mwAnon/index.php?title=File:ZweiRadMuseumNSU_NSU-SportMax_1955.JPG *License*: GNU Free Documentation License *Contributors*: w:de:Benutzer:Joachim KöhlerJoachim Köhler

Image:1997SuzukiGS500E-001.jpg *Source*: http://bibliocm.bibliolabs.com/mwAnon/index.php?title=File:1997SuzukiGS500E-001.jpg *License*: Creative Commons Attribution 2.5 *Contributors*: User:RichN

File:TPHCM-Motorcycle.JPG *Source*: http://bibliocm.bibliolabs.com/mwAnon/index.php?title=File:TPHCM-Motorcycle.JPG *License*: Creative Commons Attribution-Sharealike 3.0 *Contributors*: User:Albert Nguyen

File:Sunbeam motorcycle Owners Rally 3.JPG *Source*: http://bibliocm.bibliolabs.com/mwAnon/index.php?title=File:Sunbeam_motorcycle_Owners_Rally_3.JPG *License*: Creative Commons Attribution 3.0 *Contributors*: Mike Hope (Sunbeam Owners Fellowship)

File:Hells Angels Mural - Southampton.jpg *Source*: http://bibliocm.bibliolabs.com/mwAnon/index.php?title=File:Hells_Angels_Mural_-_Southampton.jpg *License*: GNU Free Documentation License *Contributors*: User:Ian Dunster

File:IndiaMotorcycle.jpg *Source*: http://bibliocm.bibliolabs.com/mwAnon/index.php?title=File:IndiaMotorcycle.jpg *License*: Creative Commons Attribution 2.0 *Contributors*: judepics

Image:Action-w.jpg *Source*: http://bibliocm.bibliolabs.com/mwAnon/index.php?title=File:Action-w.jpg *License*: Creative Commons Attribution-Sharealike 2.5 *Contributors*: Original uploader was Jeff dean at en.wikipedia

Image:2009-02-14 Kawasaki Vulcan 900 Custom and Yamaha FZ6.jpg *Source*: http://bibliocm.bibliolabs.com/mwAnon/index.php?title=File:2009-02-14_Kawasaki_Vulcan_900_Custom_and_Yamaha_FZ6.jpg *License*: GNU Free Documentation License *Contributors*: User:Specious

Image:Kittpeak600.jpg *Source*: http://bibliocm.bibliolabs.com/mwAnon/index.php?title=File:Kittpeak600.jpg *License*: unknown *Contributors*: -

Image:Lenride.jpg *Source*: http://bibliocm.bibliolabs.com/mwAnon/index.php?title=File:Lenride.jpg *License*: Attribution *Contributors*: Original uploader was Jeff dean at en.wikipedia

Image:Motor Cycle EB.jpg *Source*: http://bibliocm.bibliolabs.com/mwAnon/index.php?title=File:Motor_Cycle_EB.jpg *License*: unknown *Contributors*: -

Image:Werner 230 cc 1904.jpg *Source*: http://bibliocm.bibliolabs.com/mwAnon/index.php?title=File:Werner_230_cc_1904.jpg *License*: unknown *Contributors*: -

Image:Copeland stoomfiets 1894.jpg *Source*: http://bibliocm.bibliolabs.com/mwAnon/index.php?title=File:Copeland_stoomfiets_1894.jpg *License*: unknown *Contributors*: -

Image:Fn-1913.jpg *Source*: http://bibliocm.bibliolabs.com/mwAnon/index.php?title=File:Fn-1913.jpg *License*: Attribution *Contributors*: Original uploader was Jeff dean at en.wikipedia

Image:R32-pn.jpg *Source*: http://bibliocm.bibliolabs.com/mwAnon/index.php?title=File:R32-pn.jpg *License*: unknown *Contributors*: -

Image:ZweiRadMuseumNSU Triumph Bonneville.JPG *Source*: http://bibliocm.bibliolabs.com/mwAnon/index.php?title=File:ZweiRadMuseumNSU_Triumph_Bonneville.JPG *License*: unknown *Contributors*: -

File:Honda CB750a.JPG *Source*: http://bibliocm.bibliolabs.com/mwAnon/index.php?title=File:Honda_CB750a.JPG *License*: unknown *Contributors*: -

Image:Scooters Bangkok Nana.jpg *Source*: http://bibliocm.bibliolabs.com/mwAnon/index.php?title=File:Scooters_Bangkok_Nana.jpg *License*: unknown *Contributors*: -

File:gottliebdaimler1.jpg *Source*: http://bibliocm.bibliolabs.com/mwAnon/index.php?title=File:Gottliebdaimler1.jpg *License*: Public Domain *Contributors*: Denniss, Jak, Morio

Image:Stuttgart-cannstatt-daimler-gewaechshaus.jpg *Source*: http://bibliocm.bibliolabs.com/mwAnon/index.php?title=File:Stuttgart-cannstatt-daimler-gewaechshaus.jpg *License*: Creative Commons Attribution-Sharealike 2.5 *Contributors*: user:Enslin

Image:ZweiRadMuseumNSU Reitwagen.JPG *Source*: http://bibliocm.bibliolabs.com/mwAnon/index.php?title=File:ZweiRadMuseumNSU_Reitwagen.JPG *License*: GNU Free Documentation License *Contributors*: w:de:Benutzer:Joachim KöhlerJoachim Köhler

File:Wilhelm-maybach-1900.jpg *Source*: http://bibliocm.bibliolabs.com/mwAnon/index.php?title=File:Wilhelm-maybach-1900.jpg *License*: unknown *Contributors*: -

Image:Daimler Reitwagen at the Mercedes Benz museum 2009.jpg *Source*: http://bibliocm.bibliolabs.com/mwAnon/index.php?title=File:Daimler_Reitwagen_at_the_Mercedes_Benz_museum_2009.jpg *License*: unknown *Contributors*: -

Image:Ural-engine-600.jpg *Source*: http://bibliocm.bibliolabs.com/mwAnon/index.php?title=File:Ural-engine-600.jpg *License*: unknown *Contributors*: -

Image:Sokol 995 cc zijklep v-twin.jpg *Source*: http://bibliocm.bibliolabs.com/mwAnon/index.php?title=File:Sokol_995_cc_zijklep_v-twin.jpg *License*: unknown *Contributors*: -

Image:Abc-engine.jpg *Source*: http://bibliocm.bibliolabs.com/mwAnon/index.php?title=File:Abc-engine.jpg *License*: unknown *Contributors*: -

File:BMW R1200GS paralever.jpg *Source*: http://bibliocm.bibliolabs.com/mwAnon/index.php?title=File:BMW_R1200GS_paralever.jpg *License*: unknown *Contributors*: -

Image:Absbrakes.jpg *Source*: http://bibliocm.bibliolabs.com/mwAnon/index.php?title=File:Absbrakes.jpg *License*: unknown *Contributors*: -

file:A scooter, crusier and sportbikes.jpg *Source*: http://bibliocm.bibliolabs.com/mwAnon/index.php?title=File:A_scooter,_crusier_and_sportbikes.jpg *License*: unknown *Contributors*: -

file:Vintage Yamaha sportbike and Vespa scooter.jpg *Source*: http://bibliocm.bibliolabs.com/mwAnon/index.php?title=File:Vintage_Yamaha_sportbike_and_Vespa_scooter.jpg *License*: unknown *Contributors*: -

file:05.USSS.UD.Motorcycle.NHQ.NW.WDC.18jun08.jpg *Source*: http://bibliocm.bibliolabs.com/mwAnon/index.php?title=File:05.USSS.UD.Motorcycle.NHQ.NW.WDC.18jun08.jpg *License*: unknown *Contributors*: -

File:Rattle the Runway Ride 2009-1.jpg *Source*: http://bibliocm.bibliolabs.com/mwAnon/index.php?title=File:Rattle_the_Runway_Ride_2009-1.jpg *License*: unknown *Contributors*: -

File:Suzuki GSX-R at Deals Gap.jpg *Source*: http://bibliocm.bibliolabs.com/mwAnon/index.php?title=File:Suzuki_GSX-R_at_Deals_Gap.jpg *License*: unknown *Contributors*: -

File:Hond GL1800 Goldwing in Paris.jpg *Source*: http://bibliocm.bibliolabs.com/mwAnon/index.php?title=File:Hond_GL1800_Goldwing_in_Paris.jpg *License*: unknown *Contributors*: -

File:BMW R1100RS on twisty road.jpg *Source*: http://bibliocm.bibliolabs.com/mwAnon/index.php?title=File:BMW_R1100RS_on_twisty_road.jpg *License*: Creative Commons Attribution-Sharealike 2.0 *Contributors*: Geoff from UK

File:Ducati Monster 696 at Ducati Tour 09.jpg *Source*: http://bibliocm.bibliolabs.com/mwAnon/index.php?title=File:Ducati_Monster_696_at_Ducati_Tour_09.jpg *License*: Creative Commons Attribution 2.0 *Contributors*: m.caimary from Sant Boi, Catalunya

File:Loaded R1200 GS in traffic circle.jpg *Source*: http://bibliocm.bibliolabs.com/mwAnon/index.php?title=File:Loaded_R1200_GS_in_traffic_circle.jpg *License*: unknown *Contributors*: -

File:DumontDunes 2005-04-25 paddle-tire.jpg *Source*: http://bibliocm.bibliolabs.com/mwAnon/index.php?title=File:DumontDunes_2005-04-25_paddle-tire.jpg *License*: unknown *Contributors*: -

File:Motorcycle trials bike uphill.jpg *Source*: http://bibliocm.bibliolabs.com/mwAnon/index.php?title=File:Motorcycle_trials_bike_uphill.jpg *License*: Creative Commons Attribution 2.0 *Contributors*: Bengt Nyman

File:Zero Z-Force.jpg *Source*: http://bibliocm.bibliolabs.com/mwAnon/index.php?title=File:Zero_Z-Force.jpg *License*: unknown *Contributors*: -

File:Zero Motorcycles, Detail Motor und Lithium-Ionen-Batterie.jpg *Source*: http://bibliocm.bibliolabs.com/mwAnon/index.php?title=File:Zero_Motorcycles,_Detail_Motor_und_Lithium-Ionen-Batterie.jpg *License*: unknown *Contributors*: -

Image:E-max electric scooter.JPG *Source*: http://bibliocm.bibliolabs.com/mwAnon/index.php?title=File:E-max_electric_scooter.JPG *License*: unknown *Contributors*: -

Image:Yamaha fc aqel 2007.JPG *Source*: http://bibliocm.bibliolabs.com/mwAnon/index.php?title=File:Yamaha_fc_aqel_2007.JPG *License*: unknown *Contributors*: -

Image:City cut out.jpg *Source*: http://bibliocm.bibliolabs.com/mwAnon/index.php?title=File:City_cut_out.jpg *License*: unknown *Contributors*: -

Image:Parking Electric Scooters Chengdu.jpg *Source*: http://bibliocm.bibliolabs.com/mwAnon/index.php?title=File:Parking_Electric_Scooters_Chengdu.jpg *License*: unknown *Contributors*: -

Image:Electrocat - electric motorcycle.JPG *Source*: http://bibliocm.bibliolabs.com/mwAnon/index.php?title=File:Electrocat_-_electric_motorcycle.JPG *License*: unknown *Contributors*: -

File:VM 5577 Lanzhou.jpg *Source*: http://bibliocm.bibliolabs.com/mwAnon/index.php?title=File:VM_5577_Lanzhou.jpg *License*: Creative Commons Attribution-Sharealike 3.0 *Contributors*: User:Vmenkov

Image:Motorbikes.jpg *Source*: http://bibliocm.bibliolabs.com/mwAnon/index.php?title=File:Motorbikes.jpg *License*: unknown *Contributors*: -

Image:Trike.6.arp.jpg *Source*: http://bibliocm.bibliolabs.com/mwAnon/index.php?title=File:Trike.6.arp.jpg *License*: unknown *Contributors*: -

File:US Navy 040708-N-8970J-002 Motorcycle safety class instructor Chief Aviation Electronics Technician Dan Ganet shows a student where he should have stopped, during motorcycle driver training at Naval Auxiliary Landing Field (NAL.jpg *Source*: http://bibliocm.bibliolabs.com/mwAnon/index.php?title=File:US_Navy_040708-N-8970J-002_Motorcycle_safety_class_instructor_Chief_Aviation_Electronics_Technician_Dan_Ganet_shows_a_si *License*: unknown *Contributors*: -

File:Harley riders on I4.jpg *Source*: http://bibliocm.bibliolabs.com/mwAnon/index.php?title=File:Harley_riders_on_I4.jpg *License*: unknown *Contributors*: -

Image:Cows-500.jpg *Source*: http://bibliocm.bibliolabs.com/mwAnon/index.php?title=File:Cows-500.jpg *License*: unknown *Contributors*: -

File:Rider in black textile suit and blue helmet on Honda CBR600.jpg *Source*: http://bibliocm.bibliolabs.com/mwAnon/index.php?title=File:Rider_in_black_textile_suit_and_blue_helmet_on_Honda_CBR600.jpg *License*: unknown *Contributors*: -

Image:Swisherhelmet1.jpg *Source*: http://bibliocm.bibliolabs.com/mwAnon/index.php?title=File:Swisherhelmet1.jpg *License*: unknown *Contributors*: -

File:Half helmet Harley-Davidson rider.jpg *Source*: http://bibliocm.bibliolabs.com/mwAnon/index.php?title=File:Half_helmet_Harley-Davidson_rider.jpg *License*: unknown *Contributors*: -

Image:BikeModel.jpg *Source*: http://bibliocm.bibliolabs.com/mwAnon/index.php?title=File:BikeModel.jpg *License*: unknown *Contributors*: -

Image:Ravensburg Rutenfest 2005 Festzug Draisine.jpg *Source*: http://bibliocm.bibliolabs.com/mwAnon/index.php?title=File:Ravensburg_Rutenfest_2005_Festzug_Draisine.jpg *License*: unknown *Contributors*: -

Image:Bicycle dimensions.svg *Source*: http://bibliocm.bibliolabs.com/mwAnon/index.php?title=File:Bicycle_dimensions.svg *License*: unknown *Contributors*: -

Image:Gyroscope wheel-text.png *Source*: http://bibliocm.bibliolabs.com/mwAnon/index.php?title=File:Gyroscope_wheel-text.png *License*: unknown *Contributors*: -

File:K1200lt.jpg *Source*: http://bibliocm.bibliolabs.com/mwAnon/index.php?title=File:K1200lt.jpg *License*: unknown *Contributors*: -

File:1200gsfr.jpg *Source*: http://bibliocm.bibliolabs.com/mwAnon/index.php?title=File:1200gsfr.jpg *License*: unknown *Contributors*: -

Image:Bmw-cruiser.jpg *Source*: http://bibliocm.bibliolabs.com/mwAnon/index.php?title=File:Bmw-cruiser.jpg *License*: unknown *Contributors*: -

Image:2000JackalV11.jpg *Source*: http://bibliocm.bibliolabs.com/mwAnon/index.php?title=File:2000JackalV11.jpg *License*: unknown *Contributors*: -

File:Montesa Cota.jpg *Source*: http://bibliocm.bibliolabs.com/mwAnon/index.php?title=File:Montesa_Cota.jpg *License*: Public Domain *Contributors*: Original uploader was Don Williams at en.wikipedia

Image:Motorcycle phillip island03.jpg *Source*: http://bibliocm.bibliolabs.com/mwAnon/index.php?title=File:Motorcycle_phillip_island03.jpg *License*: unknown *Contributors*: -

File:Honda-logo.svg *Source*: http://bibliocm.bibliolabs.com/mwAnon/index.php?title=File:Honda-logo.svg *License*: unknown *Contributors*: -

File:Honda aoyama.JPG *Source*: http://bibliocm.bibliolabs.com/mwAnon/index.php?title=File:Honda_aoyama.JPG *License*: unknown *Contributors*: -

File:2008 Honda Accord.jpg *Source*: http://bibliocm.bibliolabs.com/mwAnon/index.php?title=File:2008_Honda_Accord.jpg *License*: unknown *Contributors*: -

File:06-08 Honda Civic Ph.jpg *Source*: http://bibliocm.bibliolabs.com/mwAnon/index.php?title=File:06-08_Honda_Civic_Ph.jpg *License*: Creative Commons Attribution 3.0 *Contributors*: User:Mike384

File:2004supercub.jpg *Source*: http://bibliocm.bibliolabs.com/mwAnon/index.php?title=File:2004supercub.jpg *License*: GNU Free Documentation License *Contributors*: User Humbleradio on en.wikipedia

File:HONDA ASIMO.jpg *Source*: http://bibliocm.bibliolabs.com/mwAnon/index.php?title=File:HONDA_ASIMO.jpg *License*: unknown *Contributors*: -

File:2009 Honda Civic NGV--DC.jpg *Source*: http://bibliocm.bibliolabs.com/mwAnon/index.php?title=File:2009_Honda_Civic_NGV--DC.jpg *License*: unknown *Contributors*: -

File:Honda Civic Clean Models USA & BRA.jpg *Source*: http://bibliocm.bibliolabs.com/mwAnon/index.php?title=File:Honda_Civic_Clean_Models_USA_&_BRA.jpg *License*: unknown *Contributors*: -

File:2010 Honda Insight--DC.jpg *Source*: http://bibliocm.bibliolabs.com/mwAnon/index.php?title=File:2010_Honda_Insight--DC.jpg *License*: unknown *Contributors*: -

File:FCX Clarity.jpg *Source*: http://bibliocm.bibliolabs.com/mwAnon/index.php?title=File:FCX_Clarity.jpg *License*: Creative Commons Attribution 3.0 *Contributors*: Original uploader was Bbqjunkie at en.wikipedia

Image:Kibo_PM_and_ELM-PS.jpg *Source*: http://bibliocm.bibliolabs.com/mwAnon/index.php?title=File:Kibo_PM_and_ELM-PS.jpg *License*: Public Domain *Contributors*: NASA

File:JR East Shinkansen lineup at Niigata Depot 200910.jpg *Source*: http://bibliocm.bibliolabs.com/mwAnon/index.php?title=File:JR_East_Shinkansen_lineup_at_Niigata_Depot_200910.jpg *License*: unknown *Contributors*: -

Image:MARCtrainBWIAirport.JPG *Source*: http://bibliocm.bibliolabs.com/mwAnon/index.php?title=File:MARCtrainBWIAirport.JPG *License*: unknown *Contributors*: -

Image:Kobe Kawasaki Shipbuilding Co02ds3200.jpg *Source*: http://bibliocm.bibliolabs.com/mwAnon/index.php?title=File:Kobe_Kawasaki_Shipbuilding_Co02ds3200.jpg *License*: unknown *Contributors*: -

Image:KawasakiFS03N.jpg *Source*: http://bibliocm.bibliolabs.com/mwAnon/index.php?title=File:KawasakiFS03N.jpg *License*: unknown *Contributors*: -

Image:Randy de Puniet 2006 Sep.jpg *Source*: http://bibliocm.bibliolabs.com/mwAnon/index.php?title=File:Randy_de_Puniet_2006_Sep.jpg *License*: unknown *Contributors*: -

Image:Kobe Crystal Tower (2006.10.22).jpg *Source*: http://bibliocm.bibliolabs.com/mwAnon/index.php?title=File:Kobe_Crystal_Tower_(2006.10.22).jpg *License*: unknown *Contributors*: -

Image:Suzuki Suzulight 01.jpg *Source*: http://bibliocm.bibliolabs.com/mwAnon/index.php?title=File:Suzuki_Suzulight_01.jpg *License*: GNU Free Documentation License *Contributors*: User:Mytho88

Image:Esztergom Suzuki plant.JPG *Source*: http://bibliocm.bibliolabs.com/mwAnon/index.php?title=File:Esztergom_Suzuki_plant.JPG *License*: Public Domain *Contributors*: User:Villy

Image:Maruti Suzuki Swift 4456.JPG *Source*: http://bibliocm.bibliolabs.com/mwAnon/index.php?title=File:Maruti_Suzuki_Swift_4456.JPG *License*: Creative Commons Attribution-Sharealike 3.0 *Contributors*: User:Premkudva

Image:2004.suzuki.grand.vitara.2point0td.arp.jpg *Source*: http://bibliocm.bibliolabs.com/mwAnon/index.php?title=File:2004.suzuki.grand.vitara.2point0td.arp.jpg *License*: Public Domain *Contributors*: Arpingstone, MB-one, MartinHansV, Milkmandan, Thomas doerfer, 1 anonymous edits

File:SuzukiHayabusa2008.jpg *Source*: http://bibliocm.bibliolabs.com/mwAnon/index.php?title=File:SuzukiHayabusa2008.jpg *License*: GNU Free Documentation License *Contributors*: PekePON, Thermos, 1 anonymous edits

File:Harley Davidson founders.jpg *Source*: http://bibliocm.bibliolabs.com/mwAnon/index.php?title=File:Harley_Davidson_founders.jpg *License*: Public Domain *Contributors*: USGov-DOL

Image:1907 Harley Davidson.jpg *Source*: http://bibliocm.bibliolabs.com/mwAnon/index.php?title=File:1907_Harley_Davidson.jpg *License*: unknown *Contributors*: -

Image:Harley-Davidson 1000 cc HT 1916.jpg *Source*: http://bibliocm.bibliolabs.com/mwAnon/index.php?title=File:Harley-Davidson_1000_cc_HT_1916.jpg *License*: unknown *Contributors*: -

Image:RalphHepburn1922.jpg *Source*: http://bibliocm.bibliolabs.com/mwAnon/index.php?title=File:RalphHepburn1922.jpg *License*: unknown *Contributors*: -

Image:Harley-Davidson 1000 cc HT 1923.jpg *Source*: http://bibliocm.bibliolabs.com/mwAnon/index.php?title=File:Harley-Davidson_1000_cc_HT_1923.jpg *License*: unknown *Contributors*: -

File:Harley-Davidson 1200 cc SV 1931.jpg *Source*: http://bibliocm.bibliolabs.com/mwAnon/index.php?title=File:Harley-Davidson_1200_cc_SV_1931.jpg *License*: unknown *Contributors*: -

File:Harley-Davidson 10.jpg *Source*: http://bibliocm.bibliolabs.com/mwAnon/index.php?title=File:Harley-Davidson_10.jpg *License*: unknown *Contributors*: -

Image:xa-600.jpg *Source*: http://bibliocm.bibliolabs.com/mwAnon/index.php?title=File:Xa-600.jpg *License*: unknown *Contributors*: -

Image:HD Liberator.jpg *Source*: http://bibliocm.bibliolabs.com/mwAnon/index.php?title=File:HD_Liberator.jpg *License*: unknown *Contributors*: -

Image:Harley-Davidson Hummer.jpg *Source*: http://bibliocm.bibliolabs.com/mwAnon/index.php?title=File:Harley-Davidson_Hummer.jpg *License*: unknown *Contributors*: -

File:Aermacchi Turismo Veloce 1971 crop.jpg *Source*: http://bibliocm.bibliolabs.com/mwAnon/index.php?title=File:Aermacchi_Turismo_Veloce_1971_crop.jpg *License*: unknown *Contributors*: -

Image:ZweiRadMuseumNSU EasyRider.JPG *Source*: http://bibliocm.bibliolabs.com/mwAnon/index.php?title=File:ZweiRadMuseumNSU_EasyRider.JPG *License*: GNU Free Documentation License *Contributors*: w:de:Benutzer:Joachim KöhlerJoachim Köhler

Image:Harley-Davidson 6.jpg *Source*: http://bibliocm.bibliolabs.com/mwAnon/index.php?title=File:Harley-Davidson_6.jpg *License*: unknown *Contributors*: -

Image:Ford-F150-Harley.jpg *Source*: http://bibliocm.bibliolabs.com/mwAnon/index.php?title=File:Ford-F150-Harley.jpg *License*: unknown *Contributors*: -

Image:Harley Davidson.jpg *Source*: http://bibliocm.bibliolabs.com/mwAnon/index.php?title=File:Harley_Davidson.jpg *License*: unknown *Contributors*: -

Image:harley.electraglide.750pix.jpg *Source*: http://bibliocm.bibliolabs.com/mwAnon/index.php?title=File:Harley.electraglide.750pix.jpg *License*: unknown *Contributors*: -

Image:Sportster moving.jpg *Source*: http://bibliocm.bibliolabs.com/mwAnon/index.php?title=File:Sportster_moving.jpg *License*: unknown *Contributors*: -

Image:Vrod.jpg *Source*: http://bibliocm.bibliolabs.com/mwAnon/index.php?title=File:Vrod.jpg *License*: Public Domain *Contributors*: Dédélembrouille, Kronoman, Liftarn

Image:HD 883 Hugger.JPG *Source*: http://bibliocm.bibliolabs.com/mwAnon/index.php?title=File:HD_883_Hugger.JPG *License*: unknown *Contributors*: -

Image:PolizeiHarley.JPG *Source*: http://bibliocm.bibliolabs.com/mwAnon/index.php?title=File:PolizeiHarley.JPG *License*: unknown *Contributors*: -

File:HD museum panorama.jpg *Source*: http://bibliocm.bibliolabs.com/mwAnon/index.php?title=File:HD_museum_panorama.jpg *License*: unknown *Contributors*: -

File:Magnify-clip.png *Source*: http://bibliocm.bibliolabs.com/mwAnon/index.php?title=File:Magnify-clip.png *License*: unknown *Contributors*: -

Image:Harley Rider.JPG *Source*: http://bibliocm.bibliolabs.com/mwAnon/index.php?title=File:Harley_Rider.JPG *License*: unknown *Contributors*: -

File:BMW R32 vl TCE.jpg *Source*: http://bibliocm.bibliolabs.com/mwAnon/index.php?title=File:BMW_R32_vl_TCE.jpg *License*: unknown *Contributors*: -

File:BMW 1200 GS right side view.jpg *Source*: http://bibliocm.bibliolabs.com/mwAnon/index.php?title=File:BMW_1200_GS_right_side_view.jpg *License*: unknown *Contributors*: -

CPSIA information can be obtained at www.ICGtesting.com
Printed in the USA
LVOW122152170412

278074LV00004B/24/P